Taste of Home Easy Everyday Cooking

TASTE OF HOME BOOKS • RDA ENTHUSIAST BRANDS, LLC • MILWAUKEE, WI

© 2024 RDA Enthusiast Brands, LLC.
1610 N. 2nd St., Suite 102, Milwaukee WI 53212-3906

Visit us at tasteofhome.com for other Taste of Home books and products.

International Standard Book Number:
979-8-88977-012-1

Content Director: Mark Hagen
Creative Director: Raeann Thompson
Senior Editor: Christine Rukavena
Editor: Hazel Wheaton
Senior Art Director: Courtney Lovetere
Assistant Art Director: Jazmin Delgado
Designer: Sierra Schuler
Deputy Editor, Copy Desk: Dulcie Shoener
Copy Editor: Rayan Naqash

Photographer: Dan Roberts
Set Stylist: Stacey Genaw
Food Stylist: Josh Rink

Pictured on front cover:
Pasta & Veggies in Garlic Sauce, p. 142

Pictured on title page:
Chicken & Rice Casserole, p. 223

Pictured on back cover:
Sausage Potato Skillet, p. 151; Smash Burgers, p. 84; Sweetened Ricotta with Berries, p. 285; Green Bean, Corn & Buttermilk Salad, p. 100; Beefy French Onion Potpie, p. 148

Printed in China
1 3 5 7 9 10 8 6 4 2

GUACAMOLE CHICKEN SALAD SANDWICHES P. 86

SHEEPHERDER'S
BREAKFAST P. 48

Contents

JALAPENO POPPER STUFFED
CHICKEN BREASTS P. 166

Icons in this book

🕐 These **fast-to-fix recipes** are table-ready in just 30 minutes or less.

🍲 A **slow cooker**—one of the most convenient kitchen tools—does the cooking while you do other things.

🍲 The handy **Instant Pot®** electric pressure cooker icon signals that these recipes are real timesavers.

🍤 For the flavor and crispness of fried but without added fat, try these **air fryer** recipes.

5️⃣ Dishes that use **five or fewer ingredients** save on time and budget. (They may also call for water, salt, pepper, canola or olive oil, or optional items.)

🍎 Our **healthiest recipes**, these dietitian-approved dishes are lower in calories, fat and sodium.

❄️ All our **freezer-friendly** items include directions for freezing and reheating.

PM With prep done the night before, these **overnight** dishes are easy to fit into your schedule.

STRAWBERRY
SHORTCAKE SALAD P. 118

30-Day Meal Planner

DAY 1
Mom's Roast Chicken, p. 181
SERVE WITH
• Corn Pudding with Bacon & Cheddar, p. 244
• Garlic & Artichoke Roasted Potatoes, p. 126

DAY 2
Spinach Ravioli Bake, p. 186
SERVE WITH
• Pesto Twists, p. 11
• Heirloom Tomato Salad, p. 103

DAY 3
Taco Skillet Pizza with Cornbread Crust, p. 275
SERVE WITH
Green Chile Corn Fritters, p. 108

DAY 4
Super Quick Chicken Fried Rice, p. 189
SERVE WITH
• Easy Egg Rolls, p. 248
• Szechuan Sugar Snap Peas, p. 111

DAY 5
Chicken & Rice Casserole, p. 223
SERVE WITH
Sesame Almond Slaw, p. 121

DAY 11
Buffalo Chicken Chili, p. 78
SERVE WITH
Spinach Salad with Hot Bacon Dressing, p. 113

DAY 12
Pressure-Cooker German Goulash, p. 218
SERVE WITH
Swiss Potato Pancake, p. 118

DAY 13
Spicy Chicken Nuggets, p. 179
SERVE WITH
Rosemary Sweet Potato Fries, p. 106

DAY 14
BBQ Meat Loaf Minis, p. 174
SERVE WITH
• Freezer Mashed Potatoes, p. 223
• Creamed Peas, p. 125

DAY 15
Beef Osso Bucco, p. 231
SERVE WITH
Dreamy Polenta, p. 126

DAY 21
Broiled Parmesan Tilapia, p. 130
SERVE WITH
• Mashed cauliflower
• Italian Tomato Cucumber Salad, p. 107

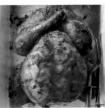
DAY 22
Sweet & Spicy Chipotle Chicken, p. 182
SERVE WITH
Saucy Mac & Cheese, p. 148

DAY 23
One-Pot Dutch Oven Pasta Bake, p. 276
SERVE WITH
Green Chile Prosciutto Rolls, p. 34

DAY 24
Spinach Pizza Quesadillas, p. 75
SERVE WITH
Mexican-Inspired Chicken Soup, p. 74

DAY 25
Flaky Chicken Wellington, p. 240
SERVE WITH
Ramen Corn Chowder, p. 80

When making a meal plan, look to new recipes as well as cherished standbys. To shake things up, consider incorporating meatless Mondays, taco Tuesdays, or fish on Fridays. Mom's Roast Chicken (Day 1) makes a great meal on its own or can provide the basis for fried rice (Day 4) or a chicken casserole (Day 5). Or, freeze leftover shredded chicken to toss into future tacos, casseroles or soups. The possibilities are endless!

DAY 6 Cilantro-Topped Salmon, p. 161 **SERVE WITH** French Potato Salad, p. 103	**DAY 7** Pizza Monkey Bread, p. 37 **SERVE WITH** Zucchini Fries, p. 122	**DAY 8** Rosemary-Apricot Pork Tenderloin, p. 181 **SERVE WITH** Walnut Cranberry Orzo, p. 108	**DAY 9** Eggplant Casserole, p. 227 **SERVE WITH** Buttered noodles or rice	**DAY 10** Easy Shrimp Tacos, p. 134 **SERVE WITH** Southwestern Rice, p. 258

DAY 16 White Bean, Sweet Potato & Pepper Ragout, p. 256 **SERVE WITH** Garlic bread	**DAY 17** Air-Fryer Fish Tacos, p. 219 **SERVE WITH** • Avocado Salsa, p. 228 • Classic Wilted Lettuce Salad, p. 99	**DAY 18** Best Ever Grilled Cheese Sandwiches, p. 89 **SERVE WITH** Basil Tomato Soup with Orzo, p. 89	**DAY 19** Chicken & Vegetable Curry Couscous, p. 165 **SERVE WITH** • Toasted pita bread • Radish Cucumber Salad, p. 113	**DAY 20** Veg Jambalaya, p. 253 **SERVE WITH** Grapefruit Lettuce Salad, p. 104

DAY 26 Pork Schnitzel with Sauce, p. 130 **SERVE WITH** Skillet Cabbage, p. 121	**DAY 27** Honey-Mustard Glazed Salmon, p. 168 **SERVE WITH** Syrian Green Beans with Fresh Herbs, p. 117	**DAY 28** Chicken Thai Pizza, p. 136 **SERVE WITH** Thai Salad with Peanut Dressing, p. 114	**DAY 29** Roast Leg of Lamb with Rosemary, p. 185 **SERVE WITH** • Harvard Beets, p. 107 • Balsamic Brussels Sprouts with Pears, p. 99	**DAY 30** Garlic Lime Shrimp, p. 155 **SERVE WITH** Zucchini Patties, p. 114

1

Appetizers & Beverages

Snack time with the family, game-day gatherings or an
evening in with a close circle of friends—you'll find the perfect
dishes to serve for every occasion in this collection of dips,
spreads, beverages and small-plate appetizers.

PIZZA MONKEY BREAD
P. 37

FETA CHEESE &
POMEGRANATE
GUACAMOLE

BABA GANOUSH

Also spelled *baba ghanoush* or *baba ghanouj*, this smoky-flavored Lebanese dip is made with roasted eggplant. It's typically served as a starter with pita bread or fresh vegetables.
—*Nithya Narasimhan, Chennai, India*

- -

Prep: 15 min. • **Bake:** 20 min + cooling
Makes: 8 servings (1 cup)

  1   medium eggplant
  2   Tbsp. olive oil, divided
  1   tsp. salt, divided
  ½   tsp. paprika
  2   Tbsp. tahini
  1   garlic clove, minced
  1   tsp. lemon juice
      Chopped fresh parsley

1. Preheat oven to 450°. Cut the eggplant in half lengthwise. Place halves cut side up on an ungreased baking sheet. Brush 1 Tbsp. olive oil over cut sides. Sprinkle with ½ tsp. salt and paprika. Bake until dark golden brown, 20-25 minutes. Remove from pan to a wire rack to cool.
2. Peel skin from the eggplant; discard. Place flesh in a food processor and pulse to mash; transfer to bowl. Stir in tahini, garlic, lemon juice and the remaining ½ tsp. salt. Spoon into serving dish. Drizzle with remaining 1 Tbsp. olive oil. Sprinkle with chopped fresh parsley and additional paprika.

2 TBSP.: 74 cal., 6g fat (1g sat. fat), 0 chol., 297mg sod., 5g carb. (2g sugars, 2g fiber), 1g pro.

Test Kitchen Tip

Instead of baking the eggplant, grill it whole over medium-high heat, turning occasionally, until the skin is charred, 25-35 minutes. When it's cool enough to handle, halve the eggplant and scoop out flesh.

FETA CHEESE & POMEGRANATE GUACAMOLE

Want to add a little flair to a bowl of guac? Top it off with chunks of feta and fresh pomegranate seeds. Since the cheese is so briny, we recommend cutting back on the amount of salt you use in the guacamole, or opting for reduced-sodium tortilla chips.
—Taste of Home *Test Kitchen*

- -

Takes: 15 min. • **Makes:** 6 servings

  3   medium ripe avocados,
      peeled and cubed
  2   to 3 Tbsp. fresh lime juice
  ½   to 1 tsp. kosher salt
  ½   cup pomegranate seeds
  ½   cup crumbled feta cheese

In a bowl, mash avocados until almost smooth. Stir in lime juice and ½ tsp. salt. Let stand 10 minutes to allow flavors to blend. Adjust seasoning with additional lime juice and salt if desired. Top with pomegranate seeds and feta.
¼ CUP: 146 cal., 12g fat (2g sat. fat), 5mg chol., 256mg sod., 9g carb. (2g sugars, 5g fiber), 3g pro. **DIABETIC EXCHANGES:** 2 fat, ½ starch.

BABA GANOUSH

TOSTONES

STRAWBERRY WATERMELON LEMONADE

My local hospital's nutrition department inspired this refreshing summer sipper. I tweaked the recipe slightly to create a drink full of sweet-tart flavor.
—*Dawn Lowenstein, Huntingdon Valley, PA*

Takes: 20 min. • **Makes:** 12 servings (3 qt.)

- ¼ cup sugar
- 2 cups boiling water
- ½ lb. fresh strawberries, hulled and quartered (about 2 cups)
- 12 cups cubed watermelon (about 1 medium)
- 1 can (12 oz.) frozen lemonade concentrate, thawed
- 3 Tbsp. lemon juice
    Ice cubes

Dissolve sugar in boiling water. Working in batches, place the strawberries and watermelon in a blender; cover and process until blended. Pour blended fruit through a fine-mesh strainer; transfer to a large pitcher. Stir in lemonade concentrate, lemon juice and sugar water. Serve over ice.
1 CUP: 119 cal., 0 fat (0 sat. fat), 0 chol., 7mg sod., 34g carb. (30g sugars, 1g fiber), 1g pro.

TOSTONES

I grew up eating Puerto Rican dishes, and *tostones* have always been my favorite. I still make the fried snacks when I miss my family.
—*Leah Martin, Gilbertsville, PA*

Prep: 15 min. + soaking
Cook: 5 min./batch • **Makes:** 3 dozen

- 3 garlic cloves, minced
- 1 Tbsp. garlic salt
- ½ tsp. onion powder
- 6 green plantains, peeled and cut into 1-in. slices
    Oil for deep-fat frying

SEASONING MIX
- 1 Tbsp. garlic powder
- 1½ tsp. garlic salt
- ½ tsp. onion powder
- ½ tsp. kosher salt
    Optional: Guacamole and pico de gallo

1. In a large bowl, combine the garlic, garlic salt and onion powder. Add the plantain slices; cover with cold water. Soak for 30 minutes.
2. Drain the plantains; place on paper towels and pat dry. In a deep cast-iron or electric skillet, heat oil to 375°. Add plantains, a few at a time; cook until lightly browned, 30-60 seconds. Remove with a slotted spoon; drain on paper towels.
3. Place plantain slices between 2 sheets of foil. With the bottom of a glass, flatten to ½-in. thickness. A few at a time, fry until golden brown, 2-3 minutes longer.
4. Combine next 4 ingredients; sprinkle over the tostones. Serve with guacamole and pico de gallo if desired.
1 TOSTONE: 63 cal., 3g fat (0 sat. fat), 0 chol., 103mg sod., 10g carb. (2g sugars, 1g fiber), 0 pro.

PESTO TWISTS

Make pesto with basil from your kitchen garden or buy prepared pesto from the grocery store to make these appetizers.
—*Jaye Beeler, Grand Rapids, MI*

Takes: 25 min. • **Makes:** 12 twists

- 1 pkg. (17.3 oz.) frozen puff pastry, thawed
- ½ cup prepared pesto
- ½ cup shredded Parmesan cheese
  Marinara sauce, warmed, optional

1. Preheat the oven to 400°. Unfold the puff pastry sheets on a lightly floured surface; roll each into a 12-in. square. Spread pesto onto 1 pastry sheet to within ¼ in. of edges. Sprinkle with cheese. Top with remaining pastry sheet, pressing down lightly.
2. Cut into twelve 1-in.-wide strips. Twist each strip 4 times. Place strips 2 in. apart on parchment-lined baking sheets, pressing down the ends. Bake until golden brown, 12-15 minutes. Serve the twists warm and, if desired, with marinara sauce.
1 TWIST: 265 cal., 17g fat (4g sat. fat), 6mg chol., 270mg sod., 24g carb. (0 sugars, 3g fiber), 6g pro.
CHEDDAR TWISTS: In a bowl, beat 1 large egg and 1 Tbsp. water; brush over both pastry sheets. Top 1 sheet with ¾ cup shredded cheddar cheese. Top with the remaining pastry; egg wash side down. Cut, twist and bake as directed.
SWEET ALMOND TWISTS: In a bowl, beat 1 large egg and 1 Tbsp. water; brush over both sheets of pastry. Top 1 sheet with ¼ cup almond cake and pastry filling; sprinkle with 1 cup sliced almonds. Top with the remaining pastry; egg wash side down. Cut, twist and bake as directed.

PESTO TWISTS

MANGO LASSI

Learn how to make a mango *lassi*, the perfect summer drink any mango lover will love. This sweet and refreshing treat needs only a few ingredients and comes together in a snap!

—Namrata Telugu, Terre Haute, IN

Takes: 10 min. • **Makes:** 2 servings

- 1 cup fat-free plain yogurt
- 1 medium mango, peeled and cubed
- 2 cups ice cubes
- 3 Tbsp. sugar
- 5 fresh mint leaves
- 2 cardamom pods, crushed, optional

In a blender, combine the yogurt, mango, ice, sugar, mint leaves and, if desired, cardamom pods. Cover and process for 30-60 seconds or until blended. Pour into 2 chilled glasses; serve immediately.

1½ CUPS: 226 cal., 1g fat (0 sat. fat), 3mg chol., 73mg sod., 54g carb. (48g sugars, 3g fiber), 6g pro.

Test Kitchen Tips

- This drink is best enjoyed fresh, but it will keep until the next day in a covered jar in the refrigerator.

- To make a vegan mango lassi, substitute a dairy-free option for the yogurt. We recommend using a coconut-based yogurt.

- You can adapt this recipe to other fruits as well, such as banana, strawberry, peach or cantaloupe.

MANGO LASSI

CAJUN CRAB POPPERS

My brother moved to New Orleans, and I love visiting him and his family whenever I can. These easy jalapeno poppers are stuffed with crab, Cajun seasonings and bacon. They're a little hot and spicy, just like a visit to New Orleans!

—Elizabeth Lubin, Huntington Beach, CA

Prep: 20 min. • **Bake:** 15 min.
Makes: 16 poppers

- 4 oz. cream cheese, softened
- 1 large egg, lightly beaten
- 2 Tbsp. minced fresh parsley
- 1 garlic clove, minced
- ½ tsp. Cajun seasoning
- 1½ cups shredded sharp cheddar cheese
- 1 can (8 oz.) lump crabmeat, drained
- 2 bacon strips, cooked and crumbled
- 8 jalapeno peppers

1. Preheat oven to 375°. In a small bowl, beat the first 5 ingredients until blended. Stir in shredded cheese, crab and bacon.
2. Cut jalapenos in half lengthwise and remove seeds. Spoon filling into the pepper halves. Place on an ungreased baking sheet; bake until lightly browned, 15-20 minutes. Sprinkle with additional fresh parsley.
NOTE: Wear disposable gloves when cutting hot peppers; the oil can burn skin. Avoid touching your face.
1 POPPER: 88 cal., 7g fat (4g sat. fat), 41mg chol., 187mg sod., 1g carb. (1g sugars, 0 fiber), 6g pro.

CAJUN CRAB
POPPERS

SALMON DIP WITH
CREAM CHEESE

SALMON DIP WITH CREAM CHEESE

Here's a delightful hors d'oeuvre that's excellent for any occasion. The combination of salmon, cream cheese and spices gives it terrific flavor.
—*Raymonde Hebert Bernier, Saint-Hyacinthe, QC*

Prep: 10 min. + chilling • **Makes:** 1½ cups

- 6 oz. cream cheese, softened
- 3 Tbsp. mayonnaise
- 1 Tbsp. lemon juice
- ½ tsp. salt
- ½ tsp. curry powder
- ¼ tsp. dried basil
- ⅛ tsp. pepper
- 1 can (7½ oz.) salmon, drained, bones and skin removed
- 2 green onions, thinly sliced
  Crackers and chopped vegetables

In a bowl, combine the cream cheese, mayonnaise and lemon juice. Add salt, curry powder, basil and pepper; mix well. Gently stir in salmon and onions. Cover and refrigerate for at least 1 hour. Serve with crackers and vegetables.
2 TBSP.: 78 cal., 7g fat (2g sat. fat), 17mg chol., 234mg sod., 1g carb. (0 sugars, 0 fiber), 4g pro.

Test Kitchen Tip

This dip will last for up to 5 days in the refrigerator. We do not recommend freezing it—cream cheese dips typically don't hold up well in the freezer.

APPLE MARTINI

You'll feel like a movie star when you sip this fancy martini—and guests will be impressed when you garnish each drink with a green apple slice.
—Taste of Home *Test Kitchen*

Takes: 5 min. • **Makes:** 1 serving

  Ice cubes
- 2 oz. vodka
- 1½ oz. sour apple liqueur
- 1½ tsp. lemon juice
  Optional: Green apple slice

Fill a shaker three-fourths full with ice. Add the vodka, apple liqueur and lemon juice. Cover and shake for 10-15 seconds or until condensation forms on outside of shaker. Strain into a chilled cocktail glass. If desired, garnish with apple slice.
⅔ CUP: 285 cal., 0 fat (0 sat. fat), 0 chol., 1mg sod., 17g carb. (17g sugars, 0 fiber), 0 pro.

APPLE MARTINI

BLUE CHEESE
GARLIC BREAD

CRANBERRY ENDIVE APPETIZERS

You can pack a lot of flavor into an elegant appetizer by using the right combination of ingredients. I created this blue cheese and cranberry filling for a holiday party, and everyone loved it!
—*Margee Berry, White Salmon, WA*

Takes: 20 min. • **Makes:** 2 dozen

- 4 oz. cream cheese, softened
- 2 Tbsp. apple jelly
- ⅓ cup crumbled blue cheese
- ¼ cup dried cranberries, chopped
- 24 leaves Belgian endive
- ¼ cup chopped pecans, toasted

In a large bowl, beat cream cheese and jelly until smooth. Stir in the blue cheese and cranberries. Drop filling by heaping teaspoonfuls onto each endive leaf. Sprinkle with pecans.

1 APPETIZER: 40 cal., 3g fat (1g sat. fat), 7mg chol., 41mg sod., 3g carb. (2g sugars, 0 fiber), 1g pro.

BLUE CHEESE GARLIC BREAD

This is an irresistible way to dress up an ordinary loaf of bread. Serve slices as an appetizer or with a meal.
—*Kevalyn Henderson, Hayward, WI*

Takes: 30 min. • **Makes:** 10 servings

- ½ cup butter, softened
- 4 oz. crumbled blue cheese
- 2 Tbsp. grated Parmesan cheese
- 1 Tbsp. minced chives
- 1 tsp. garlic powder
- 1 loaf (1 lb.) unsliced French bread

1. Preheat oven to 350°. In a small bowl, combine the first 5 ingredients. Cut into bread to make 1-in.-thick slices, but don't cut all the way through—leave slices attached at the bottom. Spread cheese mixture between the slices.
2. Wrap loaf in a large piece of heavy-duty foil (about 28x18 in.); fold around bread and seal tightly. Bake until heated through, about 20 minutes. Serve warm.

1 PIECE: 250 cal., 14g fat (8g sat. fat), 34mg chol., 546mg sod., 24g carb. (1g sugars, 1g fiber), 7g pro.

CRANBERRY ENDIVE
APPETIZERS

CREAMY CRAB WONTONS

CREAMY CRAB WONTONS

How about a fast appetizer for two that melts in your mouth? These hot, crispy little bites boast a creamy filling with a hint of crab. Serve with plum sauce or sweet-and-sour sauce for dipping.
—*Robin Boynton, Harbor Beach, MI*

Takes: 20 min. • **Makes:** 2 servings

- 2 oz. cream cheese, softened
- 2 Tbsp. canned crabmeat, drained, flaked and cartilage removed
- 2 tsp. chopped green onion
- 6 wonton wrappers
  Oil for frying
  Sweet-and-sour sauce, optional

1. In a small bowl, combine the cream cheese, crab and onion. Place 1 rounded tsp. filling in the center of each wonton wrapper. Moisten the wrapper edges with water. Fold in half lengthwise away from you, forming a rectangle; press firmly to seal.
2. Keeping filling in the center, moisten bottom left corner of the rectangle with water. Curve wonton rectangle toward you, bringing bottom right corner over bottom left corner; press firmly to seal.
3. In a deep cast-iron or electric skillet, heat 1 in. oil to 375°. Fry wontons on each side until golden brown, 1-2 minutes. Drain on paper towels. Serve warm, with sauce if desired.
3 WONTONS: 226 cal., 16g fat (6g sat. fat), 39mg chol., 274mg sod., 16g carb. (1g sugars, 0 fiber), 6g pro.

Test Kitchen Tip
If you prefer, you can cook these wontons in an air fryer, fry them in a pan or bake them in the oven. Just make sure you coat them with cooking spray if air-frying or baking.

SPARKLING GINGER LEMONADE

Chill out with this delightful cooler, perfect for springtime bridal showers or hot summer days on the deck. It's a quick fix you'll stir up time and again.
—*Jodi Blubaugh, Eagle Mountain, UT*

Prep: 20 min. + cooling
Makes: 5 servings

- 2 cups water
- 1 cup honey
- 2 Tbsp. minced fresh gingerroot
- 2 cups club soda, chilled
- 1 cup lemon juice
  Optional: Lemon slices and fresh mint

1. In a saucepan, bring the water, honey and ginger to a boil. Remove from heat; cover and steep for 10 minutes. Strain, discarding ginger. Cool completely.
2. Transfer to a pitcher; stir in soda and lemon juice. Serve over ice. Garnish with lemon slices and fresh mint if desired.
1 CUP: 217 cal., 0 fat (0 sat. fat), 0 chol., 23mg sod., 59g carb. (56g sugars, 0 fiber), 0 pro.

Test Kitchen Tip
The flavor of fresh ginger is preferred, but if you don't have it on hand, you can use 1¼ tsp. ground ginger instead of the 2 Tbsp. fresh ginger.

SPARKLING GINGER LEMONADE

- Pico de Gallo -

This simple and quick-to-make classic salsa is a celebration of flavor!
Use the freshest, highest-quality ingredients for the best results.

In a medium bowl, combine
6 chopped **plum tomatoes**,
1 finely chopped **small onion**,
½ cup chopped **fresh cilantro**,
1-2 seeded and finely chopped
jalapeno peppers, 3 Tbsp. **lime
juice**, 1 Tbsp. finely chopped
cilantro stems, 1 minced
garlic clove and ¼ tsp. **salt**.
Cover and refrigerate for
1-2 hours before serving.

AIR-FRYER
THAI CHICKEN
MEATBALLS

AIR-FRYER THAI CHICKEN MEATBALLS

These meatballs make a great game-day snack. We also like to serve them as a main dish over stir-fried veggies.
—*Merry Graham, Newhall, CA*

Prep: 10 min. • **Cook:** 10 min./batch
Makes: 12 servings

- ½ cup sweet chili sauce
- 2 Tbsp. lime juice
- 2 Tbsp. ketchup
- 1 tsp. soy sauce
- 1 large egg, lightly beaten
- ¾ cup panko bread crumbs
- 1 green onion, finely chopped
- 1 Tbsp. minced fresh cilantro
- ½ tsp. salt
- ½ tsp. garlic powder
- 1 lb. lean ground chicken

1. Preheat air fryer to 350°. In a small bowl, combine chili sauce, lime juice, ketchup and soy sauce. In a large bowl, combine egg, bread crumbs, green onion, cilantro, salt, garlic powder and 4 Tbsp. chili sauce mixture (reserve remaining ½ cup for serving). Add chicken; mix lightly but thoroughly. Shape into 12 balls.
2. In batches, arrange meatballs in a single layer on greased tray in the air-fryer basket. Cook until lightly browned, 4-5 minutes. Turn and cook until lightly browned and cooked through, 4-5 minutes longer. Serve with the reserved sauce; sprinkle with additional cilantro.
1 MEATBALL: 98 cal., 3g fat (1g sat. fat), 43mg chol., 369mg sod., 9g carb. (6g sugars, 0 fiber), 9g pro.

BLUEBERRY ICED TEA

I enjoy coming up with new ways to use my slow cooker. If it's going to take up space, it needs to earn its keep! Pour this refreshing tea over plenty of ice, and garnish with blueberries if desired. For extra fun, freeze blueberries in the ice cubes.
—*Colleen Delawder, Herndon, VA*

Prep: 10 min. • **Cook:** 3 hours + cooling
Makes: 11 servings

- 12 cups water
- 2 cups fresh blueberries
- 1 cup sugar
- ¼ tsp. salt
- 4 family-sized tea bags
  Ice cubes
  Optional: Additional blueberries, lemon slices and fresh mint leaves

1. In a 5-qt. slow cooker, combine water, blueberries, sugar and salt. Cook, covered, on low heat for 3 hours.
2. Turn off slow cooker; add tea bags. Cover and let stand for 5 minutes. Discard tea bags; let cool for 2 hours. Strain; discard the blueberries. Pour tea into pitcher; serve over ice cubes. If desired, top each serving with additional blueberries, lemon slices and fresh mint leaves.
1 CUP: 73 cal., 0 fat (0 sat. fat), 0 chol., 61mg sod., 19g carb. (18g sugars, 0 fiber), 0 pro.

BRIE WITH ALMONDS

This nut-topped cheese is elegant and impressive for holiday occasions. No one will guess that the recipe is actually a snap to prepare.
—*Mildred Aydt, Chanhassen, MN*

Takes: 15 min. • **Makes:** 8 servings

- 1 round Brie cheese (8 oz.)
- 2 Tbsp. butter, melted
- ¼ cup sliced almonds
- 1 Tbsp. brandy, optional
  Assorted crackers or fresh vegetables

1. Preheat oven to 400°. Place the Brie in a small ungreased cast-iron skillet or shallow 1-qt. baking dish. Combine the butter, almonds and, if desired, brandy; pour over the Brie.
2. Bake, uncovered, until the cheese is softened, 10-12 minutes. Serve with crackers or vegetables.
1 SERVING: 141 cal., 12g fat (7g sat. fat), 36mg chol., 199mg sod., 1g carb. (0 sugars, 0 fiber), 7g pro.

BRIE WITH ALMONDS

AIR-FRYER CALAMARI

You can make the same kind of crispy calamari you'd find at your favorite Italian restaurants, thanks to the air fryer! A quick coat in crunchy panko bread crumbs and a few minutes in the air fryer are all it takes to make this special appetizer.
—*Peggy Woodward, Shullsburg, WI*

Prep: 20 min. • **Cook:** 7 min./batch
Makes: 5 dozen

- ½ cup all-purpose flour
- ½ tsp. salt
- 1 large egg, lightly beaten
- ½ cup 2% milk
- 1 cup panko bread crumbs
- ½ tsp. seasoned salt
- ¼ tsp. pepper
- 8 oz. cleaned fresh or frozen calamari (squid), thawed and cut into ½-in. rings
  Cooking spray

1. Preheat air fryer to 400°. In a shallow bowl, combine flour and salt. In another shallow bowl, whisk the egg and milk. In a third shallow bowl, combine the bread crumbs, seasoned salt and pepper. Coat calamari with the flour mixture, then dip into the egg mixture and coat with bread crumb mixture.
2. Working in batches, place calamari in a single layer on a greased tray in air-fryer basket; spritz with cooking spray. Cook for 4 minutes. Turn; spritz with cooking spray. Cook until golden brown, 3-5 minutes longer.
1 PIECE: 11 cal., 0 fat (0 sat. fat), 10mg chol., 28mg sod., 1g carb. (0 sugars, 0 fiber), 1g pro.

AIR-FRYER CALAMARI

EASY PIMIENTO CHEESE

Every authentic Southerner has their own version of pimiento cheese. It's wonderful on crackers, in a sandwich with a fresh summer tomato, inside a grilled cheese sandwich or plain with some crackers.

—Josh Carter, Birmingham, AL

- -

Prep: 15 min. + chilling
Makes: 16 servings

- 1⅓ cups mayonnaise
- 2 jars (4 oz. each) pimiento strips, chopped
- 1½ tsp. Worcestershire sauce
- ¼ tsp. cayenne pepper
- ¼ tsp. pepper
- 1 block (8 oz.) sharp cheddar cheese, shredded
- 1 block (8 oz.) extra-sharp cheddar cheese, shredded

In a large bowl, combine the first 5 ingredients. Add cheeses and stir to combine. Refrigerate, covered, at least 1 hour.

¼ CUP: 238 cal., 23g fat (7g sat. fat), 29mg chol., 286mg sod., 2g carb. (1g sugars, 0 fiber), 7g pro.

STUFFED PIZZA ROLLS

After trying a similar dish at a local restaurant, I came up with my own version. It's easy, delicious and fun for potlucks or parties.

—Sarah Gilbert, Beaverton, OR

- -

Takes: 30 min. • **Makes:** 1 dozen

- 1 tube (13.8 oz.) refrigerated pizza crust
- ¼ cup prepared ranch salad dressing
- 6 oz. pepperoni, finely chopped
- 1 cup shredded pepper jack cheese
- ¼ cup shredded Romano cheese
- ¼ cup thinly sliced green onions
- ¼ cup chopped green pepper
- 4 cooked bacon strips, chopped
- 2 tsp. Italian seasoning
- 1 tsp. garlic powder
  Optional: Marinara sauce or Alfredo sauce, warmed

1. Grease 12 muffin cups; set aside. On a lightly floured surface, unroll pizza crust. Spread ranch dressing to within ½ in. of edges. Sprinkle with pepperoni, cheeses, green onions, green pepper, bacon and seasonings. Roll up jelly-roll style; pinch the edge closed. Cut crosswise into 12 slices. Place each slice in a prepared muffin cup.
2. Bake at 350° until lightly browned, 20-25 minutes. Serve rolls warm, with marinara or Alfredo sauce, if desired.
1 PIZZA ROLL: 234 cal., 14g fat (6g sat. fat), 28mg chol., 664mg sod., 17g carb. (2g sugars, 1g fiber), 10g pro.

EASY
PIMIENTO CHEESE

STUFFED
PIZZA ROLLS

Taste of Home

VEGETARIAN
STUFFED MUSHROOMS

VEGETARIAN STUFFED MUSHROOMS

Soy crumbles mixed with parsley, basil, oregano and bread crumbs make a delightful vegetarian filling for these savory stuffed mushrooms.
—*Arline Aaron, Brooklyn, NY*

Prep: 15 min. • **Bake:** 25 min.
Makes: 14 servings

- 14 large fresh mushrooms
- 1 small onion, finely chopped
- 4 tsp. canola oil
- ¾ cup soft bread crumbs
- ½ cup frozen vegetarian meat crumbles, thawed
- 1 tsp. minced fresh parsley
- 1 tsp. dried basil
- ½ tsp. dried oregano
- ½ tsp. salt
- ½ tsp. pepper
  Chopped fresh basil, optional

1. Preheat oven to 350°. Remove stems from mushrooms and chop; set the caps aside. In a large nonstick skillet, saute chopped stems and onion in oil until tender. Stir in bread crumbs, crumbles and the next 5 ingredients; cook until bread crumbs are lightly browned. Let cool slightly.
2. Stuff mixture into the mushroom caps. Place stuffed caps in a 15x10x1-in. baking pan coated with cooking spray. Bake for 25-30 minutes or until heated through and mushroom caps are tender. If desired, top with chopped fresh basil. Serve warm.
1 STUFFED MUSHROOM: 34 cal., 2g fat (0 sat. fat), 0 chol., 111mg sod., 3g carb. (1g sugars, 1g fiber), 2g pro. **DIABETIC EXCHANGES:** ½ starch, ½ fat.

STRAWBERRY SHAKES

Full of summer fruit, these thick berry blends are the perfect way to savor hot days. I serve them in tall glasses with sliced fresh strawberries as a garnish.
—*Ruby Williams, Bogalusa, LA*

Takes: 5 min. • **Makes:** 4 servings

- ⅔ cup 2% milk
- 3 cups strawberry ice cream
- 1 cup fresh strawberries
- 2 Tbsp. strawberry syrup

In a blender, combine all ingredients; cover and process until smooth. Pour into chilled glasses. Serve immediately.
1 CUP: 253 cal., 10g fat (6g sat. fat), 34mg chol., 81mg sod., 38g carb. (9g sugars, 1g fiber), 5g pro.

STRAWBERRY SHAKES

SAUSAGE
CHEESE BALLS

SAUSAGE CHEESE BALLS

These bite-sized meatballs are my favorite. Feel free to swap in different cheese for the cheddar or to serve with Dijon mustard instead of the barbecue and sweet-and-sour sauces.
—*Anna Damon, Bozeman, MT*

Takes: 30 min. • **Makes:** 20 servings

- ½ cup shredded cheddar cheese
- 3 Tbsp. biscuit/baking mix
- 1 Tbsp. finely chopped onion
- 1 Tbsp. finely chopped celery
- ⅛ tsp. garlic powder
- ⅛ tsp. pepper
- ¼ lb. bulk pork sausage
  Optional: Sweet-and-sour and barbecue sauces

1. Preheat oven to 375°. Combine first 6 ingredients. Crumble sausage over mixture; mix lightly but thoroughly. Shape into 1-in. balls.
2. Place in a shallow baking pan coated with cooking spray. Bake, uncovered, until golden brown and no longer pink inside, 12-15 minutes. Drain on paper towels. Serve with sauces if desired.

1 MEATBALL: 30 cal., 2g fat (1g sat. fat), 6mg chol., 64mg sod., 1g carb. (0 sugars, 0 fiber), 1g pro.

Test Kitchen Tip

To make these meatballs ahead of time, place shaped, uncooked balls in a single layer on a sheet pan in the freezer. Once frozen, transfer to a freezer-safe container and return to the freezer. When you're ready to bake the meatballs, take out as many as you need and bake from frozen until heated through, allowing a little extra baking time.

HOT ARTICHOKE-
SPINACH DIP

SAVORY CHEESE BALL

Blue cheese contributes a pleasant, tangy bite and olive a saltiness to this creamy cheese ball recipe. It can be made a day in advance and kept, covered, in the refrigerator. For the optimum taste, let it stand at room temperature for 20 minutes before serving.
—*Jan Stawara, Howell, MI*

Prep: 15 min. + chilling • **Makes:** 2 cups

    1   pkg. (8 oz.) cream cheese, softened
    1   cup crumbled blue cheese
    ¼   cup butter, softened
    1   can (4¼ oz.) chopped ripe olives
    1   Tbsp. minced chives
    ¾   cup chopped walnuts
        Assorted crackers

1. In a large bowl, beat cream cheese, blue cheese and butter until smooth. Stir in olives and chives. Cover and refrigerate for at least 1 hour.
2. Shape cheese mixture into a ball; roll in walnuts. Cover and refrigerate for at least 1 hour. Serve with crackers.
2 TBSP.: 145 cal., 14g fat (6g sat. fat), 27mg chol., 204mg sod., 2g carb. (1g sugars, 1g fiber), 3g pro.

HOT ARTICHOKE-SPINACH DIP

One taste of this outrageously delicious dip and your guests will not stop until it's all gone. The savory blend of artichokes, spinach and Parmesan cheese is really addictive! It tastes even better if you assemble it the night before and chill it in the fridge before baking.
—*Michelle Krzmarzick, Torrance, CA*

Takes: 30 min. • **Makes:** 3 cups

    1   pkg. (8 oz.) cream cheese, softened
    ½   cup grated Parmesan cheese
    ¼   cup mayonnaise
    1   garlic clove, minced
    1   tsp. dried basil
    ¼   tsp. garlic salt
    ¼   tsp. pepper
    1   can (14 oz.) water-packed artichoke hearts, rinsed, drained and chopped
    ½   cup frozen chopped spinach, thawed and squeezed dry
    ¼   cup shredded mozzarella cheese
        Assorted crackers

1. Preheat oven to 350°. In a large bowl, combine the first 7 ingredients; mix well. Stir in artichokes and spinach. Transfer to a greased 9-in. pie plate. Sprinkle with mozzarella cheese.
2. Bake, uncovered, until the dip is bubbly and the edge is lightly browned, 20-25 minutes. Serve with crackers.
2 TBSP.: 68 cal., 6g fat (3g sat. fat), 13mg chol., 139mg sod., 2g carb. (0 sugars, 0 fiber), 2g pro.

BUFFALO BITES WITH
BLUE CHEESE RANCH DIP

FROZEN MARGARITAS

One of my favorite summer drinks is a frozen margarita. What's not to love? This drink is great paired with tacos or chips and salsa.
—*Caroline Stanko, Milwaukee, WI*

Takes: 15 min. • **Makes:** 6 servings

- 6 lime wedges
  Kosher salt
- 1 cup tequila
- ½ cup Triple Sec
- ¼ cup lime juice (about 4 limes)
- ½ cup simple syrup or superfine sugar
- 6 to 9 cups ice cubes

1. Using lime wedges, moisten the rims of 6 margarita or cocktail glasses. Set aside lime wedges for garnish. Sprinkle salt on a plate; hold each glass upside down and dip rim into salt. Set aside. Discard remaining salt on plate.
2. In a blender, combine tequila, Triple Sec, lime juice, simple syrup and enough ice to reach desired consistency; cover and process until blended. Pour into prepared glasses. Garnish with lime wedges. Serve immediately.
1 CUP: 214 cal., 0 fat (0 sat. fat), 0 chol., 34mg sod., 24g carb. (22g sugars, 0 fiber), 0 pro.

Test Kitchen Tips

- If your blender isn't powerful enough to crush whole ice cubes, use pre-crushed ice instead.

- For a flavored margarita, replace a few ice cubes with frozen mangoes, strawberries or mixed berries.

BUFFALO BITES WITH BLUE CHEESE RANCH DIP

Low-carb cauliflower bites cook up fast in the air fryer, making them an easy snack or side dish. I serve them with a flavorful dip made with cottage cheese that's packed with protein compared to most dips. My teenagers happily eat their veggies with this recipe.
—*Julie Peterson, Crofton, MD*

Prep: 10 min. • **Cook:** 30 min.
Makes: 6 servings

- 1 small head cauliflower, cut into florets
- 2 Tbsp. olive oil
- 3 Tbsp. Buffalo wing sauce
- 3 Tbsp. butter, melted

DIP

- 1½ cups 2% cottage cheese
- ¼ cup fat-free plain Greek yogurt
- ¼ cup crumbled blue cheese
- 1 envelope ranch salad dressing mix
  Celery sticks, optional

1. Preheat air fryer to 350°. In a large bowl, combine cauliflower and oil; toss to coat. In batches, arrange cauliflower in a single layer in the air-fryer basket. Cook until florets are tender and edges are browned, 10-15 minutes, stirring halfway through.
2. In a large bowl, combine Buffalo sauce and melted butter. Add cauliflower; toss to coat. Transfer to a serving platter.
3. In a bowl, combine the cottage cheese, yogurt, blue cheese and salad dressing mix. Serve with the cauliflower and, if desired, celery sticks.
1 SERVING: 203 cal., 13g fat (6g sat. fat), 22mg chol., 1470mg sod., 13g carb. (4g sugars, 1g fiber), 8g pro.

FROZEN MARGARITAS

BACON
CHEESEBURGER
BALLS

BACON CHEESEBURGER BALLS

The first time I served these, my husband and kids thought they were just plain and simple meatballs. Then they cut into the flavorful filling inside!
—*Cathy Lendvoy, Boharm, SK*

Prep: 25 min. • **Cook:** 10 min.
Makes: 3 dozen

- 1 large egg
- 1 envelope onion soup mix
- 1 lb. ground beef
- 2 Tbsp. all-purpose flour
- 2 Tbsp. 2% milk
- 1 cup shredded cheddar cheese
- 4 bacon strips, cooked and crumbled

COATING
- 2 large eggs
- 1 cup crushed saltines
  (about 30 crackers)
- 5 Tbsp. canola oil

1. In a large bowl, combine egg and soup mix. Crumble beef over mixture and mix well. Divide into 36 portions; set aside. In another large bowl, combine the flour and milk until smooth. Add cheese and bacon; mix lightly but thoroughly. Shape the cheese mixture into 36 balls. Shape 1 beef portion around each cheese ball.
2. In a shallow bowl, beat the eggs for coating. Place the cracker crumbs in another bowl. Dip meatballs into the beaten eggs, then coat with crumbs.
3. Heat oil in a large cast-iron or other heavy skillet over medium heat. Cook meatballs until the meat is no longer pink and the coating is golden brown, 10-12 minutes.
1 MEATBALL: 75 cal., 5g fat (2g sat. fat), 27mg chol., 137mg sod., 2g carb. (0 sugars, 0 fiber), 4g pro.

LOBSTER TARTLETS

LOBSTER TARTLETS

I love lobster, so I created these gems. They are perfect appetizers for a cocktail party or family dinner. You can top them with chives or green onions for color.
—*Lorraine Caland, Shuniah, ON*

Takes: 25 min. • **Makes:** 25 tartlets

- ½ cup shredded white cheddar cheese
- ½ cup shredded provolone cheese
- ½ cup cooked lobster meat
  or 1 can (6½ oz.) flaked canned lobster meat, drained
- ⅓ cup finely chopped sweet red pepper
- 2 Tbsp. finely chopped green onion
  (white portion only)
- 2 Tbsp. mayonnaise
  Dash seafood seasoning
- 2 pkg. (1.9 oz. each) frozen miniature phyllo tart shells
  Paprika, optional

1. Preheat oven to 350°. In a small bowl, combine the first 7 ingredients. Spoon the mixture into tart shells.
2. Place filled shells on an ungreased baking sheet. Bake until shells are lightly browned and filling is heated through, 12-15 minutes. If desired, sprinkle with paprika before serving.
1 TARTLET: 76 cal., 4g fat (1g sat. fat), 8mg chol., 78mg sod., 6g carb. (0 sugars, 0 fiber), 3g pro.

GREEN CHILE
PROSCIUTTO ROLLS

GREEN CHILE PROSCIUTTO ROLLS

I created these for my husband, who adores green chiles. He loves the rolls so much he could eat a whole pan.
—*Paula McHargue, Richmond, KY*

- -

Takes: 25 min. • **Makes:** 14 rolls

1	tube (8 oz.) refrigerated crescent rolls
3	oz. cream cheese, softened
1	can (4 oz.) chopped green chiles, drained
1	Tbsp. sweet hot mustard
½	cup thinly sliced prosciutto, cooked and crumbled
1	large egg, beaten
3	Tbsp. grated Parmesan cheese

1. Preheat oven to 375°. Unroll crescent dough into 1 long rectangle; press the perforations to seal. In a small bowl, beat cream cheese, green chiles and mustard. Spread over dough to within ½ in. of edges. Sprinkle with prosciutto. Roll up left and right long sides toward the center, jelly-roll style, until the rolls meet in the middle. Cut into 1-in. slices.
2. Place slices on a parchment-lined baking sheet. Brush with egg; sprinkle with Parmesan. Bake until golden brown, 12-15 minutes. Top with additional grated Parmesan cheese if desired.
1 ROLL: 98 cal., 6g fat (2g sat. fat), 23mg chol., 258mg sod., 8g carb. (2g sugars, 0 fiber), 3g pro.

LONG ISLAND ICED TEA

Smooth but potent describes this drink. Adjust the tequila to suit your taste. If you like a bold flavor, use an ounce. If you like a more mellow drink, use half an ounce.
—Taste of Home *Test Kitchen*

Takes: 5 min. • **Makes:** 1 serving

- 1 to 1¼ cups ice cubes
- 1 oz. vodka
- ½ to 1 oz. tequila
- 1 oz. light rum
- 1 oz. sour mix
- 1 oz. Triple Sec
- ½ oz. cola
  Lemon slice, optional

Place ice in a Collins or highball glass. Pour the next 6 ingredients into the glass; stir. If desired, garnish with a slice of lemon.

⅔ CUP: 330 cal., 0 fat (0 sat. fat), 0 chol., 3mg sod., 30g carb. (28g sugars, 0 fiber), 0 pro.

Test Kitchen Tips

- If you're serving a crowd, you can make a pitcher of Long Island iced tea by just increasing the quantities.
- To keep things fresh, mix up a batch of liquor starter—the vodka, tequila, rum, sour mix and Triple Sec—and let each guest add the ice and cola to suit their own personal taste.

LONG ISLAND ICED TEA

CHILI-LIME AIR-FRIED CHICKPEAS

Looking for a lighter snack that's still a crowd-pleaser? You've found it! These zesty, crunchy chickpeas will have everyone happily munching.
—*Julie Ruble, Charlotte, NC*

Prep: 10 min. • **Cook:** 20 min. + cooling
Makes: 1 cup

- 1 can (15 oz.) chickpeas or garbanzo beans, rinsed, drained and patted dry
- 1 Tbsp. olive oil
- 1½ tsp. chili powder
- 1 tsp. ground cumin
- ½ tsp. grated lime zest
- 1½ tsp. lime juice
- ¼ tsp. sea salt

1. Preheat air fryer to 400°. Spread the chickpeas in a single layer on greased tray in air-fryer basket, removing any loose skins. Cook until very crunchy, 20-30 minutes, shaking basket every 5 minutes.
2. Meanwhile, whisk together remaining ingredients. Remove chickpeas from the air fryer; let cool 5 minutes. Drizzle with oil mixture; toss to coat. Cool completely.
¼ CUP: 133 cal., 6g fat (0 sat. fat), 0 chol., 287mg sod., 17g carb. (3g sugars, 5g fiber), 4g pro.

BASIL SHRIMP

FAVORITE MARINATED MUSHROOMS

Here's a great way to serve mushrooms as an appetizer. Sometimes I add them to salads for tangy flavor, or serve them as a side dish.
—*Brenda Snyder, Hesston, PA*

- -

Prep: 15 min. + marinating
Makes: 4 cups

- 2 lbs. fresh mushrooms
- 1 envelope (0.7 oz.) Italian salad dressing mix
- 1 cup water
- ½ cup olive oil
- ⅓ cup cider vinegar
- 2 Tbsp. lemon juice
- 1 Tbsp. sugar
- 1 Tbsp. minced fresh parsley
- 1 Tbsp. reduced-sodium soy sauce
- 2 tsp. crushed red pepper flakes
- 3 garlic cloves, minced
- ½ tsp. salt
- ⅛ tsp. pepper

1. Remove mushroom stems (discard or save for another use). Place caps in a large saucepan and cover with water. Bring to a boil. Reduce heat; cook for 3 minutes, stirring occasionally. Drain and cool.

2. In a small bowl, whisk the remaining ingredients. Place the mushrooms in a large bowl; add the dressing and stir to coat. Refrigerate, covered, for 8 hours or overnight.

½ CUP: 166 cal., 14g fat (2g sat. fat), 0 chol., 602mg sod., 9g carb. (5g sugars, 2g fiber), 4g pro.

BASIL SHRIMP

My husband loves shrimp and agrees that nothing beats this incredibly easy, enjoyable dish.
—*Natalie Corona, Maple Grove, MN*

- -

Takes: 30 min. • **Makes:** 2 servings

- 1 Tbsp. minced fresh basil
- 1 Tbsp. olive oil
- 1 Tbsp. butter, melted
- 1 Tbsp. Dijon mustard
- 2 tsp. lemon juice
- 1 garlic clove, minced
  Dash salt and white pepper
- 8 uncooked shrimp (16-20 per lb.), peeled and deveined

1. In a small bowl, combine the basil, oil, butter, mustard, lemon juice, garlic, salt and pepper. Pour 3 Tbsp. mixture into a small shallow dish; set the remaining marinade aside. Add shrimp to dish; turn to coat. Let stand at room temperature 15-20 minutes.

2. Drain shrimp; discard marinade in dish. Thread shrimp onto 2 metal or soaked wooden skewers. Grill, covered, over medium heat until shrimp turn pink, 2-3 minutes on each side, basting occasionally with reserved marinade. If desired, garnish with additional fresh basil.

3 OZ. COOKED SHRIMP: 159 cal., 9g fat (3g sat. fat), 133mg chol., 330mg sod., 1g carb. (0 sugars, 0 fiber), 17g pro.

Test Kitchen Tip

To use frozen shrimp for this recipe, first thaw them. Place shrimp in a colander over a bowl, covered, in the refrigerator overnight. You can also place in a resealable bag, removing as much air as possible. Place the bag in cold water until shrimp are completely thawed, 20-30 minutes, covering with a plate to keep the bag submerged. Pat shrimp dry with paper towels, then peel and devein.

PINEAPPLE SMOOTHIES

I got this recipe over 30 years ago and have been making it ever since. I've tried several diabetic recipes, and this is one of the best.
—*Margery Bryan, Moses Lake, WA*

Prep: 5 min. + freezing
Makes: 5 servings

- 1 can (20 oz.) unsweetened pineapple chunks, undrained
- 1 cup buttermilk
- 2 tsp. vanilla extract
- 2 tsp. sugar or sugar substitute

1. Drain pineapple, reserving ½ cup juice. Freeze pineapple chunks.
2. Place the reserved juice, buttermilk, vanilla, sugar and frozen pineapple in a blender; cover and process until smooth. Serve immediately.
¾ CUP: 96 cal., 0 fat (0 sat. fat), 2mg chol., 93mg sod., 19g carb. (18g sugars, 1g fiber), 3g pro. **DIABETIC EXCHANGES:** 1 starch.

> ### Test Kitchen Tip
> If you're looking to sweeten this recipe but don't want to use sugar, try raw honey or agave nectar. Fruit is naturally sweet, so first try making this smoothie without the sugar and taste to see if you like it—you might find it doesn't need sugar at all!

PIZZA MONKEY BREAD

I cannot throw a party without making this recipe. It's fast and easy, and my kids love it.
—*Courtney Wilson, Fresno, CA*

Prep: 15 min. • **Bake:** 40 min. + cooling
Makes: 16 servings

- ⅓ cup olive oil
- 1 tsp. Italian seasoning
- 1 garlic clove, minced
- ¼ tsp. crushed red pepper flakes
- 2 cans (16.3 oz. each) large refrigerated flaky biscuits (8 count)
- 2 cups shredded part-skim mozzarella cheese
- ¼ cup grated Parmesan cheese
- 20 slices pepperoni, halved
- ½ cup marinara sauce

1. Preheat the oven to 350°. In a large microwave-safe bowl, combine the first 4 ingredients; microwave, covered, on high for 30 seconds. Cool slightly.
2. Cut each biscuit into 4 pieces; add to the oil mixture and toss to coat. Add the cheeses and pepperoni; toss to combine. In a heavy 10-in. fluted tube pan coated with cooking spray, layer half the biscuit mixture; drizzle with ¼ cup marinara sauce. Repeat layers.
3. Bake for 40 minutes or until golden brown. Cool in pan for 10 minutes. Run a knife around sides and center tube of pan. Invert onto a serving plate. Serve with additional marinara sauce, warmed. If desired, top with additional grated Parmesan cheese and red pepper flakes.
1 SERVING: 288 cal., 17g fat (5g sat. fat), 12mg chol., 723mg sod., 26g carb. (6g sugars, 1g fiber), 8g pro.

PIZZA MONKEY BREAD

2

Breakfast & Brunch

Rise and shine! Streamlining kitchen time doesn't mean skipping the most important meal of the day. Turn here when you need a hot and hearty breakfast or an impressive brunch-buffet addition. Not sure what to make for supper? Consider these dishes for a breakfast-for-dinner surprise.

OAT
WAFFLES P. 59

APPLE-CINNAMON
BAKED FRENCH TOAST

APPLE-CINNAMON BAKED FRENCH TOAST

When my wife and I hosted a breakfast for our church group, we wanted to avoid the last-minute rush of cooking. So we decided to try this make-ahead French toast. Everyone loved it and requested the recipe.
—*John Cashen, Moline, IL*

Prep: 20 min. + chilling • **Bake:** 45 min.
Makes: 6 servings

- 12 slices day-old French bread (¾ in. thick)
- 6 large eggs, lightly beaten
- 2¾ cups 2% milk
- ⅔ cup sugar, divided
- 1 Tbsp. vanilla extract
- 4 medium apples, peeled and thinly sliced
- 2 tsp. ground cinnamon
- ¾ tsp. ground nutmeg
- 1 Tbsp. butter
  Optional: Whipped cream and maple syrup

1. Arrange 6 slices bread in a greased 13x9-in. baking dish. Combine eggs, milk, ⅓ cup sugar and vanilla; pour half over the bread. Top with apples. Combine cinnamon, nutmeg and the remaining ⅓ cup sugar; sprinkle over apples. Top with the remaining bread slices; pour remaining egg mixture over the bread. Dot with butter. Cover and refrigerate 8 hours or overnight.
2. Remove from refrigerator 30 minutes before baking. Preheat the oven to 350°. Bake, uncovered, until a knife inserted in center comes out clean, 45-50 minutes. Let stand for 5 minutes before serving. If desired, serve with whipped cream and syrup.

1 PIECE: 378 cal., 10g fat (5g sat. fat), 200mg chol., 352mg sod., 58g carb. (37g sugars, 3g fiber), 13g pro.

BACON & EGG GRAVY

BACON & EGG GRAVY

My husband, Ron, created this wonderful homestyle breakfast gravy. Sometimes we ladle the gravy over homemade biscuits. Served with fruit salad, it's an excellent breakfast.
—*Terry Bray, Winter Haven, FL*

Takes: 20 min. • **Makes:** 2 servings

- 6 bacon strips, diced
- 5 Tbsp. all-purpose flour
- 1½ cups water
- 1 can (12 oz.) evaporated milk
- 3 hard-boiled large eggs, sliced
  Salt and pepper to taste
- 4 slices bread, toasted

In a skillet, cook bacon over medium heat until crisp; remove to paper towels. Stir flour into the drippings until blended; cook over medium heat until browned, stirring constantly. Gradually add the water and milk. Bring to a boil; cook and stir for 2 minutes or until thickened. Add bacon, eggs, salt and pepper. Serve over toast.

1 SERVING: 905 cal., 55g fat (23g sat. fat), 396mg chol., 1066mg sod., 59g carb. (22g sugars, 2g fiber), 38g pro.

Test Kitchen Tips

- A roux is the combination of fat and flour used to thicken sauces. In this case, bacon grease is used with the flour to thicken the gravy, but you may also find butter or oil as the fat in other roux recipes.

- Bacon grease lends a savory flavor to a roux. If you'd like to save clean bacon grease to use for a future roux, refrigerate it. You can also use it to grease a casserole dish or season vegetables before baking. Try brushing some onto bread slices when making a grilled cheese sandwich.

QUICK STOVETOP
GRANOLA

PECAN PUMPKIN BISCUITS

Our two daughters love munching on these rich, pecan-studded biscuits for breakfast. I make dozens and serve them piping-hot with butter and honey.
—*Connie Bolton, San Antonio, TX*

Takes: 30 min. • **Makes:** 1 dozen

- 2   cups all-purpose flour
- ¼   cup sugar
- 4   tsp. baking powder
- ½   tsp. salt
- ½   tsp. ground cinnamon
- ½   tsp. ground nutmeg
- ½   cup cold butter
- ⅓   cup chopped pecans, toasted
- ⅔   cup canned pumpkin
- ⅓   cup half-and-half cream
      Optional: Melted butter and cinnamon sugar

1. In a large bowl, combine the first 6 ingredients. Cut in the butter until mixture resembles coarse crumbs. Stir in pecans. Combine the pumpkin and cream; stir into dry ingredients. Turn onto a floured surface; knead 4-6 times. Roll to ½-in. thickness; cut with a 2½-in. biscuit cutter.
2. Place on a greased baking sheet. Bake at 400° for 12-15 minutes or until golden brown. Serve warm, with melted butter and cinnamon sugar if desired.
1 BISCUIT: 194 cal., 11g fat (5g sat. fat), 24mg chol., 313mg sod., 22g carb. (5g sugars, 1g fiber), 3g pro.

QUICK STOVETOP GRANOLA

The fiber-rich oats in this granola will quell your cravings with just a small serving. Always keep some handy in an airtight container for times when your stomach growls. For an even longer-lasting satisfaction, pair the treat with protein-packed yogurt.
—*Taste of Home Test Kitchen*

Takes: 15 min. • **Makes:** 3 cups

- 2   cups quick-cooking oats
- 2   Tbsp. brown sugar
- 2   Tbsp. honey
- 1   Tbsp. butter
- ¼   cup slivered almonds
- 2   Tbsp. golden raisins
- 2   Tbsp. sweetened shredded coconut

1. In a large nonstick skillet, toast oats over medium heat until golden brown. Remove and set aside. In the same skillet, cook and stir the brown sugar, honey and butter over medium-low heat until bubbly, 1-2 minutes.
2. Stir in the almonds, raisins, coconut and oats until coated. Cool. Store in an airtight container.
¼ CUP: 102 cal., 3g fat (1g sat. fat), 3mg chol., 14mg sod., 16g carb. (6g sugars, 2g fiber), 3g pro. **DIABETIC EXCHANGES:** 1 starch, ½ fat.

PECAN PUMPKIN
BISCUITS

BLUEBERRY CANTALOUPE SALAD

BLUEBERRY CANTALOUPE SALAD

Add a fresh touch to any meal with these cute cups. The simple citrus dressing really jazzes up the fruit.
—*R. Jean Rand, Edina, MN*

- -

Takes: 10 min. • **Makes:** 4 servings

- ¾ cup orange yogurt
- 1½ tsp. lemon juice
- ¾ tsp. poppy seeds
- ½ tsp. grated orange zest
- 2 cups diced cantaloupe
- 1 cup fresh blueberries

In a bowl, mix yogurt, lemon juice, poppy seeds and orange zest. To serve, divide cantaloupe and blueberries among 4 dishes; top with yogurt dressing.

¾ CUP WITH 3 TBSP. DRESSING: 76 cal., 1g fat (0 sat. fat), 1mg chol., 24mg sod., 17g carb. (15g sugars, 1g fiber), 2g pro. **DIABETIC EXCHANGES:** 1 fruit.

Test Kitchen Tip

Blueberries contain more antioxidants than just about any other fruit. Eating them raw helps ensure you get all those benefits, so add them to salads and other recipes that don't require baking or cooking.

GINGERBREAD COFFEE CAKE

At our house, we love gingerbread that's not too sweet. If you like things a bit sweeter, however, mix confectioners' sugar, milk and vanilla extract for an icing to drizzle on top.
—*Barbara Humiston, Tampa, FL*

Prep: 20 min. • **Bake:** 20 min. + cooling
Makes: 8 servings

- 1 cup all-purpose flour
- ½ cup plus 1 Tbsp. sugar, divided
- 1¾ tsp. ground cinnamon, divided
- 1 tsp. ground ginger
- ¼ tsp. salt
- ¼ tsp. ground allspice
- ¼ cup cold butter
- ¾ tsp. baking powder
- ½ tsp. baking soda
- 1 large egg, room temperature
- ½ cup buttermilk
- 2 Tbsp. molasses

1. Preheat oven to 350°. In a large bowl, mix flour, ½ cup sugar, ¾ tsp. cinnamon, ginger, salt and allspice; cut in the butter until crumbly. Reserve ⅓ cup for topping.
2. Stir baking powder and baking soda into the remaining flour mixture. In a small bowl, whisk egg, buttermilk and molasses. Add to the flour mixture; stir just until moistened. Transfer batter to a greased 8-in. round baking pan.
3. Add remaining 1 Tbsp. sugar and 1 tsp. cinnamon to reserved topping; sprinkle over batter. Bake 20-25 minutes or until a toothpick inserted in the center comes out clean. Cool completely in pan on a wire rack.

1 PIECE: 195 cal., 7g fat (4g sat. fat), 39mg chol., 283mg sod., 31g carb. (19g sugars, 1g fiber), 3g pro. **DIABETIC EXCHANGES:** 2 starch, 1½ fat.

OPTIONAL VANILLA ICING AND GINGER TOPPING: Mix ¾ cup confectioners' sugar, 1 Tbsp. 2% milk and ½ tsp. vanilla extract. Drizzle over cooled cake. Sprinkle with 2 Tbsp. finely chopped crystallized ginger.

CINNAMON
BREAKFAST BITES

CINNAMON BREAKFAST BITES

These quick early-morning treats with a sweet, crispy coating are baked in the oven instead of deep-fried.
—*Ruth Hastings, Louisville, IL*

Takes: 30 min. • **Makes:** 1½ dozen

- 1⅓ cups all-purpose flour
- 1 cup crisp rice cereal, coarsely crushed
- 2 Tbsp. plus ½ cup sugar, divided
- 1 Tbsp. baking powder
- ½ tsp. salt
- ¼ cup butter-flavored shortening
- ½ cup 2% milk
- 1 tsp. ground cinnamon
- ¼ cup butter, melted

1. Preheat oven to 425°. In a large bowl, combine the flour, cereal, 2 Tbsp. sugar, baking powder and salt; cut in shortening until mixture resembles coarse crumbs. Stir in milk just until moistened. Shape into 1-in. balls.
2. In a shallow bowl, combine the remaining ½ cup sugar and cinnamon. Dip balls in the melted butter, then roll in the cinnamon-sugar mix.
3. Arrange balls in a single layer in an 8-in. cast-iron skillet or round baking pan. Bake until browned and a toothpick inserted in centers comes out clean, 15-18 minutes.

1 PIECE: 118 cal., 5g fat (2g sat. fat), 7mg chol., 178mg sod., 16g carb. (8g sugars, 0 fiber), 1g pro.

"My entire family loved these! I will definitely be making them again soon."
—JERRYSELENA, TASTEOFHOME.COM

BREAKFAST ENCHILADAS

BREAKFAST ENCHILADAS

Draped in gooey cheese and a savory sauce, these enchiladas are a popular option at any brunch. Chorizo gives the hearty filling a southwestern kick.
—*Tahnia Fox, Trenton, MI*

Prep: 25 min. • **Bake:** 25 min.
Makes: 8 enchiladas

- ½ lb. uncooked chorizo or spicy pork sausage
- 1 small onion, finely chopped
- ½ medium green pepper, finely chopped
- 2 tsp. butter
- 6 large eggs, beaten
- ¾ cup shredded cheddar cheese, divided
- ¾ cup shredded pepper Jack cheese, divided
- 1 can (10 oz.) enchilada sauce
- 8 flour tortillas (6 in.), room temperature
- 1 green onion, finely chopped

1. Preheat oven to 350°. Crumble chorizo into a large skillet; add the onion and green pepper. Cook over medium heat for 6-8 minutes or until the sausage is fully cooked; drain.

2. In another skillet, heat butter over medium heat. Add the eggs; cook and stir until almost set. Remove from the heat; stir in the chorizo mixture and ⅓ cup each cheddar and pepper Jack.

3. Spread ½ cup enchilada sauce into a greased 11x7-in. baking dish. Spoon 3 Tbsp. egg mixture down the center of each tortilla. Roll up and place seam side down in prepared baking dish.

4. Pour remaining enchilada sauce over the top; sprinkle with remaining cheeses.

5. Bake, uncovered, for 25-30 minutes or until heated through. Sprinkle with green onion.

1 ENCHILADA: 369 cal., 23g fat (10g sat. fat), 189mg chol., 1028mg sod., 20g carb. (2g sugars, 1g fiber), 20g pro.

AUNT EDITH'S BAKED PANCAKE

My aunt made a mighty breakfast that revolved around a really big pancake. I always enjoyed watching as she poured the batter into her huge iron skillet, then baked the confection to perfection in the oven.
—*Marion Kirst, Troy, MI*

Prep: 15 min. • **Bake:** 20 min.
Makes: 4 servings

- 3 large eggs, room temperature
- ½ tsp. salt
- ½ cup all-purpose flour
- ½ cup 2% milk
- 2 Tbsp. butter, softened
  Confectioners' sugar
  Lemon wedges

1. Preheat oven to 450°. In a bowl, beat eggs until very light. Add salt, flour and milk; beat well. Thoroughly rub bottom and sides of a 10-in. cast-iron or other heavy ovenproof skillet with butter. Pour batter into skillet.

2. Bake for 15 minutes. Reduce heat to 350° and bake until set, 5 minutes longer. If desired, remove pancake from skillet and place on a large hot platter. Dust with confectioners' sugar and serve immediately, with lemon wedges on side.

1 PIECE: 180 cal., 10g fat (5g sat. fat), 158mg chol., 407mg sod., 14g carb. (2g sugars, 0 fiber), 7g pro.

AUNT EDITH'S BAKED PANCAKE

PUMPKIN CHEESE COFFEE CAKE

PUMPKIN CHEESE COFFEE CAKE

This is one of my favorite recipes, especially in autumn. It is much easier to make than a traditional pumpkin roll—and it's always a crowd-pleaser!
—*Carlene Jessop, Hildale, UT*

Prep: 15 min. • **Bake:** 35 min.
Makes: 15 servings

- 2 cups sugar
- 2 large eggs
- 1¼ cups canned pumpkin
- ¼ cup canola oil
- ½ tsp. vanilla extract
- 2¼ cups all-purpose flour
- 2 tsp. ground cinnamon
- 1 tsp. baking soda
- ½ tsp. salt

FILLING
- 1 pkg. (8 oz.) cream cheese, softened
- 1 large egg
- 1 Tbsp. sugar

TOPPING
- ¾ cup sweetened shredded coconut
- ½ cup chopped pecans
- ¼ cup packed brown sugar
- ¼ tsp. ground cinnamon

1. Preheat oven to 350°. In a large bowl, beat sugar, eggs, pumpkin, oil and vanilla. Combine flour, cinnamon, baking soda and salt; add to the egg mixture and mix well. Pour into a greased 13x9-in. baking dish.
2. In a small bowl, beat the cream cheese, egg and sugar until smooth. Drop by tablespoonfuls over the batter; cut through batter with a knife to swirl. Combine topping ingredients; sprinkle over top. Bake for 35-40 minutes or until a toothpick inserted in the center comes out clean. Cool on a wire rack.
1 PIECE: 344 cal., 15g fat (6g sat. fat), 59mg chol., 234mg sod., 50g carb. (33g sugars, 2g fiber), 5g pro.

SHEEPHERDER'S BREAKFAST

My sister-in-law would always make this delicious breakfast dish when we were camping. Served with toast, juice, and milk or coffee, it's a sure hit with the breakfast crowd. One-dish casseroles like this were a big help while I was raising my nine children, and now I've passed this recipe on to them.
—*Pauletta Bushnell, Albany, OR*

Takes: 30 min. • **Makes:** 8 servings

- ¾ lb. bacon strips, finely chopped
- 1 medium onion, chopped
- 1 pkg. (30 oz.) frozen shredded hash brown potatoes, thawed
- 8 large eggs
- ½ tsp. salt
- ¼ tsp. pepper
- 1 cup shredded cheddar cheese

1. In a large skillet, cook bacon and onion over medium heat until bacon is crisp. Drain, reserving ¼ cup drippings in pan.
2. Stir in hash browns. Cook, uncovered, over medium heat until the bottom is golden brown, about 10 minutes. Turn potatoes. With the back of a spoon, make 8 evenly spaced wells in the potato mixture. Carefully break 1 egg into each well. Sprinkle with salt and pepper.
3. Cook, covered, on low until eggs are set and potatoes are tender, about 10 minutes. Sprinkle with cheese; let stand until cheese is melted.
1 SERVING: 354 cal., 22g fat (9g sat. fat), 222mg chol., 617mg sod., 22g carb. (2g sugars, 1g fiber), 17g pro.

Test Kitchen Tip

This top-rated breakfast recipe can easily be adjusted to suit your taste. Feel free to use country pork sausage instead of bacon, or make it vegetarian by eliminating the meat and replacing the bacon drippings with oil or butter.

SHEEPHERDER'S
BREAKFAST

BLUEBERRY CREAM MUFFINS

When most people think of Maine, they immediately think of lobster. But we who live here know of something equally as good: wild blueberries. Their flavor is unmatched, and they're especially enjoyable in these blueberry muffins with sour cream.
—*Lillian Van der Harst, Center Lovell, ME*

Prep: 15 min. • **Bake:** 20 min.
Makes: 2 dozen

- 4 large eggs
- 2 cups sugar
- 1 cup canola oil
- 1 tsp. vanilla extract
- 4 cups all-purpose flour
- 1 tsp. salt
- 1 tsp. baking soda
- 2 tsp. baking powder
- 2 cups sour cream
- 2 cups fresh blueberries

1. Preheat oven to 400°. In a bowl, beat eggs. Gradually add sugar. While beating, slowly pour in oil; add vanilla. Combine the next 4 ingredients; add alternately with the sour cream to the egg mixture. Gently fold in blueberries.
2. Fill 24 greased muffin cups three-fourths full. Bake until a toothpick inserted in center comes out clean, 18-20 minutes. Cool 5 minutes before removing from pans to wire racks.
1 MUFFIN: 282 cal., 14g fat (4g sat. fat), 45mg chol., 210mg sod., 35g carb. (19g sugars, 1g fiber), 4g pro.

BUFFET SCRAMBLED EGGS
My favorite scrambled eggs! The white sauce flavored with chicken bouillon keeps the eggs creamy and moist. It's a tasty twist on a morning mainstay.
—*Elsie Beachy, Plain City, OH*

- -

Takes: 20 min. • **Makes:** 8 servings

8 Tbsp. butter, divided
¼ cup all-purpose flour
2 cups whole milk
4 tsp. chicken bouillon granules
16 large eggs, lightly beaten
  Optional: Minced fresh parsley, tarragon and chives

1. In a small saucepan, melt 2 Tbsp. butter. Stir in the flour until smooth. Gradually add the milk and bouillon. Bring to a boil; cook and stir until thickened, about 2 minutes.
2. In a large skillet, melt the remaining 6 Tbsp. butter. Add the eggs; cook over medium heat until eggs begin to set, stirring occasionally. Stir in the white sauce. Cook until eggs are completely set. If desired, sprinkle with parsley, tarragon and chives.
¾ CUP: 304 cal., 24g fat (11g sat. fat), 464mg chol., 692mg sod., 7g carb. (4g sugars, 0 fiber), 15g pro.

COLORFUL BRUNCH FRITTATA
A friend called and asked me for a special recipe he could serve at his daughter's wedding brunch. I created this recipe for the occasion, and he loved it. Loaded with colorful veggies, the dish looks beautiful on a buffet.
—*Kristin Arnett, Elkhorn, WI*

- -

Prep: 15 min. • **Bake:** 50 min. + standing
Makes: 12 servings

1 lb. fresh asparagus, trimmed and cut into 1-in. pieces
½ lb. sliced fresh mushrooms
1 medium sweet red pepper, diced
1 medium sweet yellow pepper, diced
1 small onion, chopped
3 green onions, chopped
3 Tbsp. olive oil
2 garlic cloves, minced
3 plum tomatoes, seeded and chopped
14 large eggs, lightly beaten
2 cups half-and-half cream
2 cups shredded Colby-Monterey Jack cheese
3 Tbsp. minced fresh parsley
3 Tbsp. minced fresh basil
½ tsp. salt
¼ tsp. pepper
½ cup shredded Parmesan cheese

1. Preheat oven to 350°. In a large skillet, saute asparagus, mushrooms, peppers and onions in oil until tender. Add garlic; cook 1 minute longer. Add the tomatoes; set aside.
2. In a large bowl, whisk eggs, cream, Colby-Monterey Jack cheese, parsley, basil, salt and pepper; stir into the vegetable mixture.
3. Pour into a greased 13x9-in. baking dish. Bake, uncovered, 45 minutes.
4. Sprinkle with Parmesan cheese. Bake 5 minutes longer or until a knife inserted in the center comes out clean. Let stand 10 minutes before cutting.
1 PIECE: 270 cal., 19g fat (10g sat. fat), 256mg chol., 377mg sod., 7g carb. (4g sugars, 1g fiber), 16g pro.

COLORFUL BRUNCH FRITTATA

Place 2 cups **unseasoned croutons** and 1 cup **shredded cheddar cheese** in a greased 11-x-7-in. baking dish. Combine 4 **large eggs**, 2 cups **2% milk**, ½ tsp. **salt**, ½ tsp. **ground mustard**, ⅛ tsp. **onion powder** and a dash **pepper**; pour into baking dish. Sprinkle with 4 strips cooked crumbled **bacon**. Bake at 325° for 1 hour or until set.

- Brunch Egg Casserole -

This meal-in-one dish makes breakfast a snap. It's perfect for overnight guests, busy holiday mornings or any time you need an easy, hearty fix early in the day.

PM

BROCCOLI & CHICKEN CHEESE STRATA

On our dairy farm, chores often delay dinner. That's when this strata comes in handy. I'll prepare it beforehand and later pop it in the oven for a quick and easy meal. Breakfast-for-dinner ease!
—*Margery Moore, Richfield Springs, NY*

Prep: 15 min. + chilling • **Bake:** 1 hour
Makes: 8 servings

- 12 slices bread
- 2¼ cups shredded cheddar cheese, divided
- 3 cups frozen chopped broccoli, thawed and drained
- 2 cups diced cooked chicken
- 1 Tbsp. butter, melted
- 6 large eggs
- 3 cups 2% milk
- 2 Tbsp. finely chopped onion
- ¾ tsp. salt
- ½ tsp. ground mustard
- ¼ tsp. pepper

1. Using a doughnut cutter, cut 12 rings and holes from the bread; set aside. Tear the remaining bread scraps and place in a greased 13x9-in. baking dish. Sprinkle with 2 cups cheese, broccoli and chicken. Arrange bread rings and holes on top; brush with melted butter.
2. Whisk together the remaining 6 ingredients; pour over top. Refrigerate, covered, for 8 hours or overnight.
3. Remove strata from the refrigerator 30 minutes before baking. Preheat oven to 325°. Bake, uncovered, 55-60 minutes. Sprinkle with remaining ¼ cup cheese; bake until a knife inserted in the center comes out clean, about 5 minutes longer. Let stand 5-10 minutes before cutting.
1 PIECE: 440 cal., 22g fat (10g sat. fat), 213mg chol., 794mg sod., 30g carb. (8g sugars, 3g fiber), 31g pro.

CARAMEL BUBBLE RING

Lots of caramel topping make this quick pull-apart bread oh so gooey and delicious. It truly is a finger-lickin' good baked treat.
—*Laura Clifton, Wenatchee, WA*

Prep: 15 min. • **Bake:** 20 min.
Makes: 16 servings

- ¾ cup sugar
- 4 tsp. ground cinnamon
- ½ cup caramel ice cream topping
- 2 Tbsp. maple syrup
- ⅓ cup chopped pecans, divided
- 2 tubes (11 oz. each) refrigerated breadsticks
- ⅓ cup butter, melted

1. Preheat oven to 350°. Combine sugar and cinnamon; set aside. Combine the caramel topping and syrup; set aside. Sprinkle half the pecans into a greased 10-in. fluted tube pan. Drizzle with a third of the caramel mixture.
2. Open the tubes of breadstick dough (do not unroll). Cut each into 6 slices; dip each slice in melted butter, then roll in cinnamon sugar. Place half in the pan; sprinkle with remaining pecans. Drizzle with half the remaining caramel mixture. Top with remaining dough. Drizzle with remaining caramel mixture.
3. Bake for 20-25 minutes or until golden brown. Cool for 2 minutes. Invert onto a serving platter; serve warm.
1 SERVING: 176 cal., 7g fat (3g sat. fat), 10mg chol., 220mg sod., 28g carb. (18g sugars, 1g fiber), 2g pro.

CARAMEL BUBBLE RING

BACON-CHEESE
PUFF PIE

CORNED BEEF HASH & EGGS

Sunday breakfasts have always been special in our house. It's fun to get in the kitchen and cook with the kids. No matter how many new recipes we try, the kids always rate this No. 1!
—*Rick Skildum, Maple Grove, MN*

Prep: 15 min. • **Bake:** 20 min.
Makes: 8 servings

- 1 pkg. (32 oz.) frozen cubed hash browns
- 1½ cups chopped onion
- ½ cup canola oil
- 4 to 5 cups chopped cooked corned beef
- ½ tsp. salt
- 8 large eggs
  Salt and pepper to taste
- 2 Tbsp. minced fresh parsley

1. Preheat the oven to 325°. In a large ovenproof skillet, cook hash browns and onion in oil until potatoes are browned and onion is tender. Remove from the heat; stir in the corned beef and salt.
2. Make 8 wells in the hash browns. Carefully break 1 egg into each well. Sprinkle with salt and pepper. Bake, covered, for 20-25 minutes or until the eggs reach desired doneness. Garnish with parsley.
1 SERVING: 442 cal., 30g fat (6g sat. fat), 242mg chol., 895mg sod., 24g carb. (3g sugars, 2g fiber), 20g pro.

Test Kitchen Tip

You can make corned beef hash and eggs without an ovenproof skillet. Instead of transferring the pan to the oven after cracking the eggs into the hash, keep it on the stovetop. Simply put a lid on it and cook until the egg whites are set and the yolks reach the desired doneness.

BACON-CHEESE PUFF PIE

This recipe comes from my grandma, and it's one of my family's favorites—we love the combination of bacon, tomatoes and cheese. It's outstanding for brunch at any time of year.
—*Sherry Lee, Sheridan, IN*

Prep: 20 min. + cooling • **Bake:** 45 min.
Makes: 6 servings

- 1 pie crust, unbaked
- 1 lb. sliced bacon, cooked and crumbled
- 1 large tomato, peeled and sliced
- 1 cup shredded cheddar cheese
- 3 large eggs, separated
- ¾ cup sour cream
- ½ cup all-purpose flour
- ½ tsp. salt
  Paprika

1. Preheat oven to 450°. Line unpricked pie crust with a double thickness of heavy-duty foil. Bake for 5 minutes. Remove foil. Bake 5 minutes longer. Cool completely.
2. Sprinkle bacon over the crust. Top with tomato and cheese. In a large bowl, beat the egg yolks, sour cream, flour and salt until smooth. In another large bowl, beat the egg whites until stiff. Fold into sour cream mixture; spread over the cheese. Sprinkle with the paprika.
3. Bake at 350° until a knife inserted in the center comes out clean, about 45 minutes. Let stand 5-10 minutes before cutting.
1 PIECE: 518 cal., 35g fat (17g sat. fat), 176mg chol., 901mg sod., 29g carb. (4g sugars, 1g fiber), 19g pro.

CORNED BEEF HASH
& EGGS

FESTIVE
FRENCH PANCAKES

FESTIVE FRENCH PANCAKES

Not quite as thin as true crepes, these light-as-a-feather pancakes are topped with preserves and a sweet dusting of confectioners' sugar. So easy to make, they have an elegant and delicious French flair!
—*Diane Aune, Nine Mile Falls, WA*

Takes: 15 min. • **Makes:** 4 servings

- ⅔ cup 2% milk
- 2 large eggs
- ⅓ cup water
- ½ tsp. vanilla extract
- ¾ cup all-purpose flour
- 2 Tbsp. confectioners' sugar
- 1 tsp. baking powder
- ½ tsp. salt
  Preserves of your choice, optional

1. In a blender, combine the milk, eggs, water and vanilla; cover and process until well blended. Combine the flour, confectioners' sugar, baking powder and salt; add to egg mixture. Cover and process until smooth.
2. Heat a lightly greased 8-in. nonstick skillet over medium heat; pour 2 Tbsp. batter into the center of the skillet. Lift and tilt the pan to coat bottom evenly. Cook until top appears dry; turn and cook 15-20 seconds longer. Remove to a wire rack.
3. Repeat with the remaining batter, greasing skillet as needed. If desired, spread preserves over crepes; roll up. Sprinkle with additional confectioners' sugar if desired.
2 CREPES: 158 cal., 3g fat (1g sat. fat), 96mg chol., 470mg sod., 24g carb. (6g sugars, 1g fiber), 7g pro. **DIABETIC EXCHANGES:** 1½ starch, 1 medium-fat meat.

HAM & EGG POCKETS

Refrigerated crescent roll dough makes these savory breakfast pockets a snap to prepare.
—Taste of Home *Test Kitchen*

Takes: 20 min. • **Makes:** 2 pockets

- 1 large egg
- 2 tsp. 2% milk
- 2 tsp. butter
- 1 oz. thinly sliced deli ham, chopped
- 2 Tbsp. shredded cheddar cheese
- 1 tube (4 oz.) refrigerated crescent rolls

1. Preheat oven to 375°. In a small bowl, combine egg and milk. In a small skillet heat butter until hot. Add egg mixture; cook and stir over medium heat until egg is completely set. Remove from the heat. Fold in ham and cheese.
2. On a greased baking sheet, separate the crescent dough into 2 rectangles. Seal perforations; spoon half the filling down the center of each rectangle. Fold in ends and sides; pinch to seal. Bake until golden brown, 10-14 minutes.
1 POCKET: 345 cal., 22g fat (8g sat. fat), 132mg chol., 756mg sod., 23g carb. (5g sugars, 0 fiber), 12g pro.

HAM & EGG POCKETS

EARLY-RISER
OVEN OMELET

EARLY RISER OVEN OMELET

Everyone will rush to the table when you serve this big fluffy omelet. Packed with tomato, broccoli, ham and cheese, it makes a hearty brunch dish that easily serves a crowd.
—*Wendy Fawcett, Gillam, MB*

Prep: 15 min. • **Bake:** 35 min.
Makes: 6 servings

- 10 large egg whites
- 5 large eggs
- 1 cup fat-free milk
- ¼ tsp. seasoned salt
- ¼ tsp. pepper
- 1½ cups cubed fully cooked ham
- 1 cup chopped fresh broccoli
- 1 cup shredded reduced-fat cheddar cheese
- 1 medium tomato, seeded and chopped
- 3 Tbsp. finely chopped onion

1. In a bowl, beat egg whites, eggs, milk, seasoned salt and pepper. Pour into a greased 10-in. cast-iron or other ovenproof skillet. Sprinkle with ham, broccoli, cheese, tomato and onion.
2. Bake, uncovered, at 350° until the eggs are almost set, 30-35 minutes. Broil 4-6 in. from the heat until the eggs are set and top is lightly browned, 1-2 minutes.
1 PIECE: 216 cal., 10g fat (4g sat. fat), 183mg chol., 805mg sod., 6g carb. (4g sugars, 1g fiber), 25g pro. **DIABETIC EXCHANGES:** 3 medium-fat meat, 1 vegetable.

OAT WAFFLES

These family favorites have more fiber and less fat than standard waffles. My 2-year-old daughter loves them with fresh berries.
—*Karen Hayes, Danville, VA*

Takes: 10 min.
Makes: 8 servings

- 1 cup all-purpose flour
- 1 cup oat flour
- 4 tsp. baking powder
- 1 Tbsp. sugar
- ½ tsp. salt
- 2 large eggs
- 1¾ cups fat-free milk
- 2 Tbsp. canola oil
- 1 tsp. vanilla extract
  Optional: Fresh fruit, maple syrup and powdered sugar

1. In a large bowl, combine the first 5 ingredients. In another bowl, combine the eggs, milk, oil and vanilla; stir into the dry ingredients just until combined.
2. Pour the batter by ½ cupfuls into a preheated waffle maker; bake according to manufacturer's directions until golden brown. Garnish with toppings as desired.
1 WAFFLE: 178 cal., 6g fat (1g sat. fat), 54mg chol., 307mg sod., 24g carb. (0 sugars, 2g fiber), 7g pro. **DIABETIC EXCHANGES:** 1½ starch, 1 lean meat.

Test Kitchen Tip

As a substitute for 1 cup oat flour, you can process 1¼ cups quick-cooking or old-fashioned oats until finely ground.

OAT WAFFLES

MUSHROOM ASPARAGUS QUICHE

❄ MUSHROOM ASPARAGUS QUICHE

Loads of asparagus pieces add color and flavor to this hearty, creamy quiche. And the easy crescent roll crust means you'll have breakfast ready in a snap!
—*Sharon Fujita, Fontana, CA*

- -

Prep: 20 min. • **Bake:** 25 min. + standing
Makes: 8 servings

- 1 tube (8 oz.) refrigerated crescent rolls
- 2 tsp. prepared mustard
- 1½ lbs. fresh asparagus, trimmed and cut into ½-in. pieces
- 1 medium onion, chopped
- ½ cup sliced fresh mushrooms
- ¼ cup butter, cubed
- 2 large eggs, lightly beaten
- 2 cups shredded part-skim mozzarella cheese
- ½ tsp. salt
- ½ tsp. pepper
- ¼ tsp. garlic powder
- ¼ tsp. each dried basil, oregano, parsley and rubbed sage

1. Preheat oven to 375°. Separate the crescent dough into 8 triangles. Place in an ungreased 9-in. pie plate with points toward the center. Press dough onto the bottom and up the sides to form a crust; seal perforations. Spread with mustard; set aside.
2. In a large skillet, saute asparagus, onion and mushrooms in butter until asparagus is crisp-tender. In a large bowl, combine remaining ingredients; stir in the asparagus mixture. Pour into crust.
3. Bake for 25-30 minutes or until a knife inserted in the center comes out clean. Let stand for 10 minutes before cutting.
FREEZE OPTION: Cover and freeze the unbaked quiche. To use, remove from freezer 30 minutes before baking (do not thaw). Place quiche on a baking sheet; cover edge loosely with foil. Bake as directed, increasing time as necessary for a knife inserted in the center to come out clean.
1 PIECE: 272 cal., 18g fat (8g sat. fat), 84mg chol., 580mg sod., 16g carb. (5g sugars, 1g fiber), 12g pro.

CINNAMON SWIRL QUICK BREAD

While cinnamon bread is a natural for breakfast, we love it any time of the day. This one is a nice twist on traditional cinnamon swirl yeast breads.
—*Helen Richardson, Shelbyville, MI*

- -

Prep: 15 min. • **Bake:** 45 min. + cooling
Makes: 16 pieces

- 2 cups all-purpose flour
- 1½ cups sugar, divided
- 1 tsp. baking soda
- ½ tsp. salt
- 1 cup buttermilk
- 1 large egg, room temperature
- ¼ cup canola oil
- 3 tsp. ground cinnamon

GLAZE
- ¼ cup confectioners' sugar
- 1½ to 2 tsp. 2% milk

1. Preheat oven to 350°. In a large bowl, combine flour, 1 cup sugar, baking soda and salt. Combine buttermilk, egg and oil; stir into dry ingredients just until moistened. In a small bowl, combine cinnamon and remaining ½ cup sugar.
2. Grease only the bottom of a 9x5-in. loaf pan. Pour half the batter into pan; sprinkle with half the cinnamon sugar. Carefully spread with the remaining batter and sprinkle with the remaining cinnamon sugar; cut through the batter with a knife to swirl.
3. Bake for 45-50 minutes or until a toothpick inserted in the center comes out clean. Let cool for 10 minutes before removing from pan to a wire rack to cool completely.
4. For the glaze, combine confectioners' sugar and enough milk to reach desired consistency; drizzle over cooled loaf.
1 PIECE: 179 cal., 4g fat (1g sat. fat), 14mg chol., 173mg sod., 34g carb. (21g sugars, 1g fiber), 3g pro.

CINNAMON SWIRL
QUICK BREAD

HAM & SWISS
BREAD PUDDING

HAM & SWISS BREAD PUDDING

This rich and hearty brunch dish is loaded with ham, mushrooms and cheese, plus layers of French bread. It's a terrific choice for when you have overnight guests.
—*Kelly Williams, Forked River, NJ*

Prep: 30 min. • **Bake:** 50 min.
Makes: 9 servings

¼   cup plus 3 Tbsp. butter, melted, divided
18 slices day-old French bread (¾ in. thick)
½   cup stone-ground mustard
1½ cups cubed fully cooked ham
1   cup sliced fresh mushrooms
2   garlic cloves, minced
¼   cup chopped green onions
2   cups shredded Swiss cheese
8   large eggs
4   cups heavy whipping cream
½   tsp. salt
½   tsp. pepper
2   Tbsp. minced fresh parsley
    Warm maple syrup, optional

1. Preheat oven to 325°. Pour ¼ cup melted butter into a 13x9-in. baking dish; set aside. Spread both sides of the bread slices with mustard. Arrange 9 bread slices in the baking dish.
2. In a large skillet, saute the ham, mushrooms and garlic in the remaining butter until mushrooms are tender. Add the onions; cook until crisp-tender, about 1 minute longer. Spoon ham mixture over the bread; sprinkle with cheese. Arrange remaining bread slices on top. In a large bowl, beat the eggs, cream, salt and pepper. Stir in parsley; pour over bread.
3. Place dish in a larger roasting pan; add 1 in. hot water to larger pan. Bake until a knife inserted in the center comes out clean, 50-60 minutes. Let stand for 5 minutes before serving. Drizzle with maple syrup if desired.
1 PIECE: 858 cal., 69g fat (41g sat. fat), 415mg chol., 1152mg sod., 28g carb. (3g sugars, 3g fiber), 31g pro.

RED PEPPER
CORNMEAL SOUFFLE

RED PEPPER CORNMEAL SOUFFLÉ

I use the vegetables from our garden in all my cooking. Doing so adds an unbeatable fresh, from-scratch flavor. Dotted with parsley and red pepper, this souffle is a favorite.
—*Janet Eckhoff, Woodland, CA*

Prep: 20 min. • **Bake:** 35 min.
Makes: 10 servings

1   large onion, chopped
1   cup chopped sweet red pepper
¼   cup butter
3   cups whole milk
⅔   cup cornmeal
1   cup shredded sharp cheddar cheese
2   Tbsp. minced fresh parsley
1   tsp. salt, divided
½   tsp. white pepper
2   large egg yolks, beaten
7   large egg whites, room temperature
½   tsp. cream of tartar

1. Preheat oven to 375°. In a large saucepan, saute onion and red pepper in butter until tender. Add milk. Bring to a boil. Gradually whisk in the cornmeal; whisk constantly until thickened, about 5 minutes. Add cheese, parsley, ½ tsp. salt and pepper. Add 1 cup cornmeal mixture to the egg yolks; mix well. Return all to saucepan.
2. In a large bowl, beat the egg whites, cream of tartar and the remaining ½ tsp. salt until stiff peaks form. Fold into the cornmeal mixture. Bake until golden brown, 35-40 minutes.
1 SERVING: 193 cal., 11g fat (7g sat. fat), 77mg chol., 427mg sod., 14g carb. (5g sugars, 1g fiber), 9g pro.

PEANUT BUTTER
BANANA OATMEAL

2 large eggs
¾ cup water
¾ cup 2% milk
2 Tbsp. butter, melted
½ tsp. vanilla extract
1 cup all-purpose flour
1 Tbsp. sugar
½ tsp. salt

BANANA FILLING
3 Tbsp. butter
3 Tbsp. brown sugar
3 medium firm bananas,
  cut into ¼-in. slices

SOUR CREAM FILLING
1 cup sour cream
2 Tbsp. confectioners' sugar
½ cup slivered almonds, toasted

1. In a small bowl, whisk the eggs, water, milk, butter and vanilla. In another bowl, mix the flour, sugar and salt; add to the egg mixture and mix well. Refrigerate, covered, 1 hour.
2. Heat a lightly greased 8-in. nonstick skillet over medium heat. Stir batter. Fill a ¼-cup measure three-fourths full with batter; pour into center of pan. Quickly lift and tilt pan to coat bottom evenly. Cook until top appears dry; turn crepe over and cook until bottom is cooked, 15-20 seconds longer. Remove to a wire rack. Repeat with the remaining batter, greasing pan as needed. When crepes are cool, stack them between pieces of waxed paper or paper towels.
3. In a small skillet, heat butter and brown sugar over medium heat until sugar is dissolved. Add bananas; toss to coat. Remove from heat; keep warm.
4. In a small bowl, combine sour cream and confectioners' sugar. Spread over half of each crepe. Top with banana filling and almonds; fold over filling. If desired, sprinkle with additional confectioners' sugar and almonds.
2 CREPES: 429 cal., 25g fat (12g sat. fat), 99mg chol., 327mg sod., 46g carb. (22g sugars, 3g fiber), 9g pro.

PEANUT BUTTER BANANA OATMEAL
The classic flavors of peanut butter and banana come together in an oatmeal that's loved by kids and adults alike. My family has enjoyed this dish on many chilly mornings.
—Deborah Purdue, Westland, MI

- -

Takes: 15 min. • **Makes:** 4 servings

3 cups fat-free milk or water
¼ tsp. salt
1½ cups quick-cooking oats
2 large bananas, sliced
2 Tbsp. peanut butter
½ tsp. vanilla extract

Place milk and salt in a large saucepan; bring just to a boil. Stir in oats; cook until thickened, 1-2 minutes, stirring occasionally. Remove from heat; stir in remaining ingredients.
1 CUP: 284 cal., 7g fat (1g sat. fat), 4mg chol., 260mg sod., 47g carb. (19g sugars, 5g fiber), 13g pro.

CREAMY BANANA CREPES
My husband and I enjoy taking turns fixing weekend breakfasts. These crepes are frequently on our menus. The sweet-and-sour banana filling is delicious. You'll want to serve them for lunch, dinner and dessert!
—Parrish Smith, Lincoln, NE

- -

Prep: 10 min. + chilling • **Cook:** 10 min.
Makes: 6 servings

CREAMY BANANA CREPES

FLUFFY PANCAKES

FLUFFY PANCAKES

I found this fluffy pancake recipe among our old family favorites, and adapted it to make a small amount. It's quick and easy to prepare, but we still consider it a special treat on Sunday mornings.
—*Eugene Presley, Council, VA*

Takes: 15 min. • **Makes:** 8 pancakes

- 1 cup all-purpose flour
- 1 Tbsp. sugar
- 2 tsp. baking powder
- ½ tsp. salt
- 1 large egg, room temperature
- ¾ cup 2% milk
- ¼ cup shortening or butter, melted

1. In a small bowl, combine flour, sugar, baking powder and salt. Combine egg, milk and shortening; stir into the dry ingredients just until moistened.
2. Pour batter by ¼ cupfuls onto a greased hot griddle. Turn when bubbles form on top of pancakes; cook until the second side is golden brown.
2 PANCAKES: 274 cal., 15g fat (9g sat. fat), 82mg chol., 664mg sod., 29g carb. (5g sugars, 1g fiber), 6g pro.
CHOCOLATE CHIP PANCAKES: Stir ½ cup miniature chocolate chips into batter. Proceed as recipe directs.
MAPLE PANCAKES: Omit sugar. Add 1 Tbsp. maple syrup to milk mixture. Proceed as recipe directs.

SAUSAGE & EGG GRITS

SAUSAGE & EGG GRITS

I always eat my sausage, grits and eggs together, so I thought it would be fun to mix them up in the same skillet. The resulting breakfast bombshell is loaded with down-home flavor—and it doesn't even use any butter!
—*Jeannine Quiller, Raleigh, NC*

Prep: 15 min. • **Cook:** 20 min.
Makes: 6 servings

- 4 breakfast turkey sausage links, casings removed
- 1½ cups egg substitute
- 1¼ cups whole milk, divided
- 3 cups water
- ⅛ tsp. salt
- 1 cup quick-cooking grits
- ¾ cup shredded reduced-fat cheddar cheese, divided
- 2 green onions, chopped
- ⅛ tsp. pepper

1. Crumble sausage into a large skillet; cook over medium heat until no longer pink. Remove to paper towels with a slotted spoon. Whisk egg substitute and ¼ cup milk; add to same skillet. Cook and stir until set; remove from the heat.
2. Meanwhile, in a Dutch oven, bring water, salt and the remaining 1 cup milk to a boil. Slowly stir in the grits. Reduce the heat; cook and stir until thickened, 5-7 minutes.
3. Stir in half the cheese. Add sausage, eggs, green onions and pepper; heat through. Serve in bowls; sprinkle with the remaining cheese.
1 CUP: 208 cal., 6g fat (3g sat. fat), 25mg chol., 369mg sod., 24g carb. (4g sugars, 1g fiber), 16g pro. **DIABETIC EXCHANGES:** 2 lean meat, 1½ starch.

3

Favorite Soups & Sandwiches

Whether you team them up for a lunch-counter classic combo meal or serve them solo, you'll love discovering these cozy soups and irresistible sandwiches.

GUACAMOLE
CHICKEN SALAD SANDWICHES
P. 86

QUICK TANGY
SLOPPY JOES

QUICK TANGY SLOPPY JOES

I adjusted and combined three recipes to come up with this one. Kids like the tangy taste so much, they request the sandwiches for birthday parties.
—*Anna Adams, Chatsworth, CA*

Takes: 20 min. • **Makes:** 6 servings

- 1 lb. ground beef
- 1 cup finely chopped onion
- ¾ cup finely chopped sweet red or green pepper
- ¼ cup finely chopped celery
- ½ cup ketchup
- 1 Tbsp. white vinegar
- 2 tsp. chili powder
- 1½ tsp. Worcestershire sauce
- 1 tsp. sugar
- 1 tsp. salt
- 6 hamburger buns, split

1. In a large cast-iron or other heavy skillet, cook and stir beef, onion, red pepper and celery over medium heat until meat is no longer pink and the vegetables are crisp-tender; drain.
2. In a small bowl, combine ketchup, vinegar, chili powder, Worcestershire sauce, sugar and salt; stir into the beef mixture. Simmer, uncovered, for 10 minutes, stirring occasionally. Serve on buns.
1 SLOPPY JOE: 314 cal., 12g fat (4g sat. fat), 50mg chol., 935mg sod., 32g carb. (8g sugars, 3g fiber), 20g pro.

ITALIAN SAUSAGE BEAN SOUP

ITALIAN SAUSAGE BEAN SOUP

During the frigid months, I like to put on a big pot of this soothing soup. It cooks away while I do other things, such as baking bread, crafting or even cleaning.
—*Glenna Reimer, Gig Harbor, WA*

Prep: 20 min. • **Cook:** 1½ hours
Makes: 8 servings (3 qt.)

- 1 lb. bulk Italian sausage
- 1 medium onion, finely chopped
- 3 garlic cloves, sliced
- 4 cans (14½ oz. each) reduced-sodium chicken broth
- 2 cans (15 oz. each) pinto beans, rinsed and drained
- 1 can (14½ oz.) diced tomatoes, undrained
- 1 cup medium pearl barley
- 1 large carrot, sliced
- 1 celery rib, sliced
- 1 tsp. minced fresh sage
- ½ tsp. minced fresh rosemary or ⅛ tsp. dried rosemary, crushed
- 6 cups chopped fresh kale

1. In a Dutch oven, cook and stir sausage and onion over medium heat until meat is no longer pink, 6-7 minutes. Add garlic; cook 1 minute longer. Drain.
2. Stir in broth, beans, tomatoes, barley, carrot, celery, sage and rosemary. Bring to a boil. Reduce heat; simmer, covered, for 45 minutes.
3. Stir in kale; return to a boil. Reduce heat; cover and simmer until vegetables are tender, 25-30 minutes.
1½ CUPS: 339 cal., 9g fat (3g sat. fat), 23mg chol., 1100mg sod., 48g carb. (7g sugars, 11g fiber), 19g pro.

REUBEN SANDWICHES

SPRING PEA SOUP

Sauteed potatoes add body to this easy soup with superb fresh pea flavor. Truly one for the pea lover, the recipe originated with an old cookbook with advice about eating better to live longer.
—*Denise Patterson, Bainbridge, OH*

Prep: 10 min. • **Cook:** 30 min.
Makes: 6 servings

- 2 cups cubed peeled potatoes
- 2 Tbsp. butter
- 6 cups chicken broth
- 2 cups fresh or frozen peas, thawed
- 2 Tbsp. minced chives
   Microgreens, optional

1. In a large saucepan, saute potatoes in butter until lightly browned. Stir in broth; bring to a boil. Reduce heat; cover and simmer until the potatoes are tender, 10-15 minutes. Add peas; cook until peas are tender, 5-8 minutes. Cool slightly.
2. In a blender, process the soup in batches until smooth. Return all to the pan; heat through. Sprinkle with chives and, if desired, microgreens.
1 CUP: 133 cal., 5g fat (2g sat. fat), 15mg chol., 1012mg sod., 18g carb. (4g sugars, 3g fiber), 5g pro.

Test Kitchen Tip

This recipe makes a smooth, light springtime soup that is on the thinner side. If you prefer a thicker soup, you can reduce the amount of chicken stock you use.

REUBEN SANDWICHES

My daughter shared this recipe with me. It's become a favorite of our entire family.
—*Kathryn Binder, Pickett, WI*

Takes: 20 min. • **Makes:** 10 servings

- ¾ cup mayonnaise
- 3 Tbsp. chili sauce
- 2 cups shredded Swiss cheese
- 1 can (14 oz.) sauerkraut, rinsed and well drained
- 12 oz. sliced deli corned beef
- 20 slices rye bread
- ½ cup butter, softened
   Thousand Island salad dressing, optional

1. In a large bowl, combine mayonnaise and chili sauce until blended. Stir in the cheese and sauerkraut. Spread over all 20 bread slices, about 2 Tbsp. per slice. Place corned beef on 10 bread slices; top with the remaining bread, spread side down. Spread outsides of sandwiches with butter.
2. On a griddle, toast sandwiches over medium heat until golden brown and cheese is melted, 4-5 minutes on each side. If desired, serve with dressing.
1 SANDWICH: 486 cal., 32g fat (13g sat. fat), 69mg chol., 1308mg sod., 34g carb. (4g sugars, 5g fiber), 17g pro.

SPRING
PEA SOUP

MEXICAN-INSPIRED CHICKEN SOUP

BARBECUED CHICKEN SALAD SANDWICHES

An impromptu picnic inspired this dish. The dressed-up sandwiches are instant summertime favorites, and have become a mainstay at our house.
—*Linda Orme, Battleground, WA*

Prep: 15 min. + marinating
Grill: 15 min. + cooling
Makes: 8 servings

- 1½ lbs. boneless skinless chicken breasts
- ½ cup barbecue sauce
- 1 cup mayonnaise
- ½ cup finely chopped onion
- ½ cup chopped celery
- ¼ tsp. salt
- ¼ tsp. crushed red pepper flakes
- 8 kaiser rolls, split
- 8 tomato slices
- 8 lettuce leaves

1. Place the chicken in a shallow baking dish; add barbecue sauce. Turn to coat; cover. Refrigerate overnight.
2. Grill chicken, covered, over medium-high heat for 6-8 minutes on each side or until a thermometer reads 165°. Cool; cover and refrigerate chicken until chilled.
3. Chop chicken; place in a large bowl. Stir in mayonnaise, onion, celery, salt and pepper flakes. Serve on rolls with tomato and lettuce.
1 SANDWICH: 481 cal., 27g fat (4g sat. fat), 57mg chol., 712mg sod., 34g carb. (6g sugars, 2g fiber), 24g pro.

MEXICAN-INSPIRED CHICKEN SOUP

This zesty soup is loaded with chicken, corn and black beans in a mildly spicy red broth. As a busy mom of three young children, I'm always looking for dinner recipes that can be prepared in the morning. The kids love the taco taste of this easy soup.
—*Marlene Kane, Lainesburg, MI*

Prep: 10 min. • **Cook:** 3 hours
Makes: 6 servings (2¼ qt.)

- 1½ lbs. boneless skinless chicken breasts, cubed
- 2 tsp. canola oil
- ½ cup water
- 1 envelope reduced-sodium taco seasoning
- 3 cans (11½ oz. each) V8 juice
- 1 jar (16 oz.) salsa
- 1 can (15 oz.) black beans, rinsed and drained
- 1 pkg. (10 oz.) frozen corn, thawed
  Optional: Shredded cheddar cheese, sour cream and chopped fresh cilantro

1. In a large nonstick skillet, saute chicken in oil until no longer pink. Add water and taco seasoning; simmer, uncovered, until chicken is well coated.
2. Transfer to a 5-qt. slow cooker. Stir in V8 juice, salsa, beans and corn. Cook, covered, on low for 3-4 hours or until heated through. Garnish as desired.
1½ CUPS: 304 cal., 5g fat (1g sat. fat), 63mg chol., 1199mg sod., 35g carb. (11g sugars, 5g fiber), 29g pro.

RUSSIAN BORSCHT

Loaded with beets, carrots and cabbage, this recipe is terrific for gardeners. Not only is it delicious, but its brilliant colors are eye-catching on the table.
—Ginny Bettis, Montello, WI

Prep: 15 min. • **Cook:** 1 hour
Makes: 8 servings (2 qt.)

- 2 cups chopped fresh beets
- 2 cups chopped carrots
- 2 cups chopped onion
- 4 cups beef or vegetable broth
- 1 can (16 oz.) diced tomatoes, undrained
- 2 cups chopped cabbage
- ½ tsp. salt
- ½ tsp. dill weed
- ¼ tsp. pepper
  Sour cream, optional

1. In a large saucepan, combine beets, carrots, onion and broth; bring to a boil. Reduce heat; cover and simmer for 30 minutes.
2. Add tomatoes and cabbage; cover and simmer until the cabbage is tender, 30 minutes longer. Stir in salt, dill and pepper. Top each serving with sour cream if desired.

1 CUP: 71 cal., 1g fat (0 sat. fat), 0 chol., 673mg sod., 14g carb. (9g sugars, 4g fiber), 3g pro.

> *"My family is from Russia. This is a good, basic recipe for borscht. I like adding stew beef, and I let it simmer until fork tender. Back in the day, not everyone could afford beef in Russia, so this was typical. It's easy and so good!"*
> **—DIANEINFV, TASTEOFHOME.COM**

SPINACH PIZZA QUESADILLAS

This simple five-ingredient dinner is special to me because my daughter and I created it together. You can make variations with other veggies you might have at home. It's a smart way to get kids to eat healthier.
—Tanna Mancini, Gulfport, FL

Takes: 20 min. • **Makes:** 6 servings

- 6 whole wheat tortillas (8 in.)
- 3 cups shredded part-skim mozzarella cheese
- 3 cups chopped fresh spinach
- 1 can (8 oz.) pizza sauce

1. Preheat oven to 400°. On half of each tortilla, layer ½ cup cheese, ½ cup spinach and about 2 Tbsp. sauce. Fold tortilla in half over the filling. Place on baking sheets coated with cooking spray.
2. Bake until the cheese is melted, 10-12 minutes. If desired, serve with additional pizza sauce.

1 QUESADILLA: 301 cal., 13g fat (7g sat. fat), 36mg chol., 650mg sod., 29g carb. (3g sugars, 4g fiber), 19g pro. **DIABETIC EXCHANGES:** 2 starch, 2 medium-fat meat.

SPINACH PIZZA QUESADILLAS

ROASTED SWEET POTATO & CHICKPEA PITAS

ROASTED SWEET POTATO & CHICKPEA PITAS

Here's a hearty take on Mediterranean pita pocket sandwiches, this time with sweet potatoes tucked inside.
—*Beth Jacobson, Milwaukee, WI*

Takes: 30 min. • **Makes:** 6 servings

- 2 medium sweet potatoes (about 1¼ lbs.), peeled and cubed
- 2 cans (15 oz. each) chickpeas or garbanzo beans, rinsed and drained
- 1 medium red onion, chopped
- 3 Tbsp. canola oil, divided
- 2 tsp. garam masala
- ½ tsp. salt, divided
- 2 garlic cloves, minced
- 1 cup plain Greek yogurt
- 1 Tbsp. lemon juice
- 1 tsp. ground cumin
- 2 cups arugula or baby spinach
- 12 whole wheat pita pocket halves, warmed
- ¼ cup minced fresh cilantro

1. Preheat oven to 400°. Place the potatoes in a large microwave-safe bowl; microwave, covered, on high for 5 minutes. Stir in chickpeas and onion; toss with 2 Tbsp. oil, the garam masala and ¼ tsp. salt.
2. Spread into a 15x10x1-in. pan. Roast until the potatoes are tender, about 15 minutes. Cool slightly.
3. Place minced garlic and remaining 1 Tbsp. oil in a small microwave-safe bowl; microwave on high until the garlic is lightly browned, 1-1½ minutes. Stir in yogurt, lemon juice, cumin and the remaining ¼ tsp. salt.
4. Toss the potato mixture with arugula. Spoon into the pitas; top with the sauce and cilantro.

2 FILLED PITA HALVES: 462 cal., 15g fat (3g sat. fat), 10mg chol., 662mg sod., 72g carb. (13g sugars, 12g fiber), 14g pro.

STROGANOFF SOUP

STROGANOFF SOUP

My husband and I share a love for all kinds of soup and came up with this delicious recipe together. It really does taste like beef Stroganoff!
—*Karen Shiveley, Springfield, MN*

Prep: 15 min. • **Cook:** 25 min.
Makes: 6 servings

- 1 Tbsp. butter
- ½ lb. beef top sirloin steak or beef tenderloin, cut into thin strips
- ½ cup chopped onion
- 2 cups water
- ¼ cup tomato paste
- 1½ cups 2% milk
- 1 can (8 oz.) mushroom stems and pieces, drained
- 2 tsp. beef bouillon granules
- 1 tsp. salt
- ⅛ tsp. pepper
- ⅓ cup all-purpose flour
- 1 can (12 oz.) evaporated milk
- 2 cups cooked wide egg noodles
- ½ cup sour cream
  Minced fresh thyme, optional

1. In a large saucepan, melt butter over medium heat. Add beef and onion; cook and stir until the beef is almost cooked through, 3-5 minutes. In a small bowl, whisk the water and tomato paste until blended; stir into saucepan. Add 2% milk, mushrooms, bouillon, salt and pepper; bring to a boil.
2. In a small bowl, whisk the flour and evaporated milk until smooth. Gradually stir into saucepan. Return to a boil; cook and stir until thickened, 1-2 minutes. Add the noodles; cook until heated through. Top each serving with sour cream and, if desired, thyme.

1 CUP: 314 cal., 13g fat (8g sat. fat), 78mg chol., 935mg sod., 28g carb. (12g sugars, 2g fiber), 17g pro.

GRILLED CHEESE &
PEPPERONI SANDWICH

GRILLED CHEESE & PEPPERONI SANDWICH

Who doesn't love a good grilled cheese sandwich? This super decadent version comes fully loaded with pepperoni and five types of cheese!
—*Josh Rink, Milwaukee, WI*

- -

Takes: 25 min. • **Makes:** 4 servings

6 Tbsp. butter, softened, divided
8 slices sourdough bread
½ cup shredded sharp white cheddar cheese
½ cup shredded Monterey Jack cheese
½ cup shredded Gruyere cheese
3 Tbsp. mayonnaise
3 Tbsp. finely shredded Manchego or Parmesan cheese
⅛ tsp. onion powder
24 slices pepperoni
4 oz. Brie cheese, rind removed and sliced

1. Spread 3 Tbsp. butter on 1 side of bread slices. Toast bread, butter side down, in a large cast-iron skillet or an electric griddle over medium-low heat until golden brown, 2-3 minutes; remove from heat. In a small bowl, combine the cheddar, Monterey Jack and Gruyere. In another bowl, mix together remaining 3 Tbsp. butter, mayonnaise, Manchego cheese and onion powder.
2. To assemble sandwiches, top toasted side of 4 bread slices with the pepperoni; add sliced Brie. Sprinkle cheddar cheese mixture evenly over the Brie. Top with the remaining bread slices, toasted sides facing inward. Spread the butter-mayonnaise mixture on the outsides of each sandwich.
3. Place sandwiches in the same skillet; toast until bread is golden brown and cheese is melted, 5-6 minutes on each side. Serve immediately.
1 SANDWICH: 719 cal., 55g fat (29g sat. fat), 134mg chol., 1207mg sod., 30g carb. (3g sugars, 1g fiber), 27g pro.

BUFFALO CHICKEN CHILI

This recipe is rich in the best way. Cream cheese, blue cheese and tangy hot sauce join forces for a dinner everyone will love.
—*Peggy Woodward, Shullsburg, WI*

- -

Prep: 10 min. • **Cook:** 5½ hours
Makes: 6 servings (2 qt.)

1 can (15½ oz.) navy beans, rinsed and drained
1 can (14½ oz.) chicken broth
1 can (14½ oz.) fire-roasted diced tomatoes
1 can (8 oz.) tomato sauce
½ cup Buffalo wing sauce
½ tsp. onion powder
½ tsp. garlic powder
1 lb. boneless skinless chicken breast halves
1 pkg. (8 oz.) cream cheese, cubed and softened
Optional: Crumbled blue cheese, chopped celery and chopped green onions

1. In a 4- or 5-qt. slow cooker, combine the first 7 ingredients. Add the chicken. Cover and cook on low until the chicken is tender, 5-6 hours.
2. Remove chicken; shred with 2 forks. Return to slow cooker. Stir in cream cheese. Cover and cook on low until cheese is melted, about 30 minutes. Stir until blended. Serve with toppings as desired.
1¼ CUPS: 337 cal., 16g fat (8g sat. fat), 80mg chol., 1586mg sod., 25g carb. (5g sugars, 5g fiber), 25g pro.

Test Kitchen Tip

Cream cheese can curdle when frozen, so keep leftovers of this chili in the refrigerator, not the freezer!

BUFFALO CHICKEN
CHILI

SUNDAY SUPPER SANDWICHES

Here's a terrific way to make a traditional dinner with little hands-on time. You can prepare the meat in the slow cooker as well: Cook all the ingredients except the bread and cheese, covered, on low in a 4-quart slow cooker for 8 to 10 hours.
—*Elizabeth Godecke, Chicago, IL*

Prep: 25 min. • **Bake:** 2½ hours
Makes: 8 servings

- 1 can (14 oz.) sauerkraut, rinsed and well drained
- 1 boneless pork shoulder butt roast (2½ to 3 lbs.)
- ½ tsp. salt
- ¼ tsp. pepper
- ¼ cup stone-ground mustard, divided
- 1 cup apple cider or unsweetened apple juice
- ¼ cup sweetened applesauce
- 8 slices rye bread, toasted
- 1 cup shredded Swiss cheese

1. Preheat oven to 325°. Place sauerkraut in an ovenproof Dutch oven. Sprinkle the pork with salt and pepper; brush with 2 Tbsp. mustard. Place over sauerkraut. Add cider and applesauce.
2. Bake, covered, until pork is tender, 2½-3 hours. Remove the roast; cool slightly. Drain the sauerkraut mixture; set aside. Shred the pork with 2 forks.
3. Place toast on an ungreased baking sheet. Spread with the remaining 2 Tbsp. mustard. Top with pork, then sauerkraut mixture; sprinkle with cheese. Broil 4-6 in. from the heat until cheese is melted, 2-3 minutes.
1 OPEN-FACED SANDWICH: 403 cal., 20g fat (8g sat. fat), 96mg chol., 966mg sod., 25g carb. (8g sugars, 4g fiber), 31g pro.

RAMEN CORN CHOWDER

This tastes so good, as if it simmered for hours, but it's ready in 15 minutes. I thought the original recipe was lacking in flavor, so I jazzed it up with extra corn and bacon bits.
—*Darlene Brenden, Salem, OR*

Takes: 15 min. • **Makes:** 4 servings

- 2 cups water
- 1 pkg. (3 oz.) chicken ramen noodles
- 1 can (15¼ oz.) whole kernel corn, drained
- 1 can (14¾ oz.) cream-style corn
- 1 cup 2% milk
- 1 tsp. dried minced onion
- ¼ tsp. curry powder
- ¾ cup shredded cheddar cheese
- ⅓ cup cubed cooked bacon
- 1 Tbsp. minced fresh parsley
- 1 Tbsp. minced chives

1. In a small saucepan, bring water to a boil. Break noodles into large pieces. Add noodles and contents of seasoning packet to water. Reduce heat to medium. Cook, uncovered, until noodles are tender, 2-3 minutes.
2. Stir in corn, cream-style corn, milk, onion and curry powder; heat through. Stir in the cheese, bacon, parsley and chives until blended. If desired, top with additional cheddar cheese and additional minced fresh chives.
1 CUP: 333 cal., 9g fat (5g sat. fat), 17mg chol., 1209mg sod., 49g carb. (13g sugars, 4g fiber), 13g pro.

SUNDAY SUPPER SANDWICHES

VEGGIE BROWN RICE WRAPS

Salsa gives a bit of zip to the hearty brown rice and bean filling in these meatless tortilla wraps.
—*Lisa Sullivan, St. Marys, OH*

Takes: 20 min. • **Makes:** 6 servings

- 1 medium sweet red or green pepper, diced
- 1 cup sliced fresh mushrooms
- 1 Tbsp. olive oil
- 2 garlic cloves, minced
- 2 cups cooked brown rice
- 1 can (16 oz.) kidney beans, rinsed and drained
- 1 cup frozen corn, thawed
- ¼ cup chopped green onions
- ½ tsp. ground cumin
- ½ tsp. pepper
- ¼ tsp. salt
- 6 flour tortillas (8 in.), warmed
- ½ cup shredded reduced-fat cheddar cheese
- ¾ cup salsa

1. In a large cast-iron or other heavy skillet, saute pepper and mushrooms in oil until tender. Add garlic; cook 1 minute. Add the rice, beans, corn, green onions, cumin, pepper and salt. Cook and stir until heated through, 4-6 minutes.

2. Spoon ¾ cup rice mixture onto each tortilla. Sprinkle with the cheese; drizzle with salsa. Fold sides of tortilla over the filling; roll up. Serve immediately.

1 WRAP: 377 cal., 8g fat (2g sat. fat), 7mg chol., 675mg sod., 62g carb. (4g sugars, 7g fiber), 15g pro.

Test Kitchen Tip
Green peppers are unripened versions of red, yellow or orange peppers. Use a red or yellow pepper if you prefer more sweetness.

VEGGIE BROWN RICE WRAPS

Spread 2 Tbsp. **creamy peanut butter** over 1 slice of **bread**. (We like artisanal bakery variety for its texture.) Top with ½ **medium banana**, sliced, and 1 **bacon strip**, cooked and crumbled.

- The Elvis Sandwich -

The surprising combo of rich peanut butter, sweet banana and crisp, smoky bacon really is a meal fit for a king.

CREAMY GARLIC & MUSHROOM SOUP

Cool, crisp winter evenings call for comforting bowls of rich and creamy soup. It makes a terrific first course at holiday meals.
—*Mandy Howison, Renfrew, PA*

Prep: 15 min. • **Cook:** 30 min.
Makes: 13 servings (3¼ qt.)

- 1 lb. medium fresh mushrooms, sliced
- 1 lb. sliced baby portobello mushrooms
- ½ lb. sliced fresh shiitake mushrooms
- 7 Tbsp. butter
- 12 garlic cloves, minced
- 2 green onions, chopped
- ½ cup all-purpose flour
- 2 cans (14½ oz. each) chicken broth
- 3⅓ cups 2% milk
- 1⅔ cups heavy whipping cream
- 4 tsp. minced fresh thyme or 1½ tsp. dried thyme
- 2 tsp. minced fresh basil or ¾ tsp. dried basil
- 1 tsp. salt
- 1 tsp. pepper
  Minced fresh parsley

1. In a Dutch oven, saute mushrooms in butter in batches until tender. Return all to the pan; add garlic and green onions. Cook and stir for 2 minutes. Sprinkle with flour; stir until blended.
2. Gradually stir in broth and milk. Bring to a boil; cook and stir until thickened, about 2 minutes. Stir in cream, thyme, basil, salt and pepper; heat through. Sprinkle each serving with parsley.
1 CUP: 246 cal., 20g fat (12g sat. fat), 66mg chol., 539mg sod., 13g carb. (5g sugars, 1g fiber), 6g pro.

CHICKEN MUSHROOM STEW

CHICKEN MUSHROOM STEW

The flavors blend beautifully in this dish of chicken, vegetables and herbs as it simmers in a slow cooker. Folks with busy schedules will love this convenient and satisfying recipe.
—*Kenny Van Rheenen, Mendota, IL*

Prep: 20 min. • **Cook:** 4 hours
Makes: 6 servings (2 qt.)

- 6 boneless skinless chicken breast halves (4 oz. each)
- 2 Tbsp. canola oil, divided
- 8 oz. fresh mushrooms, sliced
- 1 medium onion, diced
- 3 cups diced zucchini
- 1 cup chopped green pepper
- 4 garlic cloves, minced
- 3 medium tomatoes, chopped
- 1 can (6 oz.) tomato paste
- ¾ cup water
- 2 tsp. each dried thyme, oregano, marjoram and basil
  Chopped fresh thyme, optional

1. Cut chicken into 1-in. cubes; brown in 1 Tbsp. oil in a large skillet. Transfer to a 3-qt. slow cooker. In the same skillet, saute the mushrooms, onion, zucchini and green pepper in remaining 1 Tbsp. oil until crisp-tender. Add garlic; cook 1 minute longer.
2. Place vegetable mixture in the slow cooker. Add tomatoes, tomato paste, water and seasonings. Cook, covered, on low until the meat is no longer pink and vegetables are tender, 4-5 hours. If desired, top with chopped fresh thyme.
1⅓ CUPS: 237 cal., 8g fat (1g sat. fat), 63mg chol., 82mg sod., 15g carb. (7g sugars, 3g fiber), 27g pro. **DIABETIC EXCHANGES:** 3 lean meat, 1 starch, 1 fat.

SIMPLE SHRIMP CHOWDER

SMASH BURGERS

Now is not the time to cut calories or skimp on salt. Go for ground chuck that's at least 80/20. If you can find a blend with ground brisket or short rib, all the better. The best burger comes from being liberal with kosher salt—it's beef's best friend, trust me.
—James Schend, Pleasant Prairie, WI

- -

Takes: 15 min. • **Makes:** 4 servings

1   lb. ground beef (preferably 80% lean)
1   tsp. canola oil
1   tsp. kosher salt, divided
1   tsp. coarsely ground pepper, divided
4   hamburger buns, split
    Optional: Mayonnaise, sliced
    American cheese, sliced tomato,
    dill pickle slices, lettuce, ketchup
    and yellow mustard

1. Place a 9-in. cast-iron skillet over medium heat. Meanwhile, gently shape beef into 4 balls, shaping just enough to keep together (do not compact).
2. Increase the burner temperature to medium-high; add oil. Add 2 beef balls. With a heavy metal spatula, flatten each to ¼-½-in. thickness; sprinkle each with ⅛ tsp. salt and ⅛ tsp. pepper. Cook until edges start to brown, about 1½ minutes. Turn the burgers and sprinkle each with an additional ⅛ tsp. salt and ⅛ tsp. pepper. Cook until well browned and a thermometer reads at least 160°, about 1 minute. Repeat with the remaining beef.
3. Serve burgers on buns with toppings as desired.
1 BURGER: 339 cal., 16g fat (5g sat. fat), 70mg chol., 760mg sod., 22g carb. (3g sugars, 1g fiber), 24g pro.

SIMPLE SHRIMP CHOWDER

Shrimp fans will be bowled over by this tasty take on chowder. The creamy broth is chock-full of vegetables. Chop up some leftover cooked potatoes or use canned ones.
—Carolyn Schmeling, Brookfield, WI

- -

Takes: 30 min. • **Makes:** 5 servings

½   cup each chopped onion, celery,
    carrot and sweet red pepper
¼   cup butter, cubed
¼   cup all-purpose flour
2   cups 2% milk
½   lb. cooked shrimp (41-50 per lb.),
    peeled and deveined
1   can (14½ oz.) diced potatoes, drained
1   cup vegetable broth
1   cup frozen corn, thawed
2   tsp. seafood seasoning
1   tsp. minced fresh thyme
    or ½ tsp. dried thyme

1. In a large saucepan, saute the onion, celery, carrot and red pepper in butter until tender, about 5 minutes. Stir in the flour until blended; gradually add milk. Bring to a boil; cook and stir mixture until thickened, about 2 minutes.
2. Add the shrimp, potatoes, broth, corn, seafood seasoning and thyme. Reduce heat; cover and simmer until heated through, about 10 minutes. If desired, top with additional thyme.
1 CUP: 268 cal., 12g fat (7g sat. fat), 120mg chol., 901mg sod., 25g carb. (7g sugars, 2g fiber), 16g pro.

SMASH
BURGERS

GUACAMOLE CHICKEN SALAD SANDWICHES

This is inspired by a local restaurant's truly inventive guacamole, studded with pomegranate seeds. It's simple to make since rotisserie chicken is used. I serve the salad on homemade tomato bread that provides a great contrast in flavor and color. You can serve it on lettuce leaves instead of bread too.

—Debra Keil, Owasso, OK

Takes: 20 min. • **Makes:** 10 servings

- 1 rotisserie chicken, skin removed, cubed
- 2 medium ripe avocados, peeled and mashed
- ¾ cup pomegranate seeds
- 6 green onions, chopped
- 8 cherry tomatoes, halved
- 1 jalapeno pepper, seeded and minced
- ¼ cup fresh cilantro leaves, chopped
- 3 Tbsp. mayonnaise
- 2 Tbsp. lime juice
- 1 garlic clove, minced
- ½ tsp. salt
- ½ tsp. ground cumin
- ¼ tsp. pepper
- 20 slices multigrain bread, toasted

In a large bowl, combine all ingredients except the toasted bread. Spread over 10 bread slices; top with the remaining bread.

NOTE: Wear disposable gloves when cutting hot peppers; the oil can burn skin. Avoid touching your face.

1 SANDWICH: 295 cal., 12g fat (2g sat. fat), 35mg chol., 370mg sod., 28g carb. (6g sugars, 6g fiber), 19g pro. **DIABETIC EXCHANGES:** 2 starch, 2 lean meat, 2 fat.

NORTHWEST SALMON CHOWDER

I've lived on a farm in the Yakima Valley all my life. I have a big garden, and by the end of fall, my cellar shelves are full of canned fruits and vegetables. This recipe uses some of the root vegetables I grow—along with the delicious salmon that is so plentiful here.

—Josephine Parton, Granger, WA

Prep: 10 min. • **Cook:** 1 hour
Makes: 8 servings (2 qt.)

- ½ cup each chopped celery, onion and green pepper
- 1 garlic clove, minced
- 3 Tbsp. butter
- 1 can (14½ oz.) chicken broth
- 1 cup uncooked diced peeled potatoes
- 1 cup shredded carrots
- 1½ tsp. salt
- ½ tsp. pepper
- ¼ to ¾ tsp. dill weed
- 1 can (14¾ oz.) cream-style corn
- 2 cups half-and-half cream
- 1¾ to 2 cups fully cooked salmon chunks or 1 can (14¾ oz.) salmon, drained, flaked, bones and skin removed
   Optional: Crumbled cooked bacon, chives and cracked black pepper

1. In a large saucepan, saute the celery, onion, green pepper and garlic in butter until the vegetables are tender. Add the broth, potatoes, carrots, salt, pepper and dill; bring to a boil.
2. Reduce heat; cover and simmer for 40 minutes or until the vegetables are nearly tender.
3. Stir in the corn, cream and salmon. Simmer for 15 minutes or until heated through. If desired, garnish with bacon, chives and cracked black pepper.
1 CUP: 274 cal., 15g fat (8g sat. fat), 84mg chol., 1095mg sod., 18g carb. (5g sugars, 2g fiber), 16g pro.

GUACAMOLE CHICKEN SALAD SANDWICHES

HEARTY BEEF & BARLEY SOUP

Barley soup is a popular menu item in our house throughout the year. Everyone savors the flavor.
—*Elizabeth Kendall, Carolina Beach, NC*

Prep: 20 min. • **Cook:** 1½ hours
Makes: 9 servings (2¼ qt.)

- 1 Tbsp. canola oil
- 1 lb. beef top round steak, cut into ½-in. cubes
- 3 cans (14½ oz. each) beef broth
- 2 cups water
- ⅓ cup medium pearl barley
- ¾ tsp. salt
- ⅛ tsp. pepper
- 1 cup chopped carrots
- ½ cup chopped celery
- ¼ cup chopped onion
- 3 Tbsp. minced fresh parsley
- 1 cup frozen peas

1. In a large saucepan, heat the oil over medium heat. Brown beef on all sides; drain. Stir in broth, water, barley, salt and pepper. Bring to a boil. Reduce heat; cover and simmer for 1 hour.
2. Add carrots, celery, onion and parsley; cover and simmer until the meat and vegetables are tender, 30-40 minutes. Stir in peas; heat through.
1 CUP: 133 cal., 4g fat (1g sat. fat), 28mg chol., 859mg sod., 10g carb. (2g sugars, 2g fiber), 14g pro. **DIABETIC EXCHANGES:** 2 lean meat, ½ starch, ½ fat.

Test Kitchen Tip
To make this soup in a slow cooker, combine all ingredients and cook on low until both the beef and the barley are tender, 4-5 hours.

DUTCH OVEN BARBECUED PORK SANDWICHES

DUTCH OVEN BARBECUED PORK SANDWICHES

These fabulous pulled pork sandwiches have a sweet, tangy flavor. If you want a smokier taste, add a little liquid smoke to the pulled pork before returning it to the Dutch oven.
—*Taste of Home Test Kitchen*

Prep: 15 min. • **Cook:** 3 hours
Makes: 8 servings

- 1 can (8 oz.) tomato sauce
- 1 large onion, chopped
- 1 cup barbecue sauce
- 3 tsp. chili powder
- 1 tsp. ground cumin
- ½ tsp. ground cinnamon
- 1 boneless pork sirloin roast (2 lbs.)
- 8 seeded hamburger buns, split

1. In a Dutch oven, combine the first 6 ingredients; add the pork. Spoon some of the sauce over pork. Bring to a boil; reduce heat and simmer, covered, until meat is tender, 3-4 hours.
2. Remove meat; shred with 2 forks. Return to pan and heat through. Spoon ½ cup meat mixture onto each bun.
1 SANDWICH: 357 cal., 9g fat (3g sat. fat), 68mg chol., 771mg sod., 40g carb. (16g sugars, 2g fiber), 28g pro.

BEST EVER
GRILLED CHEESE
SANDWICHES

BEST EVER GRILLED CHEESE SANDWICHES

Use your imagination to come up with other fillings for your sandwiches, such as chives, Parmesan cheese, Italian seasoning or even a spoonful of salsa.
—*Edie DeSpain, Logan, UT*

Takes: 20 min. • **Makes:** 2 servings

- 2 Tbsp. mayonnaise
- 1 tsp. Dijon mustard
- 4 slices sourdough bread
- 2 slices Swiss cheese
- 2 slices cheddar cheese
- 2 slices sweet onion
- 1 medium tomato, sliced
- 6 cooked bacon strips
- 2 Tbsp. butter, softened

1. Combine mayonnaise and mustard; spread over 2 bread slices. Layer with cheeses, onion, tomato and bacon; top with remaining bread. Spread outsides of sandwiches with softened butter.
2. In a small skillet over medium heat, toast sandwiches until cheese is melted, 2-3 minutes on each side.

1 SANDWICH: 714 cal., 48g fat (23g sat. fat), 111mg chol., 1291mg sod., 41g carb. (4g sugars, 3g fiber), 29g pro.

Test Kitchen Tip

Bacon grease is so tasty, it's worth saving for use in other dishes. Once it's slightly cooled, strain the grease through cheesecloth or a coffee filter stretched over the top of a Mason jar. Cover and refrigerate the cooled grease for up to 6 months.

BASIL TOMATO SOUP WITH ORZO

BASIL TOMATO SOUP WITH ORZO

This soup is so scrumptious that it's worth the time it takes to chop the fresh onion, garlic and basil. It's even better the next day after the flavors have had a chance to blend.
—*Tonia Billbe, Elmira, NY*

Prep: 15 min. • **Cook:** 25 min.
Makes: 16 servings (4 qt.)

- 1 large onion, chopped
- ¼ cup butter, cubed
- 2 garlic cloves, minced
- 3 cans (28 oz. each) crushed tomatoes
- 1 carton (32 oz.) chicken broth
- 1 cup loosely packed basil leaves, chopped
- 1 Tbsp. sugar
- ½ tsp. pepper
- 1¼ cups uncooked orzo pasta
- 1 cup heavy whipping cream
- ½ cup grated Romano cheese

1. In a Dutch oven, saute onion in butter for 3 minutes. Add garlic; cook until onion is tender, 1-2 minutes longer. Stir in the tomatoes, broth, basil, sugar and pepper. Bring to a boil. Reduce heat; cover and simmer for 15 minutes.
2. Meanwhile, cook the orzo according to package directions; drain. Add orzo and cream to soup; heat through (do not boil). Sprinkle servings with cheese.

1 CUP: 208 cal., 10g fat (6g sat. fat), 27mg chol., 607mg sod., 25g carb. (9g sugars, 3g fiber), 7g pro.

CHICKEN
FLORENTINE
PANINI

CANADIAN CHEESE SOUP

My family loves Canadian bacon, but I don't run across a lot of dishes that call for it. Everyone was thrilled the first time I offered this succulent soup.
—*Jolene Roudebush, Troy, MI*

Prep: 15 min. • **Cook:** 30 min.
Makes: 8 servings (2 qt.)

- 3 cups chicken broth
- 4 medium potatoes, peeled and diced
- 2 celery ribs, diced
- 1 medium carrot, diced
- 1 small onion, diced
- 6 oz. Canadian bacon, trimmed and diced
- 2 Tbsp. butter
- 2 Tbsp. all-purpose flour
- 1 cup whole milk
- 2 cups shredded cheddar cheese
- ⅛ tsp. pepper

1. In a Dutch oven or soup kettle, combine the first 5 ingredients; bring to a boil. Reduce heat; cover and simmer until vegetables are very tender, about 20 minutes. With a potato masher, mash the vegetables several times. Add bacon; continue to simmer.
2. Meanwhile, melt the butter in a small saucepan; stir in flour and cook, stirring constantly, for 1 minute. Gradually whisk in milk. Bring to a boil; boil and stir for 2 minutes (mixture will be thick). Add vegetable mixture, stirring constantly. Remove from the heat; add cheese and pepper. Stir just until cheese is melted.
1 CUP: 252 cal., 11g fat (0 sat. fat), 33mg chol., 402mg sod., 22g carb. (0 sugars, 0 fiber), 19g pro. **DIABETIC EXCHANGES:** 2 meat, 1 starch, 1 vegetable.

CHICKEN FLORENTINE PANINI

This grilled sandwich combines chicken with provolone cheese, spinach and red onion.
—*Lee Bremson, Kansas City, MO*

Takes: 25 min. • **Makes:** 4 servings

- 1 pkg. (5 oz.) fresh baby spinach
- 2 tsp. olive oil
- 8 slices sourdough bread
- ¼ cup creamy Italian salad dressing
- 8 slices provolone cheese
- ½ lb. shaved deli chicken
- 2 slices red onion, separated into rings
- ¼ cup butter, softened

1. In a large cast-iron or other heavy skillet, saute the spinach in oil until wilted, about 2 minutes. Drain; wipe the skillet clean.
2. Spread 4 bread slices with salad dressing. Layer with a cheese slice, chicken, spinach, onion and another cheese slice. Top with remaining bread. Butter outsides of sandwiches.
3. Cook in same skillet or a panini maker until the bread is golden brown and the cheese is melted.
1 SANDWICH: 582 cal., 26g fat (10g sat. fat), 62mg chol., 1688mg sod., 63g carb. (4g sugars, 5g fiber), 23g pro.

CANADIAN
CHEESE SOUP

SHRIMP PATTY SANDWICHES

Quite often when we eat at a restaurant, my husband will try something and tell me that I could make it better at home. That was the case with this shrimp patty. I made some improvements, and now it's one of my husband's favorites.
—*Tina Jacobs, Hurlock, MD*

Takes: 25 min. • **Makes:** 8 servings

- 4 large eggs
- 4 cans (6 oz. each) shrimp, rinsed and drained, or 2 cups peeled and deveined cooked shrimp (31-40 per lb.)
- ½ lb. haddock, cooked and flaked
- 1½ cups pancake mix
- 2 Tbsp. cornmeal
- ½ tsp. dried parsley flakes
- ½ tsp. celery salt
- ¼ tsp. ground mustard
- ¼ tsp. paprika
- ½ cup dry bread crumbs
- 3 to 4 Tbsp. canola oil
- 8 hamburger buns
  Optional: Lettuce leaves, tomato slices, onion slices and Sriracha mayonnaise

1. In a large bowl, beat the eggs. Add the next 8 ingredients; mix well. Shape into 8 patties. Coat with bread crumbs.
2. In a large cast-iron or other heavy skillet, cook the patties in oil over medium-high heat until golden brown, about 2 minutes on each side. Serve on hamburger buns. Top with lettuce, tomato, onion and mayonnaise as desired.

1 SANDWICH: 425 cal., 11g fat (2g sat. fat), 324mg chol., 1448mg sod., 45g carb. (4g sugars, 2g fiber), 33g pro.

ROASTED RED PEPPER SOUP

If you like cream of tomato soup, try making it with roasted red peppers instead. Using jarred roasted red peppers makes this recipe extra easy, and pureeing the soup in a blender gives it a nice, smooth texture.
—Taste of Home *Test Kitchen*

Prep: 10 min. • **Cook:** 25 min.
Makes: 6 servings

- 2 tsp. butter
- 1 large sweet onion, chopped
- 2 garlic cloves, minced
- 2 jars (15½ oz. each) roasted sweet red peppers, drained
- 2 cups vegetable broth
- ½ tsp. dried basil
- ¼ tsp. salt
- 1 cup half-and-half cream
  Optional: Additional half-and-half cream and fresh basil leaves

1. In a large saucepan, melt butter over medium heat; add onion. Cook and stir until tender, 3-5 minutes. Add garlic; cook 1 minute longer. Stir in red peppers, broth, basil and salt. Bring to a boil. Reduce heat; cover and simmer for 20 minutes. Cool slightly.
2. In a blender, cover and process soup in batches until smooth. Remove 1 cup to a small bowl; stir in cream. Return remaining puree to pan. Stir in the cream mixture; heat through (do not boil). If desired, garnish with additional cream and basil.

1 CUP: 135 cal., 6g fat (3g sat. fat), 23mg chol., 753mg sod., 21g carb. (9g sugars, 1g fiber), 2g pro.

Test Kitchen Tip

You can use an immersion blender to puree this soup instead. Be aware, though, that a traditional blender gives the silkiest texture to pureed soups. Is it worth dirtying the extra dishes? That call is up to you.

ROASTED MUSHROOM & COUSCOUS SOUP

ROASTED MUSHROOM & COUSCOUS SOUP

I love adding mushrooms to soup. They add an earthy richness, and roasting them makes them even more flavorful.
—*Robin Haas, Hyde Park, MA*

Prep: 15 min. • **Cook:** 30 min.
Makes: 6 servings (2 qt.)

- 1 lb. medium fresh mushrooms, quartered
  Cooking spray
- 2 tsp. dried oregano
- ½ tsp. kosher salt
- 1 Tbsp. butter
- 1 large onion, finely chopped
- 2 medium carrots, diced
- 2 cups diced fennel bulb
- 2 cloves garlic, minced
- 1 cup uncooked pearl (Israeli) couscous
- 6 cups chicken or vegetable broth
- 1 Tbsp. minced fresh parsley
  Lemon wedges, optional

1. Preheat oven to 425°. Arrange mushrooms in a greased 15x10x1-in. baking pan. Spritz mushrooms with cooking spray. Sprinkle with oregano and salt; toss to coat. Roast until tender and lightly browned, 15-20 minutes, stirring occasionally.
2. Meanwhile, in a large saucepan, heat butter over medium heat; saute onion, carrots and fennel until tender, 4-6 minutes. Add garlic and couscous; cook and stir 2 minutes. Stir in broth and mushrooms; bring to a boil. Reduce heat; simmer, covered, until the couscous is tender, 7-8 minutes. Sprinkle with the parsley. Serve with lemon wedges if desired.

1⅓ CUPS: 182 cal., 4g fat (1g sat. fat), 10mg chol., 1187mg sod., 31g carb. (4g sugars, 2g fiber), 7g pro.

BAKED HAM & COLBY
SANDWICHES

BAKED HAM & COLBY SANDWICHES

This yummy recipe is a winner with our friends and family. Not only are the warm sandwiches a snap to prepare, but they also smell so good when they are baking that no one has been able to resist them.
—*Sherry Crenshaw, Fort Worth, TX*

Takes: 30 min. • **Makes:** 8 servings

½ cup butter, melted
2 Tbsp. prepared mustard
1 Tbsp. dried minced onion
1 Tbsp. poppy seeds
2 to 3 tsp. sugar
8 hamburger buns, split
8 slices Colby cheese
16 thin slices deli ham (about 1 lb.)
1½ cups shredded part-skim mozzarella cheese

1. Preheat oven to 350°. In a small bowl, combine the butter, mustard, onion, poppy seeds and sugar. Place bun bottoms, cut side up, in an ungreased 15x10x1-in. baking pan. Top each with Colby cheese, ham and mozzarella. Brush with half the butter mixture.
2. Replace bun tops. Brush with remaining butter mixture. Bake, uncovered, until the cheese is melted, 10-15 minutes.
1 SANDWICH: 504 cal., 32g fat (18g sat. fat), 102mg chol., 1444mg sod., 27g carb. (5g sugars, 1g fiber), 27g pro.

Test Kitchen Tip

Turn this classic ham and cheese sandwich into a Reuben by swapping in corned beef for the ham, adding a layer of sauerkraut and substituting caraway seeds for the poppy seeds.

QUICK CHICKEN MINESTRONE

QUICK CHICKEN MINESTRONE

You'll love this flavorful soup that comes together with pantry ingredients. Dress it up by serving the dish with garlic bread.
—*Patricia Harmon, Baden, PA*

Prep: 20 min. • **Cook:** 20 min.
Makes: 8 servings (3 qt.)

1 lb. boneless skinless chicken breasts, cubed
1 large onion, chopped
1 celery rib, chopped
1 Tbsp. olive oil
1 garlic clove, minced
3 cups reduced-sodium chicken broth
2½ cups water
1 can (15 oz.) white kidney or cannellini beans, rinsed and drained
1 can (14½ oz.) diced tomatoes, undrained
1 pkg. (5.9 oz.) chicken and garlic-flavored rice and vermicelli mix
1½ cups frozen vegetable blend (broccoli, red pepper, onion)
½ cup chopped pepperoni
½ tsp. dried basil
½ tsp. dried oregano
⅔ cup shredded Parmesan cheese
Crushed red pepper flakes, optional

1. In a Dutch oven over medium heat, cook the chicken, onion and celery in oil until chicken is no longer pink. Add garlic; cook 1 minute longer. Add the broth, water, beans, tomatoes, rice and vermicelli mix, vegetables, pepperoni, basil and oregano. Bring to a boil.
2. Reduce heat; simmer, uncovered, until rice is tender, 18-20 minutes. Sprinkle each serving with cheese and, if desired, pepper flakes.
1½ CUPS: 299 cal., 10g fat (3g sat. fat), 44mg chol., 932mg sod., 31g carb. (5g sugars, 5g fiber), 22g pro.

4

Sides & Salads

When time is tight, side dishes are often an afterthought—but no longer! Whether you're looking for a hearty roasted vegetable or a cool, refreshing salad, these recipes effortlessly hold their own beside any main course.

SZECHUAN SUGAR
SNAP PEAS P. 111

CLASSIC WILTED
LETTUCE SALAD

CLASSIC WILTED LETTUCE SALAD

When we were kids, my sister and I would prepare the freshly picked lettuce for this wilted lettuce recipe, rinsing it several times and carefully drying it. As we did so, we quibbled about the portions we'd each have. Somehow, it seems she always managed to get more! We still can't get enough of this salad.
—*Doris Natvig, Jesup, IA*

Takes: 15 min. • **Makes:** 6 servings

- 4 bacon strips, cut up
- ¼ cup white vinegar
- 2 Tbsp. water
- 2 green onions, sliced
- 2 tsp. sugar
- ¼ tsp. salt
- ¼ tsp. pepper
- 8 to 10 cups torn leaf lettuce
- 1 hard-boiled large egg, chopped

1. In a large skillet, cook the bacon over medium heat until crisp. Using a slotted spoon, remove to paper towels to drain.
2. To the hot drippings, add vinegar, water, onions, sugar, salt and pepper, stirring until the sugar is dissolved.
3. Place the lettuce in a salad bowl; immediately pour dressing over top and toss lightly. Top with egg. Serve immediately.
1 CUP: 118 cal., 10g fat (4g sat. fat), 45mg chol., 227mg sod., 5g carb. (3g sugars, 2g fiber), 3g pro.
WILTED SPINACH SALAD: Substitute torn fresh spinach for the lettuce.

Test Kitchen Tip

To make this salad vegetarian, skip the bacon and make a warm vinaigrette. Add vinegar, onions, sugar, salt and pepper to olive oil, and heat it on medium until the sugar dissolves. For a smoky flavor, add liquid smoke.

BALSAMIC BRUSSELS SPROUTS WITH PEARS

BALSAMIC BRUSSELS SPROUTS WITH PEARS

One year, I decided to create a new recipe for our Thanksgiving dinner, and came up a fabulous side dish I can make any time. It requires only a few ingredients but still feels special. Apples, figs and pecans are also delicious with this recipe.
—*David Ross, Spokane Valley, WA*

Prep: 20 min. • **Bake:** 35 min.
Makes: 6 servings

- 1½ lbs. Brussels sprouts, halved
- 3 Tbsp. olive oil
- 1 tsp. kosher salt
- ½ tsp. pepper
- 1 large pear, cut into ½-in.-thick slices
- ½ cup chopped walnuts
- ¾ cup balsamic vinegar
- 1 Tbsp. minced fresh rosemary or 1 tsp. dried rosemary, crushed

1. Preheat the oven to 400°. Place the Brussels sprouts in a 15x10x1-in. baking pan; toss with oil, salt and pepper. Roast for 20 minutes, stirring halfway through. Add pear and walnuts to pan. Roast until the Brussels sprouts are lightly charred and tender, 15-20 minutes longer.
2. Meanwhile, in a small saucepan, bring vinegar to a boil. Reduce heat; simmer, uncovered, until syrupy, 8-10 minutes.
3. In a large bowl, combine Brussels sprouts mixture, balsamic syrup and rosemary; toss to combine.
⅔ CUP: 220 cal., 13g fat (2g sat. fat), 0 chol., 346mg sod., 24g carb. (14g sugars, 6g fiber), 5g pro. **DIABETIC EXCHANGES:** 2½ fat, 1 starch, 1 vegetable.

CORN STUFFING BALLS

GREEN BEAN, CORN & BUTTERMILK SALAD

I love the crunch of green beans and fresh corn, so I combined them with a buttermilk Caesar dressing. This salad is good served immediately, but it's even better after chilling for a few hours.
—Arlene Erlbach, Morton Grove, IL

Prep: 25 min. • **Cook:** 15 min. + chilling
Makes: 6 servings

- ½ cup reduced-fat mayonnaise
- ½ cup buttermilk
- ½ cup shredded Parmesan cheese
- 1 Tbsp. lemon juice
- 1 tsp. Worcestershire sauce
- ½ tsp. garlic powder
- ½ tsp. salt
- ½ tsp. pepper
- ¾ lb. fresh green beans, trimmed and cut into 1-in. pieces
- 1 Tbsp. olive oil
- 4 medium ears sweet corn

1. Whisk together the mayonnaise, buttermilk, Parmesan, lemon juice, Worcestershire sauce, garlic powder, salt and pepper. Refrigerate, covered, until serving.
2. Meanwhile, in a Dutch oven, bring 8 cups water to a boil. Add beans; cook, uncovered, just until crisp-tender, 2-3 minutes. Drain and immediately drop into ice water. Drain and pat dry; transfer to a serving bowl.
3. Cut corn from the cobs. In a large cast-iron or other heavy skillet, heat oil over medium-high heat. Add corn; cook and stir until tender, 6-8 minutes. Remove from heat and add to the beans; refrigerate, covered, until chilled.
4. Stir the mayonnaise mixture into the vegetables; toss to coat. If desired, sprinkle with additional Parmesan.
1 CUP: 201 cal., 12g fat (3g sat. fat), 13mg chol., 498mg sod., 20g carb. (8g sugars, 3g fiber), 7g pro.

CORN STUFFING BALLS

My mom had many winning recipes, and this was one of our family's favorites. I can still picture these corn stuffing balls encircling the large meat platter piled high with one of her delicious entrees.
—Audrey Groe, Lake Mills, IA

Prep: 20 min. • **Bake:** 30 min.
Makes: 12 servings

- 6 cups herb-seasoned stuffing croutons
- 1 cup chopped celery
- ½ cup chopped onion
- ¾ cup butter, divided
- 1 can (14¾ oz.) cream-style corn
- 1 cup water
- 1½ tsp. poultry seasoning
- ¾ tsp. salt
- ¼ tsp. pepper
- 3 large eggs yolks, beaten

1. Preheat oven to 375°. Place croutons in a large bowl and set aside. In a skillet, saute celery and onion in ½ cup butter. Add the corn, water, poultry seasoning, salt and pepper; bring to a boil. Remove from the heat; cool for 5 minutes. Pour over the croutons. Add egg yolks and mix gently.
2. Shape ½ cupfuls into balls; flatten slightly. Place in a greased 15x10x1-in. baking pan. Melt the remaining ¼ cup butter; drizzle over the stuffing balls. Bake, uncovered, until lightly browned, 30 minutes.
1 STUFFING BALL: 365 cal., 16g fat (7g sat. fat), 84mg chol., 1233mg sod., 47g carb. (4g sugars, 3g fiber), 10g pro.

GREEN BEAN, CORN &
BUTTERMILK SALAD

HEIRLOOM
TOMATO SALAD

HEIRLOOM TOMATO SALAD

This simple yet elegant dish always pleases my guests. Not only is it tasty, but it's healthy too. The more varied the colors of the tomatoes you choose, the prettier the salad will be.
—*Jessie Apfel, Berkeley, CA*

Prep: 20 min. + chilling
Makes: 6 servings

- 2 cups cut-up heirloom tomatoes
- 1 cup multicolored cherry tomatoes, halved
- 2 cups fresh baby spinach
- ½ cup sliced red onion

DRESSING

- 3 Tbsp. olive oil
- 2 Tbsp. white balsamic vinegar
- 1 garlic clove, minced
- ½ tsp. salt
- ¼ tsp. dried basil
- ¼ tsp. dried oregano
- ¼ tsp. dried rosemary, crushed
- ¼ tsp. dried thyme
- ¼ tsp. pepper
- ⅛ tsp. rubbed sage

Place tomatoes, spinach and onion in a large bowl. Whisk together the dressing ingredients; toss with salad. Refrigerate, covered, 2 hours. Serve with a slotted spoon.

⅔ CUP: 75 cal., 5g fat (1g sat. fat), 0 chol., 161mg sod., 7g carb. (4g sugars, 2g fiber), 1g pro. **DIABETIC EXCHANGES:** 1 vegetable, 1 fat.

FRENCH POTATO SALAD

FRENCH POTATO SALAD

French potato salad is vinegar-based instead of creamy, made with Dijon mustard, olive oil, scallions or shallots, and fresh herbs.
—*Denise Cassady, Phoenix, MD*

Takes: 25 min. • **Makes:** 6 servings

- 1 lb. baby red potatoes
- 1 lb. baby yellow potatoes
- 1 garlic clove
- ¼ cup olive oil
- 2 Tbsp. champagne vinegar or white wine vinegar
- 2 tsp. Dijon mustard
- ½ tsp. salt
- ½ tsp. pepper
- 1 shallot, finely chopped
- 1 Tbsp. each minced fresh chervil, parsley and chives
- 1 tsp. minced fresh tarragon

1. Place potatoes in a large saucepan; add water to cover. Bring to a boil. Reduce heat; cook, uncovered, until tender, 10-15 minutes. With a slotted spoon, remove potatoes to a colander; cool slightly. Return water to a boil. Add garlic; cook, uncovered, 1 minute. Remove garlic and immediately drop into ice water. Drain and pat dry; mince. Reserve ¼ cup cooking liquid.

2. Cut cooled potatoes into ¼-in. slices. Transfer potatoes to a large bowl. In a small bowl, whisk reserved cooking liquid, oil, vinegar, mustard, minced garlic, salt and pepper until blended. Pour over potatoes; toss gently to coat. Gently stir in the remaining ingredients. Serve warm or at room temperature.

1 CUP: 201 cal., 9g fat (1g sat. fat), 0 chol., 239mg sod., 29g carb. (1g sugars, 2g fiber), 3g pro. **DIABETIC EXCHANGES:** 2 starch, 2 fat.

Test Kitchen Tip

To add even more zing to this salad, try capers, either finely chopped and added to the dressing or used whole as a garnish. Capers add bold, salty flavor, along with some acidity. You can also use a variety of herbs—we suggest rosemary, thyme or dill.

GRAPEFRUIT LETTUCE SALAD

A light vinaigrette flavored with cilantro and grapefruit juice drapes this tangy salad. You can make the dressing ahead of time; it keeps well in the refrigerator.
—*Vivian Haen, Menomonee Falls, WI*

Takes: 15 min. • **Makes:** 2 servings

- 2 Tbsp. pink grapefruit juice
- 1 Tbsp. olive oil
- 1½ tsp. red wine vinegar
- ½ tsp. honey
- 1½ tsp. minced fresh cilantro
- 2 cups torn Bibb or Boston lettuce
- 1 medium pink grapefruit, peeled and sectioned
  Optional: Sliced fennel bulb, fennel fronds and pistachios

In a small bowl, whisk grapefruit juice, oil, vinegar and honey; stir in cilantro. In a salad bowl, toss lettuce, grapefruit and, if desired, sliced fennel bulb, fennel fronds and pistachios. Drizzle with the dressing; gently toss to coat.

1 CUP: 120 cal., 7g fat (1g sat. fat), 0 chol., 5mg sod., 14g carb. (0 sugars, 2g fiber), 1g pro. **DIABETIC EXCHANGES:** 2 vegetable, 1½ fat.

SWEET POTATO PONE

This recipe is my absolute favorite way to prepare sweet potatoes. Not only is it an eagerly anticipated side dish for Thanksgiving dinner, but I also make it to dress up ordinary meals. You can almost serve it as a dessert!
—*Kristine Chayes, Smithtown, NY*

Prep: 15 min. • **Bake:** 55 min. + standing
Makes: 12 servings

- 2½ lbs. large sweet potatoes (about 4 large), peeled and shredded
- ½ cup sugar
- ½ cup light corn syrup
- ½ cup butter, melted
- 1 Tbsp. grated orange zest
- ¾ cup all-purpose flour
- 1 tsp. ground nutmeg
- 1 tsp. ground cinnamon

1. Preheat the oven to 350°. Grease a 13x9-in. baking dish; set aside. In a large bowl, combine sweet potatoes, sugar, corn syrup, butter and orange zest. In another bowl, combine the flour, nutmeg and cinnamon. Add to the sweet potato mixture; mix well.
2. Transfer to prepared baking dish. Bake until sweet potatoes are bubbly and golden brown, 55-60 minutes. Let stand for 10 minutes before serving.
1 SERVING: 270 cal., 8g fat (5g sat. fat), 20mg chol., 80mg sod., 49g carb. (29g sugars, 3g fiber), 3g pro.

GRAPEFRUIT LETTUCE SALAD

SWEET POTATO PONE

ROSEMARY SWEET POTATO FRIES

ROSEMARY SWEET POTATO FRIES

A local restaurant got me hooked on sweet potato fries. I started experimenting at home, trying to make my recipe taste just like theirs, but healthier and baked, not fried. I'm thrilled with the results!
—*Jackie Gregston, Hallsville, TX*

Prep: 15 min. • **Bake:** 30 min.
Makes: 4 servings

- 3 Tbsp. olive oil
- 1 Tbsp. minced fresh rosemary
- 1 garlic clove, minced
- 1 tsp. cornstarch
- ¾ tsp. salt
- ⅛ tsp. pepper
- 3 large sweet potatoes, peeled and cut into ¼-in. julienned strips (about 2¼ lbs.)

1. Preheat the oven to 425°. In a large airtight container, combine the first 6 ingredients. Add sweet potatoes; shake to coat.
2. Arrange potatoes in a single layer on two 15x10x1-in. baking pans coated with cooking spray. Bake, uncovered, 30-35 minutes or until tender and lightly browned, turning occasionally.

1 SERVING: 256 cal., 10g fat (1g sat. fat), 0 chol., 459mg sod., 39g carb. (16g sugars, 5g fiber), 3g pro.

> *"A winner. They make the house smell as delicious as they taste."*
> **—WALLYNBOB, TASTEOFHOME.COM**

HARVARD BEETS

This pretty side dish's bright, citrusy flavors are an ideal companion for down-to-earth entrees—even for people who usually shy away from beets.
—*Jean Ann Perkins, Newburyport, MA*

Takes: 15 min. • **Makes:** 4 servings

- 1 can (16 oz.) sliced beets
- ¼ cup sugar
- 1½ tsp. cornstarch
- 2 Tbsp. vinegar
- 2 Tbsp. orange juice
- 1 Tbsp. grated orange zest

Drain beets, reserving 2 Tbsp. juice; set beets and juice aside. In a saucepan, combine sugar and cornstarch. Add vinegar, orange juice and beet juice; bring to a boil. Reduce heat and simmer until thickened, 3-4 minutes. Add beets and orange zest; heat through.
½ CUP: 93 cal., 0 fat (0 sat. fat), 0 chol., 220mg sod., 23g carb. (19g sugars, 2g fiber), 1g pro.

ITALIAN TOMATO CUCUMBER SALAD

This yummy medley of vegetables is a cool complement to zesty dishes like seasoned fish and barbecued meats and poultry.
—*Florine Bruns, Fredericksburg, TX*

Takes: 10 min. • **Makes:** 4 servings

- 2 medium cucumbers, sliced
- 1 large tomato, cut into wedges
- 1 small red onion, cut into thin strips
- ¼ cup Italian salad dressing or salad dressing of your choice

In a large bowl, combine the vegetables. Add dressing; toss to coat.
½ CUP: 93 cal., 6g fat (1g sat. fat), 0 chol., 257mg sod., 9g carb. (6g sugars, 2g fiber), 2g pro. **DIABETIC EXCHANGES:** 1 vegetable, 1 fat.

HARVARD BEETS

GREEN CHILE
CORN FRITTERS

WALNUT CRANBERRY ORZO

I came up with this delightful side dish after being fascinated by the tiny pasta! With red pepper, cranberries, walnuts and Parmesan, the dish is as colorful as it is flavorful.
—*Judith Comstock, Salado, TX*

Takes: 30 min. • **Makes:** 6 servings

- 1¼ cups uncooked orzo pasta
- 1 medium sweet red pepper, chopped
- 1 small onion, chopped
- 1½ tsp. olive oil
- ½ cup reduced-sodium chicken broth or vegetable broth
- ½ cup dried cranberries
- ¼ tsp. salt
- ½ cup chopped walnuts, toasted
- ¼ cup grated Parmesan cheese

1. Cook orzo according to the package directions. Meanwhile, saute red pepper and onion in oil until tender. Stir in the broth, cranberries and salt. Bring to a boil. Reduce heat; simmer, uncovered, for 5 minutes.
2. Drain orzo; toss with the vegetable mixture. Sprinkle with walnuts and Parmesan cheese.
⅔ CUP: 283 cal., 9g fat (1g sat. fat), 3mg chol., 216mg sod., 43g carb. (9g sugars, 3g fiber), 10g pro.

GREEN CHILE CORN FRITTERS

This is a crispy side dish, appetizer or snack to add to a Mexican meal. The fritters also go well with chili or soup. I usually have all the ingredients on hand.
—*Johnna Johnson, Scottsdale, AZ*

Prep: 20 min. • **Cook:** 5 min./batch
Makes: 2 dozen

- 1 cup yellow cornmeal
- ½ cup all-purpose flour
- 1½ tsp. baking powder
- ¾ tsp. salt
- ½ tsp. garlic powder
- ½ tsp. onion powder
- ½ tsp. paprika
- ½ tsp. pepper
- 1 large egg, room temperature
- ⅔ cup 2% milk
- 1 can (8¾ oz.) whole kernel corn, drained
- 1 can (4 oz.) chopped green chiles, drained
  Oil for deep-fat frying
  Optional: Sriracha mayonnaise or condiment of your choice

1. In a large bowl, whisk together the first 8 ingredients. In another bowl, whisk the egg and milk until blended. Add to the dry ingredients, stirring just until moistened. Let stand 5 minutes. Fold in corn and green chiles.
2. In a deep cast-iron or electric skillet, heat the oil to 375°. Drop the batter by tablespoonfuls, a few at a time, into hot oil. Fry until golden brown, 1-1½ minutes on each side. Drain on paper towels. Serve with desired condiments.
1 FRITTER: 74 cal., 4g fat (0 sat. fat), 8mg chol., 159mg sod., 9g carb. (1g sugars, 1g fiber), 1g pro.

WALNUT CRANBERRY ORZO

- Smoky Cauliflower Bites -

With a spicy, smoky flavor and an irresistible crunch, these healthy little treats work as a side dish or a fun, bite-sized appetizer.

Break 1 medium head of **cauliflower** into florets. Combine ¼ cup **olive oil**, 1 tsp. **sea salt**, 1 tsp. **paprika**, ½ tsp. **ground cumin**, ¼ tsp. **ground turmeric** and ⅛ tsp. **chili powder**. Toss with cauliflower to coat. Transfer to a 15x10x1-in. baking pan. Roast at 450° until cauliflower is tender, 15-20 minutes, stirring halfway through.

SZECHUAN SUGAR SNAP PEAS
(PICTURED ON PAGE 97)
Simple seasonings transform the crisp, sweet sugar snap peas into an unbeatable side dish your family will love. You can use chopped walnuts instead of the cashews if you prefer.
—*Jeanne Holt, St. Paul, MN*

Takes: 25 min. • **Makes:** 8 servings

- 6 cups fresh sugar snap peas
- 2 tsp. peanut oil
- 1 tsp. sesame oil
- 3 Tbsp. thinly sliced green onions
- 1 tsp. grated orange zest
- ½ tsp. minced garlic
- ½ tsp. minced fresh gingerroot
- ⅛ tsp. crushed red pepper flakes
- 1 Tbsp. minced fresh cilantro
- ¼ tsp. salt
- ⅛ tsp. pepper
- ⅓ cup salted cashew halves

1. In a Dutch oven, saute peas in the peanut oil and sesame oil until crisp-tender. Add green onions, orange zest, garlic, ginger and pepper flakes; saute 1 minute longer.
2. Remove from the heat; stir in the cilantro, salt and pepper. Sprinkle with cashews just before serving.
¾ CUP: 107 cal., 5g fat (1g sat. fat), 0 chol., 121mg sod., 10g carb. (5g sugars, 4g fiber), 5g pro. **DIABETIC EXCHANGES:** 2 vegetable, 1 fat.

ROASTED PEAR SALAD

ROASTED PEAR SALAD
Oven-roasted pears are tossed with crispy greens, dried cranberries and nuts in this dish. The dressing adds even more pear flavor, sweetened with a touch of honey.
—Taste of Home *Test Kitchen*

Prep: 15 min. • **Bake:** 15 min. + cooling
Makes: 4 servings

- 2 medium pears, halved and cored
- 4 tsp. olive oil, divided
- 2 Tbsp. cider vinegar
- 1 tsp. water
- 1 tsp. honey
- ¼ tsp. salt
- ⅛ tsp. white pepper
- 1 pkg. (10 oz.) mixed baby salad greens
- 1 cup watercress sprigs
- ¼ cup chopped hazelnuts, toasted
- ¼ cup dried cranberries

1. Preheat oven to 400°. In a small bowl, toss pears with 1 tsp. oil. Place in a 15x10x1-in. baking pan coated with cooking spray. Bake 10 minutes. Turn the pears over; bake until golden and tender, 5-7 minutes longer.
2. When cool enough to handle, peel the pears. Thinly slice 2 pear halves lengthwise and set aside. Place the remaining pear halves in a blender. Add the vinegar, water, honey, salt and white pepper; cover and process until smooth. While processing, gradually add remaining 3 tsp. oil in a steady stream.
3. In a large bowl, toss the salad greens, watercress, hazelnuts and cranberries. Arrange the reserved pear slices on top; drizzle with dressing.
1 SERVING: 174 cal., 9g fat (1g sat. fat), 0 chol., 178mg sod., 24g carb. (0 sugars, 5g fiber), 3g pro.

RADISH CUCUMBER SALAD

RADISH CUCUMBER SALAD

I put this salad together with vegetables from my garden. My family liked it so much, I started bringing it to community suppers and was often asked for the recipe. It's a refreshing side dish for any meat entree.
—*Mildred Sherrer, Fort Worth, TX*

Takes: 10 min. • **Makes:** 2 servings

- ½ medium cucumber, halved and sliced
- 2 radishes, sliced
- 2 Tbsp. chopped red onion
- 1 Tbsp. olive oil
- 1½ tsp. lemon juice
- ⅛ to ¼ tsp. garlic salt
- ⅛ tsp. lemon-pepper seasoning

In a serving bowl, combine cucumber, radishes and onion. In a second bowl, combine the remaining ingredients. Pour over vegetables and toss to coat. Serve immediately.
1 SERVING: 77 cal., 7g fat (1g sat. fat), 0 chol., 143mg sod., 4g carb. (2g sugars, 1g fiber), 1g pro. **DIABETIC EXCHANGES:** 1½ fat, 1 vegetable.

Test Kitchen Tip
We recommend serving this summer salad immediately, but you can slice the veggies and prep the lemon juice dressing beforehand to save some extra time.

SPINACH SALAD WITH HOT BACON DRESSING

I came up with this recipe after having a salad like this at a restaurant years ago. It's especially delicious when the spinach comes right from the garden to the table.
—*Wanda Cover, Mediapolis, IA*

Takes: 25 min. • **Makes:** 2 servings

- 2 cups fresh baby spinach, torn
- 2 hard-boiled large eggs, sliced
- 4 cherry tomatoes, halved
- 3 medium fresh mushrooms, sliced
- ¼ cup salad croutons
- 6 pitted ripe olives, halved
- 3 slices red onion, halved

DRESSING
- 4 bacon strips, diced
- 1 Tbsp. chopped onion
- 2 Tbsp. sugar
- 2 Tbsp. ketchup
- 1 Tbsp. red wine vinegar
- 1 Tbsp. Worcestershire sauce

1. Divide the spinach between 2 plates. Arrange eggs, tomatoes, mushrooms, croutons, olives and red onion over top.
2. In a small skillet, cook the bacon over medium heat until crisp. Using a slotted spoon, remove to paper towels; drain, reserving 2 Tbsp. drippings in the pan. Saute chopped onion in drippings until tender. Stir in the sugar, ketchup, vinegar and Worcestershire sauce. Bring to a boil. Reduce heat; simmer, uncovered, until thickened, 1-2 minutes. Sprinkle bacon over salads; drizzle with dressing.
1⅓ CUPS: 367 cal., 21g fat (6g sat. fat), 238mg chol., 1178mg sod., 29g carb. (21g sugars, 2g fiber), 17g pro.

SPINACH SALAD WITH HOT BACON DRESSING

ZUCCHINI PATTIES

My sister gave me this recipe and I, in turn, have given it to many of my friends. These patties have a nice flavor and are compatible with just about any entree.
—*Annabelle Cripe, Goshen, IN*

Prep: 15 min. • **Cook:** 20 min.
Makes: 4 servings

- 2 cups shredded zucchini
- ½ cup shredded cheddar cheese
- ⅓ cup biscuit/baking mix
- 2 Tbsp. grated onion
- ½ tsp. salt
- ½ tsp. dried basil
- ¼ tsp. pepper
- 2 large eggs, lightly beaten
- 2 Tbsp. butter

1. In a bowl, combine first 7 ingredients. Stir in eggs; mix well. Shape the mixture into 6 patties, using about ¼ cup zucchini mixture for each patty.
2. In a skillet over medium-high heat, melt butter; cook patties until lightly browned, 4-5 minutes on each side.
2 PATTIES: 195 cal., 14g fat (7g sat. fat), 122mg chol., 577mg sod., 10g carb. (2g sugars, 1g fiber), 8g pro.

Test Kitchen Tip

Excess water in the mixture can cause your zucchini patties to fall apart. Make sure to pat the shredded zucchini dry before adding it to the binding mixture.

THAI SALAD WITH PEANUT DRESSING

This Thai salad is very fresh and flavorful. The peanut garnish adds a satisfying crunch.
—*James Schend, Pleasant Prairie, WI*

Takes: 25 min. • **Makes:** 8 servings

- 2 cups spring mix salad greens
- ½ cup fresh cilantro leaves
- 1 small napa cabbage, shredded
- 1 small cucumber, sliced
- 1 small red onion, julienned
- 2 small carrots, shredded
- 2 green onions, sliced

PEANUT DRESSING
- ¼ cup creamy peanut butter
- 3 Tbsp. hot water
- 1 Tbsp. lime juice
- 1 Tbsp. sesame oil
- 1 Tbsp. fish sauce
- 1 Tbsp. rice vinegar
- ½ tsp. crushed red pepper flakes
- 1 small garlic clove, minced
- ¼ cup dry roasted peanuts
  Jalapeno pepper slices, optional

1. In a large bowl, toss salad greens and the next 6 ingredients.
2. For dressing, in a small bowl, whisk the next 8 ingredients. Add to the salad and toss to coat. Divide mixture among 4 plates; top with peanuts and, if desired, jalapeno slices.
NOTE: Wear disposable gloves when cutting hot peppers; the oils can burn skin. Avoid touching your face.
1 CUP: 111 cal., 8g fat (1g sat. fat), 0 chol., 286mg sod., 7g carb. (3g sugars, 2g fiber), 4g pro.

ZUCCHINI PATTIES

THAI SALAD WITH PEANUT DRESSING

SYRIAN GREEN BEANS
WITH FRESH HERBS

SYRIAN GREEN BEANS WITH FRESH HERBS

This is how my mom made green beans. She got the recipe from a neighbor when we lived in Turkey. Cook a double batch as they make an excellent healthy snack straight from the fridge. If you like, add a thinly sliced onion and red bell pepper. Another idea is to make them ahead to add to a salad.
—Trisha Kruse, Eagle, ID

Takes: 25 min. • **Makes:** 6 servings

- 2 Tbsp. olive oil
- 2 garlic cloves, minced
- 1 lb. fresh green beans, cut into 2-in. pieces
- ½ tsp. salt
- ¼ tsp. pepper
- 2 Tbsp. each minced fresh cilantro, parsley and mint

In a large skillet, heat oil over medium heat. Add the garlic; cook for 1 minute. Add green beans, salt and pepper. Cook, covered, until crisp-tender, 8-10 minutes, stirring occasionally. Add herbs; cook and stir just until the beans are tender, 1-2 minutes.

¾ CUP: 66 cal., 5g fat (1g sat. fat), 0 chol., 203mg sod., 6g carb. (2g sugars, 3g fiber), 2g pro. **DIABETIC EXCHANGES:** 1 vegetable, 1 fat.

STRAWBERRY VINAIGRETTE

STRAWBERRY VINAIGRETTE

I enjoy using strawberries in a variety of ways, including in this pretty, sweet-tart dressing.
—Carolyn McMunn, San Angelo, TX

Takes: 10 min. • **Makes:** 2½ cups

- 1 pkg. (16 oz.) frozen unsweetened strawberries, thawed
- 6 Tbsp. lemon juice
- ¼ cup sugar
- 2 Tbsp. cider vinegar
- 2 Tbsp. olive oil
- ⅛ tsp. poppy seeds

Place the strawberries in a blender; cover and process until pureed. Add the lemon juice and sugar; cover and process until blended. While processing, gradually add vinegar and oil in a steady stream; process until thickened. Stir in poppy seeds. Transfer to a large bowl or jar; cover and store in the refrigerator.

2 TBSP. VINAIGRETTE: 31 cal., 1g fat (0 sat. fat), 0 chol., 1mg sod., 5g carb. (4g sugars, 0 fiber), 0 pro.
BLUEBERRY VINAIGRETTE: Substitute blueberries for the strawberries.

Test Kitchen Tips

- You can make substitutions to create your own version of this strawberry dressing. Try substituting avocado oil, flaxseed oil or walnut oil for the olive oil, or adding cracked black pepper, fresh basil or Italian seasoning.

- If you want your vinaigrette to be seed-free, use a fine-mesh sieve to strain the strawberries after they've been blended and before adding the lemon juice and sugar.

STRAWBERRY
SHORTCAKE SALAD

SWISS POTATO PANCAKE

This is the classic Swiss mountain dish called *rösti*. The big potato pancake is cut into wedges and usually served with bratwurst, but I also have prepared this cheese potato dish as a meatless main course. We love the nutty flavor that the Gruyere cheese provides.
—*Sue Jurack, Mequon, WI*

Takes: 15 min. • **Makes:** 6 servings

- 2 Tbsp. butter, divided
- 2 Tbsp. canola oil, divided
- 1 pkg. (30 oz.) frozen shredded hash brown potatoes, thawed
- 1 tsp. salt, divided
- ¼ tsp. pepper, divided
- 1½ cups shredded Gruyere or Swiss cheese
  Optional: Sour cream and minced chives

1. In a 9-in. nonstick skillet, melt 1 Tbsp. butter with 1 Tbsp. oil over medium-high heat. Spread half the potatoes in an even layer in skillet. Season with ½ tsp. salt and ⅛ tsp. pepper. Sprinkle with cheese, then top with the remaining potatoes. Season with remaining ½ tsp. salt and ⅛ tsp. pepper. Press mixture gently into the skillet. Cook until bottom is browned, 7 minutes.
2. Remove from heat. Loosen pancake from side of skillet. Invert onto a plate. Return skillet to heat and heat remaining 1 Tbsp. butter and 1 Tbsp. oil. Slide potato pancake browned side up into the skillet. Cook until bottom is browned and cheese is melted, 5-7 minutes.
3. Slide the pancake into a plate and cut into wedges. If desired, serve with sour cream and chives.
1 PIECE: 296 cal., 17g fat (8g sat. fat), 35mg chol., 507mg sod., 27g carb. (2g sugars, 3g fiber), 11g pro.

STRAWBERRY
SHORTCAKE SALAD

This fabulous recipe transforms a classic dessert into a bright, refreshing twist on traditional salad. Creamy Gorgonzola, crispy pancetta and strawberry yogurt dressing make this a celebration of spring in a salad bowl.
—*Adrienne Vradenburg, Bakersfield, CA*

Takes: 25 min. • **Makes:** 4 servings

- 4 oz. chopped pancetta
- 1 Tbsp. extra virgin olive oil
- 2 individual round shortcakes, cubed
- 3 Tbsp. minced fresh parsley, divided
- ½ tsp. kosher salt, divided
- ½ cup strawberry custard-style yogurt
- 1 Tbsp. fresh lemon juice
- ¼ tsp. coarsely ground pepper
- 4 cups fresh arugula
- 1 cup fresh strawberries, sliced
- ½ cup crumbled Gorgonzola cheese
- ¼ cup pine nuts, toasted

1. In a large skillet, cook pancetta over medium-high heat until crispy, about 5 minutes. Remove to paper towels to drain, reserving drippings in pan. Add olive oil to the drippings. Add shortcake cubes; cook, stirring frequently, until golden brown, 3-4 minutes. Transfer to bowl; stir in 2 Tbsp. parsley and ¼ tsp. salt.
2. In a small bowl, stir together yogurt, lemon juice, remaining 1 Tbsp. parsley and ¼ tsp. salt, and pepper. In a salad bowl, toss the arugula, strawberries, Gorgonzola, pine nuts, pancetta and shortcake croutons. Drizzle with the dressing and serve immediately.
1 SERVING: 330 cal., 24g fat (8g sat. fat), 51mg chol., 1074mg sod., 18g carb. (11g sugars, 2g fiber), 12g pro.

SWISS POTATO PANCAKE

SESAME ALMOND SLAW

SESAME ALMOND SLAW

Crunchy veggies and noodles are coated in a tangy dressing in this pleasant slaw.
—Taste of Home *Test Kitchen*

Takes: 20 min. • **Makes:** 2 servings

- 1 pkg. (3 oz.) ramen noodles
- ¾ cup shredded cabbage
- ¾ cup shredded romaine
- 2 Tbsp. sliced green onion
- 2 tsp. slivered almonds, toasted
- 2 tsp. sesame seeds, toasted

DRESSING
- 1 Tbsp. rice vinegar
- 1½ tsp. sugar
- 1½ tsp. canola oil
- 1 tsp. water
- ½ tsp. sesame oil
- ¼ tsp. reduced-sodium soy sauce
  Dash salt
  Dash pepper

1. Split ramen noodles in half. Save the seasoning packet and half the noodles for future use. Break apart remaining noodles; place in a bowl. Add cabbage, romaine, green onion, toasted almonds and sesame seeds.
2. For dressing, in a jar with a tight-fitting lid, combine the next 8 ingredients and shake well. Add to the salad and toss to coat. Serve immediately.

1 CUP: 187 cal., 10g fat (3g sat. fat), 0 chol., 193mg sod., 20g carb. (4g sugars, 2g fiber), 4g pro. **DIABETIC EXCHANGES:** 1½ fat, 1 starch, 1 vegetable.

SKILLET CABBAGE

I use this recipe often when my schedule gets tight and I need an easy vegetable to cook. It adds plenty of substance to a simple meal.
—*Charmaine Fricke, St. Charles, IL*

Takes: 25 min. • **Makes:** 6 servings

- 2 Tbsp. butter
- 4 cups shredded cabbage
- 1 green pepper, cut into thin strips
- 2 Tbsp. water
- ½ tsp. salt
- ¼ tsp. pepper
- 3 oz. cream cheese, cubed and softened

Melt butter in a large cast-iron or other heavy skillet; add cabbage and green pepper and toss to coat. Stir in water, salt and pepper. Cover; simmer until the cabbage is tender, 8-10 minutes. Add cream cheese; stir until melted.

½ CUP: 100 cal., 9g fat (5g sat. fat), 26mg chol., 286mg sod., 4g carb. (2g sugars, 1g fiber), 2g pro.

SKILLET CABBAGE

GUACAMOLE TOSSED SALAD

The fresh blend of avocados, tomatoes, red onion and greens in my salad gets additional pizazz from crumbled bacon and a slightly spicy vinaigrette.
—*Lori Fischer, Chino Hills, CA*

Takes: 15 min. • **Makes:** 4 servings

- 2 medium tomatoes, seeded and chopped
- ½ small red onion, sliced and separated into rings
- 6 bacon strips, cooked and crumbled
- ⅓ cup canola oil
- 2 Tbsp. cider vinegar
- 1 tsp. salt
- ¼ tsp. pepper
- ¼ tsp. hot pepper sauce
- 2 large ripe avocados, peeled and cubed
- 4 cups torn salad greens

1. In a large bowl, combine the tomatoes, onion and bacon; set aside.
2. In a small bowl, whisk the oil, vinegar, salt, pepper and hot pepper sauce. Pour over tomato mixture; toss gently. Add avocados.
3. Place greens in a large salad bowl; add avocado mixture and toss to coat.
1 SERVING: 531 cal., 51g fat (7g sat. fat), 12mg chol., 868mg sod., 17g carb. (3g sugars, 10g fiber), 9g pro.

GUACAMOLE TOSSED SALAD

ZUCCHINI FRIES

These aren't anything like potato fries—in a good way! They are air-fried to crispy perfection and are so flavorful. Enjoy as an appetizer or a low-carb alternative to French fries. Don't have an air fryer? You can convection bake for the same time.
—*Jen Pahl, West Allis, WI*

Prep: 20 min. • **Cook:** 10 min./batch
Makes: 4 servings

- 2 medium zucchini
- 1 cup panko bread crumbs
- 2 tsp. dried basil, divided
- 1½ tsp. seasoned salt
- 1 tsp. garlic powder
- 1 tsp. dried oregano
- ½ cup grated Parmesan cheese plus 2 Tbsp. grated Parmesan cheese
- 2 large eggs, lightly beaten
  Cooking spray
  Marinara sauce, warmed

1. Preheat air fryer to 375°. Cut each zucchini in half lengthwise and then in half crosswise. Cut each piece lengthwise into ¼-in. slices.
2. In a shallow bowl, mix bread crumbs, 1 tsp. basil, seasoned salt, garlic powder, oregano and ½ cup Parmesan cheese. In a separate shallow bowl, place eggs and remaining 1 tsp. basil. Dip zucchini slices in the egg mixture and then in the crumb mixture, patting to help the coating adhere.
3. In batches, place zucchini pieces on greased tray in air-fryer basket; spritz with the cooking spray. Cook for 6-8 minutes or until lightly browned. Flip each piece; cook until golden brown, 3-5 minutes longer.
4. Sprinkle hot fries with the remaining 2 Tbsp. Parmesan cheese. Serve with marinara sauce.
1 CUP: 91 cal., 4g fat (2g sat. fat), 52mg chol., 389mg sod., 9g carb. (2g sugars, 1g fiber), 6g pro. **DIABETIC EXCHANGES:** 1 vegetable, 1 fat.

ZUCCHINI FRIES

CREAMED PEAS

CREAMED PEAS

I can still taste these wonderful peas in Mama's delicious white sauce. Our food was pretty plain during the week, so I always thought this white sauce made the peas "extra fancy" and fitting for a Sunday meal.
—*Imogene Hutton, Brownwood, TX*

Takes: 15 min. • **Makes:** 4 servings

- 1 pkg. (10 oz.) frozen peas
- 1 Tbsp. butter
- 1 Tbsp. all-purpose flour
- ¼ tsp. salt
- ⅛ tsp. pepper
- ½ cup whole milk
- 1 tsp. sugar

Cook the peas according to the package directions. Meanwhile, melt the butter in a small saucepan. Stir in flour, salt and pepper until blended; gradually add milk and sugar. Bring to a boil; cook and stir until thickened, 1-2 minutes. Drain peas; stir into the sauce and heat through.

½ CUP: 110 cal., 4g fat (2g sat. fat), 12mg chol., 271mg sod., 14g carb. (6g sugars, 3g fiber), 5g pro.

Test Kitchen Tip

To add extra flavor and texture to these creamed peas, try sprinkling on a simple topping, such as fried onion strips or bacon pieces.

DIRTY RICE

DIRTY RICE

This is an old Louisiana recipe that I've had longer than I can remember. It's a very popular southern dish. To turn it into a main meal, simply increase the sausage and chicken livers.
—*Lum Day, Bastrop, LA*

Takes: 30 min. • **Makes:** 12 servings

- ½ lb. bulk pork sausage
- ½ lb. chicken livers, chopped
- 3 Tbsp. butter
- 1 large onion, chopped
- 1 celery rib, chopped
- 3 green onions, chopped
- 2 Tbsp. minced fresh parsley
- 1 garlic clove, minced
- 1 can (10½ oz.) condensed chicken broth, undiluted
- ½ tsp. dried basil
- ½ tsp. dried thyme
- ½ tsp. salt
- ¼ tsp. pepper
- ¼ tsp. hot pepper sauce
- 3 cups cooked rice

1. In a large cast-iron or other heavy skillet, cook sausage for 2-3 minutes; stir in chicken livers. Cook until sausage and chicken livers are no longer pink, 5-7 minutes; drain and set aside.
2. In the same skillet, melt butter over medium heat. Add the onion, celery and green onions. Cook and stir until vegetables are tender, 3-5 minutes. Add parsley and garlic; cook 1 minute longer. Add broth, basil, thyme, salt, pepper and hot pepper sauce. Stir in rice and the sausage mixture. Heat through, stirring constantly.

1 CUP: 148 cal., 7g fat (3g sat. fat), 97mg chol., 325mg sod., 14g carb. (1g sugars, 1g fiber), 6g pro.

GARLIC & ARTICHOKE
ROASTED POTATOES

DREAMY POLENTA

I grew up eating polenta, so it's a must at my holiday gatherings. Traditional polenta recipes require constant stirring, but using my handy slow cooker allows me to turn my attention to the lineup of other foods on my spread.
—Ann Voccola, Milford, CT

Prep: 10 min. • **Cook:** 5 hours
Makes: 12 servings

- 1 Tbsp. butter
- 5 cups whole milk
- 4 cups half-and-half cream
- 12 Tbsp. butter, cubed, divided
- 2 cups yellow cornmeal
- ¾ tsp. salt
- ½ tsp. minced fresh rosemary
- ¼ tsp. pepper
- 2 cups shredded Asiago cheese

1. Generously grease a 5-qt. slow cooker with 1 Tbsp. butter. Add milk, cream, 6 Tbsp. cubed butter, cornmeal, salt, rosemary and pepper; stir to combine.
2. Cook, covered, on low until polenta is thickened, 5-6 hours, whisking every hour. Just before serving, whisk again; stir in cheese and remaining 6 Tbsp. cubed butter. Garnish with additional rosemary if desired.
¾ CUP: 444 cal., 29g fat (18g sat. fat), 100mg chol., 379mg sod., 29g carb. (9g sugars, 1g fiber), 13g pro.

GARLIC & ARTICHOKE ROASTED POTATOES

I like to put this side into the oven while I'm baking a main dish. Artichokes give it gourmet appeal.
—Marie Rizzio, Interlochen, MI

Prep: 15 min. • **Bake:** 35 min.
Makes: 10 servings

- 2½ lbs. medium red potatoes, cut into 1½-in. cubes
- 2 pkg. (8 oz. each) frozen artichoke hearts
- 8 garlic cloves, halved
- 3 Tbsp. olive oil
- ¾ tsp. salt
- ¼ tsp. pepper
- ¼ cup lemon juice
- 2 Tbsp. minced fresh parsley
- 1 tsp. grated lemon zest

1. Preheat oven to 425°. Place the potatoes, artichokes and garlic in a 15x10x1-in. baking pan coated with cooking spray. Combine the oil, salt and pepper; drizzle over vegetables and toss to coat.
2. Bake, uncovered, for 35-40 minutes or until tender, stirring occasionally. Transfer to a large bowl. Add lemon juice, parsley and lemon zest; toss to coat. Serve warm.
¾ CUP: 143 cal., 4g fat (1g sat. fat), 0 chol., 209mg sod., 24g carb. (2g sugars, 4g fiber), 4g pro. **DIABETIC EXCHANGES:** 1 starch, 1 vegetable, 1 fat.

DREAMY POLENTA

5

30-Minute Dinners

On the busiest of nights, you need to get supper on the table fast.
Skip the drive-thru or frozen dinners—with these ultra quick recipes,
you'll go from ingredients to finished dish in just half an hour!

EASY SHRIMP
TACOS P. 134

PORK SCHNITZEL WITH SAUCE

combine flour and the remaining ⅓ cup broth until smooth. Stir into skillet. Bring to a boil; cook and stir for 1-2 minutes or until thickened. Reduce the heat; stir in the sour cream, dill, salt and pepper; heat through. Serve with cutlets. If desired, garnish with dill.

1 SERVING: 341 cal., 19g fat (6g sat. fat), 157mg chol., 687mg sod., 20g carb. (3g sugars, 1g fiber), 21g pro.

BROILED PARMESAN TILAPIA

Even picky eaters will love fish when you plate up this toasty Parmesan-coated entree. I serve it with mashed cauliflower and a green salad for a low-calorie meal everyone can enjoy.
—*Trisha Kruse, Eagle, ID*

Takes: 20 min. • **Makes:** 6 servings

- 6   tilapia fillets (6 oz. each)
- ¼   cup grated Parmesan cheese
- ¼   cup reduced-fat mayonnaise
- 2   Tbsp. lemon juice
- 1   Tbsp. butter, softened
- 1   garlic clove, minced
- 1   tsp. minced fresh basil or
      ¼ tsp. dried basil
- ½   tsp. seafood seasoning

1. Place fillets on a broiler pan coated with cooking spray. In a small bowl, combine the remaining ingredients; spread over fillets.
2. Broil 3-4 in. from the heat until fish flakes easily with a fork, 10-12 minutes.
1 FILLET: 207 cal., 8g fat (3g sat. fat), 94mg chol., 260mg sod., 2g carb. (1g sugars, 0 fiber), 33g pro. **DIABETIC EXCHANGES:** 5 lean meat, 1 fat.

PORK SCHNITZEL WITH SAUCE

German-style schnitzel is usually made with veal. I substituted pork to save money without sacrificing flavor. Whenever I serve this dish, I'm asked for the recipe.
—*Diane Katzmark, Metamora, MI*

Takes: 25 min. • **Makes:** 2 servings

- 2   pork cutlets (about 5 oz. each)
- 2   Tbsp. all-purpose flour
- ¼   tsp. seasoned salt
- ⅛   tsp. pepper
- 1   large egg
- 2   Tbsp. 2% milk
- ¼   cup dry bread crumbs
- ¼   tsp. paprika
- 1   to 2 Tbsp. canola oil

SAUCE
- ⅔   cup chicken broth, divided
- 1½ tsp. all-purpose flour
- 3   Tbsp. sour cream
- ⅛   tsp. dill weed
      Salt and pepper to taste
      Snipped fresh dill, optional

1. Flatten meat to ½-in. thickness. In a shallow dish, combine the flour, seasoned salt and pepper. In another shallow bowl, combine egg and milk. Place bread crumbs and paprika in a third shallow dish. Coat meat with flour; dip in egg mixture, then coat with crumb mixture. Let stand for 5 minutes.
2. In a large skillet, cook pork in oil for 2 minutes on each side or until browned. Remove and keep warm.
3. In the same skillet, stir in ⅓ cup broth, scraping browned bits. In another bowl,

BROILED PARMESAN
TILAPIA

SALMON WITH HORSERADISH
PISTACHIO CRUST

SHRIMP PAD THAI

You can make this yummy Thai classic in no time. Find fish sauce and chili garlic sauce in the Asian foods aisle of your grocery store.
—Elise Ray, Shawnee, KS

Takes: 30 min. • **Makes:** 4 servings

- 4 oz. uncooked thick rice noodles
- ½ lb. uncooked shrimp (41-50 per lb.), peeled and deveined
- 2 tsp. canola oil
- 1 large onion, chopped
- 1 garlic clove, minced
- 1 large egg, lightly beaten
- 3 cups coleslaw mix
- 4 green onions, thinly sliced
- ⅓ cup rice vinegar
- ¼ cup sugar
- 3 Tbsp. reduced-sodium soy sauce
- 2 Tbsp. fish sauce or additional reduced-sodium soy sauce
- 2 to 3 tsp. chili garlic sauce
- 2 Tbsp. chopped salted peanuts
  Chopped fresh cilantro leaves

1. Cook noodles according to package directions. In a large nonstick skillet or wok, stir-fry shrimp in oil until shrimp turn pink; remove and set aside. Add onion and garlic to the pan. Make a well in the center of the onion mixture; add egg. Stir-fry until egg is completely set, 2-3 minutes.
2. Add the coleslaw mix, green onions, vinegar, sugar, soy sauce, fish sauce, chili garlic sauce and peanuts; heat through. Return shrimp to the pan and heat through. Drain noodles; toss with shrimp mixture. Garnish with cilantro.
1¼ CUPS: 338 cal., 7g fat (1g sat. fat), 115mg chol., 1675mg sod., 52g carb. (23g sugars, 3g fiber), 17g pro.

SALMON WITH HORSERADISH PISTACHIO CRUST

Impress everyone at your table with this elegant but easy salmon. Feel free to switch up the ingredients to suit your tastes. You can substitute scallions for the shallots or try almonds or pecans instead of pistachios. The nutty coating also plays well with chicken and pork.
—Linda Press Wolfe, Cross River, NY

Takes: 30 min. • **Makes:** 6 servings

- 6 salmon fillets (4 oz. each)
- ⅓ cup sour cream
- ⅔ cup dry bread crumbs
- ⅔ cup chopped pistachios
- ½ cup minced shallots
- 2 Tbsp. olive oil
- 1 to 2 Tbsp. prepared horseradish
- 1 Tbsp. snipped fresh dill or 1 tsp. dill weed
- ½ tsp. grated lemon or orange zest
- ¼ tsp. crushed red pepper flakes
- 1 garlic clove, minced

Preheat oven to 350°. Place salmon, skin side down, in an ungreased 15x10x1-in. baking pan. Spread sour cream over each fillet. Combine the remaining ingredients. Pat crumb-nut mixture onto tops of the salmon fillets, pressing to help coating adhere. Bake until fish just begins to flake easily with a fork, 12-15 minutes.
1 SALMON FILLET: 376 cal., 25g fat (5g sat. fat), 60mg chol., 219mg sod., 15g carb. (3g sugars, 2g fiber), 24g pro. **DIABETIC EXCHANGES:** 3 lean meat, 2 fat.

SHRIMP PAD THAI

EASY SHRIMP
TACOS

EASY SHRIMP TACOS

I love preparing these easy-to-make shrimp tacos. Hatch chiles are a staple ingredient in my home state of Texas, and this was the very first recipe that I conquered with them. Mix and match your favorite toppings—salsa and avocado would be perfect additions.
—*Deborah Jamison, Austin, TX*

Takes: 25 min. • **Makes:** 4 servings

- 1 cup plain Greek yogurt or sour cream
- ¼ cup minced fresh cilantro
- 3 Tbsp. lemon juice
- 2 Tbsp. lime juice
- ⅛ tsp. plus ¼ tsp. salt, divided
- 2 Tbsp. olive oil
- 2 medium green pepper, chopped
- 4 fresh green chiles, such as Hatch or Anaheim, seeded and chopped
- ½ cup chopped red onion
- 1 lb. uncooked shrimp (31-40 per lb.), peeled and deveined
- 4 garlic cloves, minced
- 1 tsp. ground cumin
- 8 corn tortillas (6 in.), warmed
- 2 cups torn lettuce

1. In a small bowl, combine yogurt, cilantro, lemon juice, lime juice and ⅛ tsp. salt; set aside.
2. In a large skillet, heat the oil over medium-high heat. Add the peppers, chiles and onion; cook and stir until crisp-tender, 4-5 minutes. Add the shrimp, garlic, cumin and remaining ¼ tsp. salt. Cook and stir until shrimp turn pink, 2-3 minutes.
3. Remove from heat; serve in tortillas with lettuce, yogurt sauce and, if desired, lime wedges.
2 TACOS: 359 cal., 16g fat (5g sat. fat), 153mg chol., 422mg sod., 32g carb. (6g sugars, 5g fiber), 24g pro. **DIABETIC EXCHANGES:** 3 lean meat, 3 fat, 2 starch.

QUICK FETTUCCINE ALFREDO

FRIED CHICKEN STRIPS

I recently made this recipe of Mom's for my in-laws and they said it was the best fried chicken ever. Slicing the chicken breasts into strips cuts down on cooking time and ensures every piece is crunchy and evenly coated.
—*Genny Monchamp, Redding, CA*

- -

Takes: 20 min. • **Makes:** 6 servings

2⅔ cups crushed saltines (about 80 crackers)
  1 tsp. garlic salt
  ½ tsp. dried basil
  ½ tsp. paprika
  ⅛ tsp. pepper
  1 large egg
  1 cup 2% milk
1½ lbs. boneless skinless chicken breasts, cut into ½-in. strips
    Oil for frying

1. In a shallow bowl, combine the first 5 ingredients. In another shallow bowl, beat egg and milk. Dip chicken into the egg mixture, then the cracker mixture.
2. In an electric skillet or deep-fat fryer, heat oil to 375°. Fry the chicken, a few strips at a time, for 2-3 minutes on each side or until golden brown. Drain on paper towels.
4 OZ. COOKED CHICKEN: 388 cal., 19g fat (3g sat. fat), 98mg chol., 704mg sod., 25g carb. (2g sugars, 1g fiber), 28g pro.

QUICK FETTUCCINE ALFREDO

This simple recipe combines heavy whipping cream and Parmesan and Romano cheeses for a creamy, cheesy sauce that comes together in minutes.
—*Jo Gray, Park City, MT*

- -

Takes: 20 min. • **Makes:** 4 servings

  8 oz. uncooked fettuccine
  6 Tbsp. butter, cubed
  2 cups heavy whipping cream
  ¾ cup grated Parmesan cheese, divided
  ½ cup grated Romano cheese
  2 large egg yolks, lightly beaten
  ¼ tsp. salt
  ⅛ tsp. pepper
  ⅛ tsp. ground nutmeg

1. Cook fettuccine according to package directions. Meanwhile, in a saucepan, melt the butter over medium-low heat. Stir in cream, ½ cup Parmesan cheese, Romano cheese, egg yolks, salt, pepper and nutmeg. Cook and stir sauce over medium-low heat until a thermometer reads 160° (do not boil).
2. Drain the fettuccine; serve with the Alfredo sauce and remaining ¼ cup Parmesan cheese.
1 CUP: 908 cal., 73g fat (45g sat. fat), 339mg chol., 821mg sod., 44g carb. (2g sugars, 2g fiber), 23g pro.

FAJITA-STYLE SHRIMP & GRITS

I combined two favorites—shrimp with cheesy grits, and fajitas—in this spicy one-dish meal. For more heat, you can use pepper jack cheese instead of the Mexican cheese blend.
—*Arlene Erlbach, Morton Grove, IL*

Takes: 30 min. • **Makes:** 4 servings

- 1 lb. uncooked shrimp (16-20 per lb.), peeled and deveined
- 2 Tbsp. fajita seasoning mix
- 1 cup quick-cooking grits
- 4 cups boiling water
- 1½ cups shredded Mexican cheese blend
- 3 Tbsp. 2% milk
- 2 Tbsp. canola oil
- 3 medium sweet peppers, seeded and cut into 1-in. strips
- 1 medium sweet onion, cut into 1-in. strips
- 1 jar (15½ to 16 oz.) chunky medium salsa
- ¼ cup orange juice
- ¼ cup plus 1 Tbsp. fresh cilantro leaves, divided

1. Sprinkle shrimp with fajita seasoning; toss to coat. Set aside.

2. Slowly stir the grits into boiling water. Reduce heat to medium; cook, covered, stirring occasionally, for 5-7 minutes or until thickened. Remove from heat. Stir in the cheese until melted; then stir in milk. Keep warm.

3. In a large skillet, heat oil over medium-high heat. Add peppers and onion; cook and stir until tender and pepper edges are slightly charred. Add the salsa, orange juice and shrimp. Cook, stirring constantly, until the shrimp turn pink, 4-6 minutes. Stir in ¼ cup cilantro. Remove from heat.

4. Spoon grits into serving bowls; top with shrimp mixture. Sprinkle with the remaining 1 Tbsp. cilantro.

1 SERVING: 561 cal., 23g fat (8g sat. fat), 176mg chol., 1324mg sod., 55g carb. (12g sugars, 4g fiber), 33g pro.

CHICKEN THAI PIZZA

This is a recipe I make for my friends for a girls night filled with fun and laughter. It is simple to make but is full of flavor.
—*Kimberly Knuppenburg, Menomonee Falls, WI*

Takes: 25 min. • **Makes:** 6 servings

- 1 prebaked 12-in. pizza crust
- ⅔ cup Thai peanut sauce
- 2 Tbsp. reduced-sodium soy sauce
- 2 Tbsp. creamy peanut butter
- 1 cup shredded cooked chicken breast
- 1 cup shredded part-skim mozzarella cheese
- 3 green onions, chopped
- ½ cup bean sprouts
- ½ cup shredded carrot

1. Preheat oven to 400°. Place crust on an ungreased 12-in. pizza pan or baking sheet. In a small bowl, combine peanut sauce, soy sauce and peanut butter. Add chicken; toss to coat. Spread over crust; sprinkle with cheese and onions.

2. Bake until the cheese is melted, 10-12 minutes. Top with bean sprouts and carrot.

1 PIECE: 361 cal., 15g fat (4g sat. fat), 29mg chol., 1183mg sod., 35g carb. (4g sugars, 3g fiber), 23g pro.

FAJITA-STYLE SHRIMP & GRITS

APPLE CIDER PORK CHOPS

With cider gravy, these pork chops are a must for fall family dinners. I serve them with buttered egg noodles to soak up more of that delicious sauce. The recipe is easy to double when company pops in.
—*Debiana Casterline,*
Egg Harbor Township, NJ

- -

Takes: 25 min. • **Makes:** 6 servings

- 2 Tbsp. olive oil
- 6 boneless pork loin chops (6 to 8 oz. each), about ¾ in. thick
- 1 garlic clove, minced
- 1 Tbsp. Dijon mustard
- 1 tsp. honey
- ½ tsp. apple pie spice
- ½ tsp. coarsely ground pepper
- ¼ tsp. dried thyme
- ¼ tsp. salt
- 1 cup apple cider
- 1 Tbsp. plus 1 tsp. cornstarch
- 2 Tbsp. water
   Minced fresh parsley

1. In a large skillet, heat olive oil over medium heat. Brown pork chops on both sides.
2. Meanwhile, in a small bowl, combine the next 7 ingredients; stir in apple cider. Pour over pork chops. Reduce heat to medium-low; cook, covered, until a thermometer inserted into chops reads 145°, 4-5 minutes. Remove chops from skillet; let stand for 5 minutes.
3. In a small bowl, mix cornstarch and water until smooth; stir into the cider mixture in skillet. Return to a boil, stirring constantly; cook and stir until thickened, 1-2 minutes. Pour over chops; sprinkle with fresh parsley.
1 PORK CHOP: 301 cal., 14g fat (4g sat. fat), 82mg chol., 210mg sod., 8g carb. (5g sugars, 0 fiber), 33g pro. **DIABETIC EXCHANGES:** 4 lean meat, 1 fat, ½ starch.

CHICKEN PARMESAN BURGERS

CHICKEN PARMESAN BURGERS

A restaurant-quality burger topped with marinara and loaded with cheese—what's not to love? Add fresh basil for even more flavor if you'd like.
—*Brooke Petras, Alpine, CA*

- -

Takes: 30 min. • **Makes:** 4 servings

- 3 Tbsp. olive oil, divided
- 1 small onion, finely chopped
- 2 garlic cloves, minced
- ¾ cup marinara sauce, divided
- ½ cup finely chopped or shredded part-skim mozzarella cheese
- ½ cup dry bread crumbs
- 1 tsp. Italian seasoning
- 1 tsp. dried oregano
- ½ tsp. salt
- ½ tsp. pepper
- 1 lb. ground chicken
- 4 slices part-skim mozzarella cheese
- 4 hamburger buns, split and toasted
- ¼ cup shredded Parmesan cheese
   Fresh basil leaves, optional

1. In a large skillet, heat 1 Tbsp. oil over medium-high heat. Add onion; cook and stir until tender, about 3 minutes. Add garlic; cook 1 minute longer. Remove from heat; cool slightly.
2. In a large bowl, combine ¼ cup marinara sauce with the chopped mozzarella cheese, bread crumbs, seasonings and onion mixture. Add chicken; mix lightly but thoroughly. With wet hands, shape mixture into four ½-in.-thick patties.
3. In the same skillet, heat the remaining 2 Tbsp. oil over medium heat. Cook the burgers until a thermometer reads 165°, 4-5 minutes on each side. Top with sliced mozzarella cheese; cook, covered, until the cheese is melted, 1-2 minutes.
4. Serve in buns; top with remaining ½ cup marinara sauce, Parmesan cheese and, if desired, basil leaves.
1 BURGER: 603 cal., 33g fat (10g sat. fat), 108mg chol., 1275mg sod., 41g carb. (8g sugars, 3g fiber), 38g pro.

EASY MEDITERRANEAN CHICKEN

EASY MEDITERRANEAN CHICKEN

Friends and family love this special chicken recipe. I changed a few things to make it healthier, but it tastes just as good.
—*Kara Zilis, Oak Forest, IL*

- -

Takes: 30 min. • **Makes:** 4 servings

- 4 boneless skinless chicken breast halves (4 oz. each)
- 1 Tbsp. olive oil
- 1 can (14½ oz.) no-salt-added stewed tomatoes
- 1 cup water
- 1 tsp. dried oregano
- ¼ tsp. garlic powder
- 1½ cups instant brown rice
- 1 pkg. (12 oz.) frozen cut green beans
- 12 pitted Greek olives, halved
- ½ cup crumbled feta cheese

1. In a large nonstick skillet, brown chicken in oil on each side. Stir in the tomatoes, water, oregano and garlic powder. Bring to a boil; reduce heat. Cover and simmer for 10 minutes.
2. Stir in rice and green beans. Return to a boil. Cover and simmer until a thermometer reads 165° and the rice is tender, 8-10 minutes longer. Stir in olives; sprinkle with cheese.
1 SERVING: 417 cal., 12g fat (3g sat. fat), 70mg chol., 386mg sod., 44g carb. (6g sugars, 6g fiber), 31g pro. **DIABETIC EXCHANGES:** 3 lean meat, 2 starch, 2 vegetable, 1 fat.

Test Kitchen Tip

To make this recipe your own, use ingredients or seasonings you love. Use minced garlic, try fresh tomatoes instead of canned, and add any fresh vegetable instead of frozen green beans. We suggest chopped asparagus, fresh green beans or even broccoli florets.

CHICKEN CHILES RELLENOS ALFREDO

CHICKEN CHILES RELLENOS ALFREDO

This recipe combines my daughter's love of chiles rellenos and my love of chicken Alfredo! To cut down on the spice level you could substitute plain Monterey Jack cheese for the pepper jack.
—*Jennifer Stowell, Deep River, IA*

- -

Takes: 30 min. • **Makes:** 8 servings

- 1 pkg. (16 oz.) angel hair pasta
- 1½ to 2 lbs. boneless skinless chicken breasts, cubed
- 1 Tbsp. garlic powder
- 1 Tbsp. dried cilantro
- 1 tsp. ground cumin
- ½ cup butter
- 2 cups heavy whipping cream
- ½ cup cream cheese, softened
- 1½ tsp. grated lime zest
- ½ cup pepper jack cheese
- 2 cans (4 oz. each) chopped green chiles
- 2 Tbsp. lime juice

1. Cook angel hair according to package directions. Drain.
2. Meanwhile, sprinkle chicken with garlic powder, cilantro and cumin. In a large nonstick skillet, cook and stir chicken over medium heat until no longer pink, 6-8 minutes. Remove.
3. In the same skillet, melt butter. Stir in heavy cream, cream cheese and lime zest until combined, 4-6 minutes. Stir in pepper jack until melted. Add chiles and lime juice. Return chicken to the skillet; heat through. Toss the chicken mixture with pasta.
1 CUP: 698 cal., 43g fat (26g sat. fat), 167mg chol., 354mg sod., 48g carb. (4g sugars, 3g fiber), 30g pro.

- Haddock en Papillote -

Impress your guests with this elegant, showstopping entree.
Your own little secret? It couldn't be easier to prepare!

For each serving, place a **haddock fillet** (about ⅓ lb.) on a 12-in. square of parchment. Drizzle with 1 Tbsp. **dry white wine**; sprinkle with ½ tsp. **fresh dill** and ½ tsp. **lemon zest**. Top with 2 Tbsp. each **julienned carrot** and **zucchini**. Sprinkle with 1 Tbsp. **almonds**; dot with 1 Tbsp. **butter**. Fold parchment around fish, sealing tightly. Bake on a baking sheet at 375° until fish just begins to flake easily with a fork, 10-12 minutes. Open carefully.

CHICKEN WITH
PEACH-AVOCADO SALSA

ROSEMARY GARLIC SHRIMP

Delicate shrimp take on fabulous flavor when simmered in a chicken broth mixed with garlic and ripe olives.
—*Taste of Home Test Kitchen*

Takes: 20 min. • **Makes:** 8 servings

- 1¼ cups chicken or vegetable broth
- 3 Tbsp. chopped ripe olives
- 1 small cayenne or other fresh red chile pepper, finely chopped
- 2 Tbsp. lemon juice
- 1 Tbsp. minced fresh rosemary or 1 tsp. dried rosemary, crushed
- 4 garlic cloves, minced
- 2 tsp. Worcestershire sauce
- 1 tsp. paprika
- ½ tsp. salt
- ¼ to ½ tsp. pepper
- 2 lbs. uncooked shrimp (31-40 per lb.), peeled and deveined

In a large skillet, combine all ingredients except the shrimp; bring to a boil. Cook, uncovered, until the liquid is reduced by half. Stir in the shrimp; return just to a boil. Reduce heat; simmer, uncovered, until the shrimp turn pink, 3-4 minutes, stirring occasionally.
½ CUP: 110 cal., 2g fat (0 sat. fat), 139mg chol., 473mg sod., 3g carb. (1g sugars, 0 fiber), 19g pro. **DIABETIC EXCHANGES:** 3 lean meat.

CHICKEN WITH PEACH-AVOCADO SALSA

This super-fresh dinner is pure summer—juicy peaches, creamy avocado, grilled chicken and a kick of hot sauce and lime. To get it on the table even quicker, make the salsa ahead.
—*Shannon Norris, Cudahy, WI*

Takes: 30 min. • **Makes:** 4 servings

- 1 medium peach, peeled and chopped
- 1 medium ripe avocado, peeled and cubed
- ½ cup chopped sweet red pepper
- 3 Tbsp. finely chopped red onion
- 1 Tbsp. minced fresh basil
- 1 Tbsp. lime juice
- 1 tsp. hot pepper sauce
- ½ tsp. grated lime zest
- ¾ tsp. salt, divided
- ½ tsp. pepper, divided
- 4 boneless skinless chicken breast halves (6 oz. each)

1. For salsa, in a small bowl, combine the peach, avocado, red pepper, onion, basil, lime juice, hot sauce, lime zest, ¼ tsp. salt and ¼ tsp. pepper.
2. Sprinkle chicken with the remaining ½ tsp. salt and ¼ tsp. pepper. On a lightly greased grill rack, grill chicken, covered, over medium heat for 5 minutes. Turn; grill until a thermometer reads 165°, 7-9 minutes longer. Serve with salsa.
1 CHICKEN BREAST HALF WITH ½ CUP SALSA: 265 cal., 9g fat (2g sat. fat), 94mg chol., 536mg sod., 9g carb. (4g sugars, 3g fiber), 36g pro. **DIABETIC EXCHANGES:** 5 lean meat, 1 fat, ½ starch.

SUPER QUICK SHRIMP &
GREEN CHILE QUESADILLAS

PASTA & VEGGIES IN GARLIC SAUCE

Big garlic flavor and a little heat from red pepper flakes help perk up this fresh-tasting pasta dish.
—Doris Heath, Franklin, NC

Takes: 20 min. • **Makes:** 6 servings.

- 12 ounces uncooked penne pasta
- 6 garlic cloves, minced
- ¼ teaspoon crushed red pepper flakes
- 2 tablespoons olive oil
- 1 can (15 ounces) garbanzo beans or chickpeas, rinsed and drained
- 2 medium tomatoes, seeded and cut into ½-inch pieces
- 1 package (9 ounces) fresh baby spinach
- ¼ teaspoon salt
- ¼ cup grated Parmesan cheese

1. Cook pasta according to the package directions. Meanwhile, in a large skillet, saute garlic and pepper flakes in oil for 1 minute. Add garbanzo beans and tomatoes; cook and stir for 2 minutes. Add spinach and salt; cook and stir until spinach is wilted.

2. Drain pasta; add to vegetable mixture. Sprinkle with Parmesan cheese; toss to coat. If desired, serve with additional Parmesan and red pepper flakes.

1½ CUPS: 370 cal., 8g fat (2g sat. fat), 3mg chol., 432mg sod., 62g carb. (0 sugars, 6g fiber), 15g pro. **DIABETIC EXCHANGES:** 3½ starch, 1 vegetable, 1 lean meat, 1 fat.

SUPER QUICK SHRIMP & GREEN CHILE QUESADILLAS

If I am really short on time, I head to the grocery store for prepared guacamole for this recipe. Use shredded rotisserie chicken instead of shrimp for another fun option.
—Angie Ressa, Cheney, WA

Takes: 10 min.
Makes: 4 servings (½ cup guacamole)

- 1¾ cups shredded cheddar cheese
- 1 cup peeled and deveined cooked small shrimp
- 1 can (4 oz.) chopped green chiles, drained
- 2 green onions, thinly sliced
- 8 flour tortillas (8 in.)
- 1 medium ripe avocado, peeled and pitted
- 2 Tbsp. salsa
- ¼ tsp. garlic salt

1. In a large bowl, combine the cheese, shrimp, green chiles and green onions. Place half the tortillas on a greased griddle; sprinkle with cheese mixture. Top with remaining tortillas. Cook over medium heat for 1-2 minutes on each side or until golden brown and cheese is melted.

2. Meanwhile, in a small bowl, mash the avocado with salsa and garlic salt. Serve with quesadillas.

1 QUESADILLA WITH 2 TBSP. GUACAMOLE: 676 cal., 30g fat (12 g sat fat), 178mg chol., 1186mg sod., 62g carb. (1g sugars, 6g fiber), 38g pro.

PASTA & VEGGIES
IN GARLIC SAUCE

BROCCOLI BEEF BRAIDS

1. Preheat oven to 350°. In a large skillet, cook beef and onion over medium heat 6-8 minutes or until the beef is no longer pink, breaking meat into crumbles; drain. Stir in broccoli, cheese, sour cream, salt and pepper; heat through.
2. Unroll 1 tube of crescent dough onto a greased baking sheet; form into a 12x8-in. rectangle, pressing perforations to seal. Spoon half the beef mixture lengthwise down the center of dough.
3. On each long side, cut 1-in.-wide strips at an angle, from the edge to about 3 in. into the center. Fold 1 strip from each side over filling and pinch the ends together; repeat.
4. Repeat with remaining ingredients to make a second braid. Bake until golden brown, 15-20 minutes.

2 PIECES: 396 cal., 23g fat (6g sat. fat), 48mg chol., 644mg sod., 29g carb. (8g sugars, 2g fiber), 20g pro.

> *"Really good and easy. Great recipe to use up odds and ends. I used 0% Greek yogurt instead of sour cream."*
> — DILBERT098, TASTEOFHOME.COM

BROCCOLI BEEF BRAIDS

Each slice of this fast-to-fix golden bread is like a hot sandwich packed with beef, broccoli and mozzarella.
—*Penny Lapp, North Royalton, OH*

- -

Takes: 30 min.
Makes: 2 loaves (4 servings each)

1	lb. ground beef
½	cup chopped onion
3	cups frozen chopped broccoli
1	cup shredded part-skim mozzarella cheese
½	cup sour cream
¼	tsp. salt
¼	tsp. pepper
2	tubes (8 oz. each) refrigerated crescent rolls

MEATBALL SUBMARINE CASSEROLE

We were hosting a bunch of friends, and after a comedy of errors, I had to come up with a plan B for dinner. Much-loved meatball subs are even better as a hearty casserole—so delicious!
—*Rick Friedman, Palm Springs, CA*

Takes: 30 min. • **Makes:** 4 servings

- 1 pkg. (12 oz.) frozen fully cooked Italian meatballs
- 4 slices sourdough bread
- 1½ tsp. olive oil
- 1 garlic clove, halved
- 1½ cups pasta sauce with mushrooms
- ½ cup shredded part-skim mozzarella cheese, divided
- ½ cup grated Parmesan cheese, divided

1. Preheat broiler. Microwave meatballs, covered, on high until heated through, 4-6 minutes. Meanwhile, place bread on an ungreased baking sheet; brush 1 side of bread with oil. Broil 4-6 in. from heat until golden brown, 1-2 minutes. Rub the bread with cut surface of garlic; discard garlic. Tear bread into bite-sized pieces; transfer to a greased 11x7-in. baking dish. Reduce oven setting to 350°.
2. Add pasta sauce, ¼ cup mozzarella cheese and ¼ cup Parmesan cheese to meatballs; toss to combine. Pour the mixture over bread pieces; sprinkle with the remaining ¼ cup Parmesan and ¼ cup mozzarella cheeses. Bake, uncovered, until cheeses are melted, 15-18 minutes.
1 SERVING: 417 cal., 28g fat (13g sat. fat), 59mg chol., 1243mg sod., 22g carb. (8g sugars, 3g fiber), 23g pro.

SPICY BEEF & PEPPER STIR-FRY

Think of this stir-fry as your chance to play with heat and spice. I balance the savory beef with coconut milk and a spritz of lime.
—*Joy Zacharia, Clearwater, FL*

Takes: 30 min. • **Makes:** 4 servings

- 1 lb. beef top sirloin steak, cut into thin strips
- 1 Tbsp. minced fresh gingerroot
- 3 garlic cloves, minced, divided
- ¼ tsp. pepper
- ¾ tsp. salt, divided
- 1 cup light coconut milk
- 2 Tbsp. sugar
- 1 Tbsp. Sriracha chili sauce
- ½ tsp. grated lime zest
- 2 Tbsp. lime juice
- 2 Tbsp. canola oil, divided
- 1 large sweet red pepper, cut into thin strips
- ½ medium red onion, thinly sliced
- 1 jalapeno pepper, seeded and thinly sliced
- 4 cups fresh baby spinach
- 2 green onions, thinly sliced
- 2 Tbsp. chopped fresh cilantro

1. In a large bowl, toss beef with ginger, 2 garlic cloves, pepper and ½ tsp. salt; let stand 15 minutes. Meanwhile, in a small bowl, whisk coconut milk, sugar, chili sauce, lime zest, lime juice and remaining ¼ tsp. salt until blended.
2. In a large skillet, heat 1 Tbsp. oil over medium-high heat. Add beef; stir-fry until no longer pink, 2-3 minutes. Remove from pan.
3. Stir-fry red pepper, red onion, jalapeno and the remaining clove of garlic in the remaining 1 Tbsp. oil just until vegetables are crisp-tender, 2-3 minutes. Stir in the coconut milk mixture; heat through. Add spinach and beef; cook until spinach is wilted and the beef is heated through, stirring occasionally. Sprinkle with green onions and cilantro.
¾ CUP: 312 cal., 16g fat (5g sat. fat), 46mg chol., 641mg sod., 15g carb. (10g sugars, 2g fiber), 26g pro.

SPICY BEEF & PEPPER STIR-FRY

BLUE PLATE
BEEF PATTIES

BLUE PLATE BEEF PATTIES

I discovered this recipe with a friend and now we both consider it a staple. I often fix these patties for my family and friends. We love them with mashed potatoes, rice or noodles to soak up the gravy, which gets a luscious flavor from the fresh mushrooms.
—*Phyllis Miller, Danville, IN*

Takes: 20 min. • **Makes:** 4 servings

- 1 large egg
- 2 green onions with tops, sliced
- ¼ cup seasoned bread crumbs
- 1 Tbsp. prepared mustard
- 1½ lbs. ground beef
- 1 jar (12 oz.) beef gravy
- ½ cup water
- 2 to 3 tsp. prepared horseradish
- ½ lb. fresh mushrooms, sliced
   Minced fresh parsley, optional

1. In a large bowl, beat the egg; stir in the onions, bread crumbs and mustard. Add beef and mix lightly but thoroughly. Shape into four ½-in.-thick patties.
2. In an ungreased skillet, cook patties until meat is no longer pink, 4-5 minutes on each side; drain.
3. In a small bowl, combine gravy, water and horseradish; add mushrooms. Pour over patties. Cook, uncovered, until the mushrooms are tender and heated through, about 5 minutes. If desired, sprinkle with parsley.
1 SERVING: 438 cal., 24g fat (9g sat. fat), 170mg chol., 825mg sod., 14g carb. (2g sugars, 1g fiber), 41g pro.

Test Kitchen Tip
Adding an egg to ground beef helps patties, meat loaf and meatballs hold together without overworking the meat, which can make it tough.

HEARTY VEGETABLE BEEF RAGU

HEARTY VEGETABLE BEEF RAGU

This recipe is healthy yet satisfying, and quick yet delicious. I can have a hearty meal on the table in under 30 minutes, and it's one that my children will gobble up! If you are not fond of kale, stir in baby spinach or chopped broccoli instead.
—*Kim Van Dunk, Caldwell, NJ*

Takes: 30 min. • **Makes:** 8 servings

- 4 cups uncooked whole wheat spiral pasta
- 1 lb. lean ground beef (90% lean)
- 1 large onion, chopped
- 3 garlic cloves, minced
- 2 cans (14½ oz. each) Italian diced tomatoes, undrained
- 1 jar (24 oz.) meatless spaghetti sauce
- 2 cups finely chopped fresh kale
- 1 pkg. (9 oz.) frozen peas, thawed
- ¾ tsp. garlic powder
- ¼ tsp. pepper
   Grated Parmesan cheese, optional

1. Cook pasta according to the package directions; drain. Meanwhile, in a Dutch oven, cook the beef, onion and garlic over medium heat until beef is no longer pink, 6-8 minutes, crumbling beef; drain.
2. Stir in tomatoes, spaghetti sauce, kale, peas, garlic powder and pepper. Bring to a boil. Reduce heat; simmer, uncovered, until kale is tender, 8-10 minutes. Stir pasta into sauce. If desired, serve with cheese.
1½ CUPS: 302 cal., 5g fat (2g sat. fat), 35mg chol., 837mg sod., 43g carb. (15g sugars, 7g fiber), 20g pro. **DIABETIC EXCHANGES:** 2 starch, 2 vegetable, 2 lean meat.

BEEFY FRENCH ONION POTPIE

I came up with this dish knowing my husband loves French onion soup. It makes a perfect base for the hearty, beefy potpie.
—*Sara Hutchens, Du Quoin, IL*

Takes: 30 min. • **Makes:** 4 servings

- 1 lb. ground beef
- 1 small onion, chopped
- 1 can (10½ oz.) condensed French onion soup, undiluted
- 1½ cups shredded part-skim mozzarella cheese
- 1 tube (12 oz.) refrigerated buttermilk biscuits

1. Preheat oven to 350°. In a large skillet, cook beef and onion over medium heat until beef is no longer pink, 6-8 minutes, breaking beef into crumbles; drain. Stir in soup; bring to a boil.
2. Transfer mixture to an ungreased 9-in. deep-dish pie plate; sprinkle with cheese. Bake 5 minutes or until the cheese is melted. Top with biscuits. Bake until biscuits are golden brown, 15-20 minutes longer.
1 SERVING: 553 cal., 23g fat (10g sat. fat), 98mg chol., 1550mg sod., 47g carb. (4g sugars, 1g fiber), 38g pro.

SAUCY MAC & CHEESE

I love the curly noodles in this creamy recipe. Cavatappi—also sold under the name cellentani—is a corkscrew pasta, but any type of spiral pasta will work. The dish is fun to make and looks so pretty topped with extra cheese and crunchy, golden crumbs. I like to add ground pepper to my serving.
—*Sara Martin, Brookfield, WI*

Takes: 25 min. • **Makes:** 4 servings

- 2 cups cavatappi or spiral pasta
- 3 Tbsp. butter, divided
- ⅓ cup panko bread crumbs
- 2 Tbsp. all-purpose flour
- 1½ cups 2% milk
- ¾ lb. Velveeta, cubed
- ¼ cup shredded cheddar cheese

1. Cook pasta according to package directions. Meanwhile, in a large nonstick skillet, melt 1 Tbsp. butter over medium-high heat. Add bread crumbs; cook and stir until golden brown. Remove to a small bowl and set aside.
2. In the same skillet, melt remaining 2 Tbsp. butter. Stir in flour until smooth. Gradually add the milk; bring to a boil. Cook and stir until thickened, about 2 minutes. Reduce heat. Stir in Velveeta until melted.
3. Drain pasta; add to cheese mixture. Cook and stir until heated through, 3-4 minutes. Sprinkle with cheddar cheese and bread crumbs.
1¼ CUPS: 661 cal., 36g fat (21g sat. fat), 121mg chol., 1267mg sod., 58g carb. (11g sugars, 2g fiber), 27g pro.

SAUCY MAC & CHEESE

ASPARAGUS & SHRIMP WITH ANGEL HAIR

This is terrific for romantic dinners. It's easy on the budget and perfect for two!
—*Shari Neff, Takoma Park, MD*

- -

Takes: 30 min. • **Makes:** 2 servings

- 3 oz. uncooked angel hair pasta
- ½ lb. uncooked shrimp (16-20 per lb.), peeled and deveined
- ¼ tsp. salt
- ⅛ tsp. crushed red pepper flakes
- 2 Tbsp. olive oil, divided
- 8 fresh asparagus spears, trimmed and cut into 2-in. pieces
- ½ cup sliced fresh mushrooms
- ¼ cup chopped seeded tomato, peeled
- 4 garlic cloves, minced
- 2 tsp. chopped green onion
- ½ cup white wine or chicken broth
- 1½ tsp. minced fresh basil
- 1½ tsp. minced fresh oregano
- 1½ tsp. minced fresh parsley
- 1½ tsp. minced fresh thyme
- ¼ cup grated Parmesan cheese
  Lemon wedges

1. Cook pasta according to the package directions. Meanwhile, sprinkle shrimp with salt and pepper flakes. In a large skillet or wok, heat 1 Tbsp. oil over medium-high heat. Add the shrimp; stir-fry until pink, 2-3 minutes. Remove; keep warm.

2. In same skillet, stir-fry the next 5 ingredients in the remaining 1 Tbsp. oil until vegetables are crisp-tender, about 5 minutes. Add wine and seasonings. Return shrimp to pan.

3. Drain pasta; add to shrimp mixture and toss gently. Cook and stir until heated through, 1-2 minutes. Sprinkle with Parmesan cheese. Serve with lemon wedges.

1¾ CUPS: 488 cal., 19g fat (4g sat. fat), 132mg chol., 584mg sod., 41g carb. (4g sugars, 3g fiber), 29g pro.

ASPARAGUS & SHRIMP
WITH ANGEL HAIR

SAUSAGE POTATO
SKILLET

SAUSAGE POTATO SKILLET

While I was growing up, I often went home for lunch with my Italian girlfriend. Lunch was always the same—sausage, fried potatoes, green peppers and onions—but I could never get enough of my favorite meal.
—*Amelia Bordas, Springfield, VA*

- -

Takes: 30 min. • **Makes:** 2 servings

- 2 fresh Italian sausage links
- 1 Tbsp. canola oil
- 1 small onion, sliced
- ¼ cup each sliced green and sweet red pepper
- 2 small potatoes, sliced
  Salt and pepper to taste

1. In a large skillet, brown sausage in oil until a thermometer reads 160°. Add onion and peppers; saute until the vegetables are tender.
2. Add potatoes and 2 cups water; bring to a boil. Reduce heat; cover and simmer for 15 minutes or until potatoes are tender. Drain; add salt and pepper.
1 SERVING: 416 cal., 22g fat (6g sat. fat), 45mg chol., 544mg sod., 40g carb. (6g sugars, 4g fiber), 15g pro.

Test Kitchen Tip
Feel free to toss some extra veggies into your skillet. Sausage pairs well with other veggies, such as zucchini, tomatoes and broccoli. A rice side dish, such as a rice pilaf, would be a perfect addition to your dinner.

PEAR & FENNEL PORK

PEAR & FENNEL PORK

Fresh fennel has a large bulbous base and pale green stems with wispy foliage. Often mislabeled as sweet anise, it has a sweeter and more delicate flavor than anise, and makes a terrific match for mild meats, such as pork and chicken.
—Taste of Home *Test Kitchen*

- -

Takes: 25 min. • **Makes:** 4 servings

- 4 boneless butterflied pork chops (½ in. thick and 6 oz. each)
- ½ tsp. salt
- ¼ tsp. pepper
- 1 Tbsp. olive oil
- 1 cup sliced onion
- 1 cup sliced fennel bulb
- 1 Tbsp. butter
- 2 Tbsp. cornstarch
- 2 cups pear nectar
- 3 Tbsp. maple syrup
- ½ to 1 tsp. ground nutmeg

1. Sprinkle the pork chops with salt and pepper. In a large skillet, cook chops in oil over medium-high heat until juices run clear, 4-5 minutes on each side; drain. Set chops aside and keep warm.
2. In same skillet, saute onion and fennel in butter until crisp-tender. In a small bowl, combine cornstarch, pear nectar, syrup and nutmeg until smooth; add to the skillet. Bring to a boil; cook and stir until thickened, about 2 minutes. Serve over pork chops.
1 SERVING: 431 cal., 16g fat (6g sat. fat), 90mg chol., 390mg sod., 38g carb. (30g sugars, 2g fiber), 33g pro.

PEPPER RICOTTA PRIMAVERA

PORK CHOPS WITH RHUBARB

A surprising rhubarb sauce makes these tender chops extra special. I like the fruity sauce on the tangy side, but you can always add more honey if it's too puckery for your family.
—*Bonnie Bufford, Nicholson, PA*

Takes: 25 min. • **Makes:** 2 servings

- 1 Tbsp. all-purpose flour
  Salt and pepper to taste
- 2 bone-in pork loin chops
  (½ to ¾ in. thick)
- 2 Tbsp. butter
- ½ lb. fresh or frozen rhubarb, chopped
- 1 Tbsp. honey
- ⅛ tsp. ground cinnamon
- 1½ tsp. minced fresh parsley

1. In a shallow dish, combine the flour, salt and pepper. Add pork chops; turn to coat. In a skillet, melt the butter over medium heat. Add pork chops; cook until a thermometer reads 145°, 4-5 minutes on each side. Remove and keep warm.
2. Add the rhubarb, honey and cinnamon to the skillet; cook until rhubarb is tender, about 5 minutes. Serve sauce over pork chops. Sprinkle with parsley.
1 SERVING: 492 cal., 30g fat (14g sat. fat), 142mg chol., 173mg sod., 17g carb. (10g sugars, 2g fiber), 38g pro.

PEPPER RICOTTA PRIMAVERA

Garlic, peppers and herbs top creamy ricotta cheese in this meatless skillet meal you can make in just 20 minutes.
—*Janet Boulger, Botwood, NL*

Takes: 20 min. • **Makes:** 6 servings

- 1 cup part-skim ricotta cheese
- ½ cup fat-free milk
- 4 tsp. olive oil
- 1 garlic clove, minced
- ½ tsp. crushed red pepper flakes
- 1 medium green pepper, julienned
- 1 medium sweet red pepper, julienned
- 1 medium sweet yellow pepper, julienned
- 1 medium zucchini, sliced
- 1 cup frozen peas, thawed
- ¼ tsp. dried oregano
- ¼ tsp. dried basil
- 6 oz. fettuccine, cooked and drained

1. Whisk together ricotta cheese and milk; set aside. In a large skillet, heat oil over medium heat. Add garlic and pepper flakes; saute 1 minute. Add the next 7 ingredients. Cook and stir over medium heat until vegetables are crisp-tender, about 5 minutes.
2. Add cheese mixture to fettuccine; top with vegetables. Toss to coat. Serve immediately.
1 CUP: 229 cal., 7g fat (3g sat. fat), 13mg chol., 88mg sod., 31g carb. (6g sugars, 4g fiber), 11g pro. **DIABETIC EXCHANGES:** 2 starch, 1 medium-fat meat, ½ fat.

Test Kitchen Tip

This is a mostly mild dish with a bit of a spicy kick. To punch up the flavor, use fresh herbs instead of dried and sprinkle with Parmesan cheese before serving.

TAPENADE-STUFFED CHICKEN BREASTS

I created this recipe for my husband, who absolutely loves olives. I usually make a larger batch of the tapenade and serve it with bread or crackers as a snack or appetizer.
—*Jessica Levinson, Nyack, NY*

Takes: 30 min. • **Makes:** 4 servings

- 4 oil-packed sun-dried tomatoes
- 4 pitted Greek olives
- 4 pitted Spanish olives
- 4 pitted ripe olives
- ¼ cup roasted sweet red peppers, drained
- 4 garlic cloves, minced
- 1 Tbsp. olive oil
- 2 tsp. balsamic vinegar
- 4 boneless skinless chicken breast halves (6 oz. each)
  Grated Parmesan cheese

1. Place the first 8 ingredients in a food processor; pulse until the tomatoes and olives are coarsely chopped. Cut a pocket horizontally in the thickest part of each chicken breast. Fill with olive mixture; secure with toothpicks.
2. Grill chicken, covered, on a lightly oiled grill rack over medium heat or broil 4 in. from heat 8-10 minutes on each side or until a thermometer inserted in stuffing reads 165°. Sprinkle with cheese. Discard toothpicks before serving.
1 STUFFED CHICKEN BREAST HALF: 264 cal., 11g fat (2g sat. fat), 94mg chol., 367mg sod., 5g carb. (1g sugars, 1g fiber), 35g pro. **DIABETIC EXCHANGES:** 5 lean meat, 1 fat.

CLASSIC CRAB CAKES

Our region is known for good seafood, and crab cakes are a traditional favorite. I learned to make them from a chef in a restaurant where the cakes were a bestseller. The crabmeat's sweet and mild flavor gets a spark from the other ingredients.
—*Debbie Terenzini, Lusby, MD*

Takes: 20 min. • **Makes:** 8 servings

- 1 lb. fresh or canned crabmeat, drained, flaked and cartilage removed
- 2 to 2½ cups soft bread crumbs
- 1 large egg, beaten
- ¾ cup mayonnaise
- ⅓ cup each chopped celery, green pepper and onion
- 2 tsp. lemon juice
- 1 Tbsp. seafood seasoning
- 1 Tbsp. minced fresh parsley
- 1 tsp. Worcestershire sauce
- 1 tsp. prepared mustard
- ¼ tsp. pepper
- ⅛ tsp. hot pepper sauce
  Optional: 2 to 4 Tbsp. canola oil and lemon wedges

1. In a large bowl, combine crab, bread crumbs, egg, mayonnaise, vegetables, juice and seasonings. Shape the mixture into 8 patties.
2. Broil the patties in a cast-iron or other ovenproof skillet or, if desired, cook the patties in skillet on stovetop in oil; cook for 4 minutes on each side or until golden brown. If desired, serve with lemon.
FREEZE OPTION: Freeze the cooled crab cakes in freezer containers, separating layers with waxed paper. To use, place the crab cakes on a baking sheet in a preheated 325° oven until heated through.
1 CRAB CAKE: 282 cal., 22g fat (3g sat. fat), 85mg chol., 638mg sod., 7g carb. (1g sugars, 1g fiber), 14g pro.

CLASSIC CRAB CAKES

QUICK ALMOND
CHICKEN STIR-FRY

QUICK ALMOND CHICKEN STIR-FRY

I make this dish often because it is so quick and easy to prepare. My family likes the flavor the sugar snap peas and almonds add. Sometimes I top it with chow mein noodles for extra crunch.
—*Darlene Brenden, Salem, OR*

Takes: 20 min. • **Makes:** 4 servings

- 1 cup whole unblanched almonds
- ¼ cup canola oil
- 1 lb. boneless skinless chicken breasts, cut into cubes
- 1 Tbsp. cornstarch
- ½ cup chicken broth
- 3 Tbsp. soy sauce
- 2 tsp. honey
- 1 tsp. ground ginger
- 1 pkg. (14 oz.) frozen sugar snap peas
  Hot cooked pasta or rice

1. In a large skillet over medium heat, cook almonds in oil for 3 minutes. Add chicken; cook until meat is no longer pink, 5-7 minutes.
2. In a small bowl, combine cornstarch, broth, soy sauce, honey and ginger until smooth; add to chicken mixture. Bring to a boil; cook and stir until thickened, about 2 minutes. Reduce heat; add in peas. Cook and stir until heated through. Serve with pasta or rice.

1 CUP: 526 cal., 35g fat (4g sat. fat), 63mg chol., 871mg sod., 21g carb. (8g sugars, 8g fiber), 35g pro.

GARLIC LIME SHRIMP

GARLIC LIME SHRIMP

Our son, a restaurant owner, showed me how to make this quick shrimp and noodle dish zipped up with garlic and cayenne. It's also tasty served over rice.
—*Gertraud Casbarro, Summerville, SC*

Takes: 20 min. • **Makes:** 4 servings

- 1 lb. uncooked shrimp (31-40 per lb.), peeled and deveined
- 5 garlic cloves, minced
- ½ tsp. salt
- ¼ to ½ tsp. cayenne pepper
- ½ cup butter
- 3 Tbsp. lime juice
- 1 Tbsp. minced fresh parsley
  Hot cooked pasta

In a large skillet, saute the shrimp, garlic, salt and cayenne in butter until shrimp turn pink, about 5 minutes. Stir in lime juice and parsley. Serve with pasta.

1 CUP: 309 cal., 25g fat (15g sat. fat), 199mg chol., 613mg sod., 3g carb. (0 sugars, 0 fiber), 19g pro.

> *"This is a great dish! I added more cayenne and fresh Italian parsley from my garden and yummy, yummy, yummy! Fabulous!"*
> —**SUSIEQ6969,** TASTEOFHOME.COM

GRAPEFRUIT
GREMOLATA SALMON

GRAPEFRUIT GREMOLATA SALMON

If you're looking for a simple fish dish, make this Italian-inspired recipe that combines salmon, broiled grapefruit and a fragrant gremolata. You can use halibut instead of salmon if you prefer.
—*Gilda Lester, Millsboro, DE*

Takes: 30 min. • **Makes:** 4 servings

- 2 medium grapefruit
- ¼ cup minced fresh parsley
- 1 garlic clove, minced
- 1 Tbsp. plus 1 tsp. brown sugar, divided
- 4 salmon fillets (6 oz. each)
- 1 Tbsp. cumin seeds, crushed
- ½ tsp. salt
- ½ tsp. coarsely ground pepper

1. Preheat broiler. Finely grate enough zest from grapefruit to measure 2 Tbsp. In a small bowl, mix parsley, garlic and grapefruit zest. Set aside.

2. Cut a thin slice from the top and the bottom of each grapefruit; stand the grapefruit upright on a cutting board. With a knife, cut off peel and outer membrane from grapefruit. Cut along the membrane of each segment to remove fruit. Arrange sections in a single layer on half of a foil-lined 15x10x1-in. baking pan. Sprinkle with 1 Tbsp. brown sugar.

3. Place salmon on other half of pan. Mix cumin seeds, salt, pepper and remaining 1 tsp. brown sugar; sprinkle over salmon.

4. Broil 3-4 in. from heat 8-10 minutes or until fish just begins to flake easily with a fork and grapefruit is lightly browned. Sprinkle salmon with parsley mixture; serve with grapefruit.

1 SERVING: 332 cal., 16g fat (3g sat. fat), 85mg chol., 387mg sod., 16g carb. (13g sugars, 2g fiber), 30g pro. **DIABETIC EXCHANGES:** 4 lean meat, 1 starch.

FRESH CORN & TOMATO FETTUCCINE

This recipe combines delicious whole wheat pasta with the best of fresh garden produce. It's tossed with heart-healthy olive oil, and a little feta cheese gives it bite.
—*Angela Spengler, Niceville, FL*

Takes: 30 min. • **Makes:** 4 servings

- 8 oz. uncooked whole wheat fettuccine
- 2 medium ears sweet corn, husked
- 2 tsp. plus 2 Tbsp. olive oil, divided
- ½ cup chopped sweet red pepper
- 4 green onions, chopped
- 2 medium tomatoes, chopped
- ½ tsp. salt
- ½ tsp. pepper
- 1 cup crumbled feta cheese
- 2 Tbsp. minced fresh parsley

1. In a Dutch oven, cook fettuccine according to package directions, adding corn during the last 8 minutes of the cooking time.
2. Meanwhile, in a small skillet, heat 2 tsp. oil over medium-high heat. Add red pepper and green onions; cook and stir until tender.
3. Drain pasta and corn; transfer pasta to a large bowl. Cool corn slightly; cut corn from cob and add to pasta. Add tomatoes, salt, pepper, remaining oil and the pepper mixture; toss to combine. Sprinkle with cheese and parsley.

2 CUPS: 527 cal., 17g fat (5g sat. fat), 84mg chol., 1051mg sod., 75g carb. (7g sugars, 9g fiber), 21g pro.

CHICKEN FLORENTINE PIZZA

On pizza night, we like to switch things up with this chicken and spinach version. One taste of the ricotta cheese base and you won't miss traditional sauce one bit.
—*Pam Corder, Monroe, LA*

Takes: 25 min. • **Makes:** 8 servings

- 1 tsp. Italian seasoning
- ½ tsp. garlic powder
- 3 cups cooked chicken breasts (about 1 lb.), cubed
- 1 cup whole-milk ricotta cheese
- 1 prebaked 12-in. pizza crust
- 1 pkg. (10 oz.) frozen chopped spinach, thawed and squeezed dry
- 2 Tbsp. oil-packed sun-dried tomatoes, drained and chopped
- ½ cup shredded fresh mozzarella cheese
- ¼ cup grated Parmesan cheese

Preheat oven to 425°. Stir together Italian seasoning and garlic powder; toss with chicken. Spread ricotta cheese on pizza crust. Top with chicken, spinach and tomatoes. Sprinkle with mozzarella and Parmesan cheeses. Bake until the crust is golden and cheese is melted, 10-15 minutes.

1 PIECE: 311 cal., 11g fat (5g sat. fat), 65mg chol., 423mg sod., 26g carb. (3g sugars, 2g fiber), 28g pro.

Test Kitchen Tip

For a fun appetizer at your next holiday party, cut baked pizza into bite-sized pieces. Feel free to add a few of your favorite pizza toppings; we loved tossing some chopped fresh tomatoes on this one.

CHICKEN FLORENTINE PIZZA

6

Give Me 5 or Fewer

Creating an amazing meal doesn't require a long list of ingredients! Save on time, money and energy with these recipes that need no more than five items (not including salt and pepper, oil, water and optional extras). For casual family night or showstopping feasts, these are your new go-to dishes.

HABANERO RASPBERRY
RIBS P. 169

CILANTRO-TOPPED SALMON

CILANTRO-TOPPED SALMON

A tongue-tingling cilantro-lime sauce complements tender salmon fillets in this pleasing entree. This has been a favorite with everyone who has tried it.
—Nancy Culbert, Whitehorn, CA

Takes: 30 min. • Makes: 6 servings

1½ lbs. salmon fillets
¼ cup lime juice, divided
½ cup minced fresh cilantro
3 Tbsp. thinly sliced green onions
1 Tbsp. finely chopped jalapeno pepper
1 Tbsp. olive oil
¼ tsp. salt
⅛ tsp. pepper
   Optional: Lime wedges, sliced jalapeno and cilantro sprigs

1. Preheat oven to 350°. Place salmon skin side down in a 13x9-in. baking dish coated with cooking spray. Drizzle with 1½ tsp. lime juice.
2. In a small bowl, combine cilantro, onions, jalapeno, oil, salt, pepper and remaining lime juice. Spread over the salmon. Bake, uncovered, until the fish just begins to flake easily with a fork, 20-25 minutes. If desired, serve with lime wedges, sliced jalapeno and cilantro sprigs.
NOTE: Wear disposable gloves when cutting hot peppers; the oils can burn skin. Avoid touching your face.
3 OZ. COOKED SALMON: 232 cal., 15g fat (3g sat. fat), 67mg chol., 166mg sod., 1g carb. (0 sugars, 0 fiber), 23g pro.
DIABETIC EXCHANGES: 3 lean meat, 1 fat.

Test Kitchen Tip
You can use skinless salmon fillets here, but skin-on fillets work best. The skin creates a barrier between the meat and the dish, so if the salmon sticks to the dish, it's the skin that sticks—not the meat.

FETTUCCINE WITH SAUSAGE & FRESH TOMATO SAUCE

FETTUCCINE WITH SAUSAGE & FRESH TOMATO SAUCE

Fresh homemade sauce doesn't take much more time than using jarred—and the results are so good!
—Taste of Home Test Kitchen

Prep: 15 min. • Cook: 30 min.
Makes: 4 servings

2 Tbsp. olive oil
1 pkg. (12 oz.) fully cooked Italian chicken sausage links, cut into ½-in. slices
1 large onion, finely chopped
2 lbs. plum tomatoes, chopped (about 5 cups)
½ tsp. salt
¼ tsp. pepper
8 oz. uncooked fettuccine
¼ cup thinly sliced fresh basil
1 tsp. sugar, optional
   Optional: Grated Romano cheese and additional basil

1. In a 6-qt. stockpot, heat 1 Tbsp. oil over medium heat. Brown the sausage slices; remove. Add remaining 1 Tbsp. oil and saute onion until tender, 3-5 minutes. Stir in the sausage, tomatoes, salt and pepper; bring to a boil. Reduce the heat; simmer, uncovered, until thickened, 20-25 minutes.
2. Meanwhile, cook fettuccine according to the package directions; drain.
3. Stir basil and, if desired, sugar into sauce. Serve over fettuccine. If desired, top with grated Romano cheese and additional basil.
FREEZE OPTION: Freeze cooled sauce in freezer containers. To use, partially thaw in refrigerator overnight. Heat through in a saucepan, stirring occasionally.
1 CUP PASTA WITH 1 CUP SAUCE: 457 cal., 15g fat (3g sat. fat), 65mg chol., 792mg sod., 56g carb. (9g sugars, 5g fiber), 25g pro.

GLAZED CORNISH HENS

⏱ 🕔 🍎

COCOA-CRUSTED
BEEF TENDERLOIN

My family and I have regular cooking
competitions with secret ingredients and
a 30-minute time limit. This tenderloin
recipe earned me a sweet victory.
—*Gina Myers, Spokane, WA*

Takes: 30 min. • **Makes:** 4 servings

- 4 beef tenderloin steaks
  (1½ in. thick and 6 oz. each)
- ½ tsp. salt
- ½ tsp. coarsely ground pepper
- 3 Tbsp. baking cocoa
- 3 Tbsp. finely ground coffee

1. Preheat broiler. Sprinkle steaks with
salt and pepper. In a shallow bowl, mix
cocoa and coffee. Dip the steaks in the
cocoa mixture to coat all sides; shake
off excess.
2. Place steaks on a rack of a broiler
pan. Broil 3-4 in. from heat 9-11 minutes
on each side or until meat reaches the
desired doneness (for medium-rare,
a thermometer should read 135°;
medium, 140°; medium-well, 145°).
1 STEAK: 252 cal., 10g fat (4g sat. fat),
75mg chol., 296mg sod., 1g carb.
(0 sugars, 0 fiber), 37g pro. **DIABETIC
EXCHANGES:** 5 lean meat.

🕔

GLAZED CORNISH HENS

If you want to add a touch of elegance
to your dinner table, our culinary experts
suggest these Cornish game hens topped
with a sweet apricot glaze.
—*Taste of Home Test Kitchen*

Prep: 5 min. • **Bake:** 1 hour
Makes: 4 servings

- 2 Cornish game hens (20 to 24 oz.
  each), split lengthwise
- ¼ tsp. salt
- ⅛ tsp. white pepper
- ⅓ cup apricot spreadable fruit
- 1 Tbsp. orange juice

1. Preheat oven to 350°. Place hens,
breast side up, on a rack in a shallow
roasting pan. Sprinkle with salt and
pepper. Bake, uncovered, 30 minutes.

2. In a small bowl, combine spreadable
fruit and orange juice. Spoon some of the
apricot mixture over the hens. Bake until
golden brown and the juices run clear,
30-35 minutes longer, basting several
times with remaining apricot mixture.
Let stand 5 minutes before serving.
½ HEN: 402 cal., 24g fat (7g sat. fat), 175mg
chol., 233mg sod., 14g carb. (11g sugars,
0 fiber), 30g pro.

> *"I served this on Christmas
> Eve. It was so easy to
> fix and I was out of the
> kitchen in no time flat! The
> family raved about it!"*
> —**JO-SUE, TASTEOFHOME.COM**

COCOA-CRUSTED
BEEF TENDERLOIN

BBQ COUNTRY-STYLE RIBS

BBQ COUNTRY-STYLE RIBS

Quick to prep for the slow cooker, this dinner is terrific with a salad and a fresh side. My family practically cheers whenever I make it!
—*Cheryl Mann, Winside, NE*

- -

Prep: 10 min. • **Cook:** 6 hours
Makes: 6 servings

- 3 lbs. boneless country-style pork ribs
- ½ tsp. salt
- ½ tsp. pepper
- 1 large onion, cut into ½-in. rings
- 1 bottle (18 oz.) hickory smoke–flavored barbecue sauce
- ⅓ cup maple syrup
- ¼ cup spicy brown mustard
  Thinly sliced green onions, optional

1. Sprinkle ribs with salt and pepper. Place the onion in a 6-qt. slow cooker. Top with ribs. In a large bowl, combine the barbecue sauce, maple syrup and mustard; pour over ribs. Cook, covered, on low until meat is tender, 6-8 hours.
2. Transfer the meat to a serving platter; keep warm. Pour the cooking liquid into a large saucepan; bring to a boil. Reduce heat; simmer, uncovered, 10 minutes or until sauce is thickened. Serve with pork. If desired, sprinkle with onions.
6 OZ. COOKED PORK WITH ⅓ CUP SAUCE: 598 cal., 21g fat (8g sat. fat), 131mg chol., 1443mg sod., 56g carb. (46g sugars, 1g fiber), 41g pro.

CHICKEN & VEGETABLE CURRY COUSCOUS

For my busy family, a semi-homemade one-pot meal is the easiest way to get dinner done in a hurry. Use your favorite blend of frozen veggies and serve with toasted pita bread for smiles all around.
—*Elizabeth Hokanson, Arborg, MB*

- -

Takes: 25 min. • **Makes:** 6 servings

- 1 Tbsp. butter
- 1 lb. boneless skinless chicken breasts, cut into strips
- 1 pkg. (16 oz.) frozen vegetable blend of your choice
- 1¼ cups water
- 1 pkg. (5.7 oz.) curry-flavored couscous mix
- ½ cup raisins

1. In a cast-iron or other heavy skillet, heat butter over medium-high heat. Add chicken; cook and stir until no longer pink.
2. Add vegetable blend, water and the contents of the couscous seasoning packet. Bring to a boil; stir in couscous and raisins. Remove from heat; let stand, covered, until water is absorbed, about 5 minutes. Fluff with a fork.
1 CUP: 273 cal., 4g fat (2g sat. fat), 47mg chol., 311mg sod., 39g carb. (9g sugars, 4g fiber), 21g pro. **DIABETIC EXCHANGES:** 2 starch, 2 lean meat, 1 vegetable, ½ fat.

CHICKEN & VEGETABLE CURRY COUSCOUS

JALAPENO POPPER STUFFED CHICKEN BREASTS

One of my husband's favorite snacks are jalapeno poppers, so I created this recipe. He loves chicken cooked this way, and best of all is the quick cooking with little cleanup!
—Donna Gribbins, Shelbyville, KY

Prep: 15 min. • **Cook:** 15 min./batch
Makes: 4 servings

- 4 oz. cream cheese, softened
- 1 cup shredded cheddar cheese
- 1 jalapeno pepper, seeded and finely chopped
- 4 boneless skinless chicken breast halves (6 oz. each)
- ½ tsp. salt
- ½ tsp. pepper
- 8 thick-sliced bacon strips

1. Preheat air fryer to 375°. In a small bowl, mix cream cheese, cheddar cheese and jalapeno. Cut a pocket horizontally in the thickest part of each chicken breast. Fill with cheese mixture. Sprinkle the chicken with salt and pepper. Wrap 2 bacon strips around each chicken breast; secure with toothpicks.
2. In batches, place chicken on greased tray in air-fryer basket, seam side down. Cook until a thermometer inserted into the chicken reads 165°, 14-16 minutes, turning once. Let stand 5 minutes. Discard toothpicks before serving.
NOTE: Wear disposable gloves when cutting hot peppers; the oils can burn skin. Avoid touching your face.
1 STUFFED CHICKEN BREAST: 518 cal., 33g fat (15g sat. fat), 171mg chol., 1150mg sod., 3g carb. (1g sugars, 0 fiber), 51g pro.

GRILLED RIBEYE WITH GARLIC BLUE CHEESE MUSTARD SAUCE

This simple steak gets a big flavor boost from two of my favorites: mustard and blue cheese. My husband and I make this recipe to celebrate our anniversary each year!
—Ashley Lecker, Green Bay, WI

Prep: 20 min. • **Grill:** 10 min. + standing
Makes: 4 servings

- 1 cup half-and-half cream
- ½ cup Dijon mustard
- ¼ cup plus 2 tsp. crumbled blue cheese, divided
- 1 garlic clove, minced
- 2 beef ribeye steaks (1½ in. thick and 12 oz. each)
- 1 Tbsp. olive oil
- ¼ tsp. salt
- ¼ tsp. pepper

1. In a small saucepan over medium heat, whisk together cream, mustard, ¼ cup blue cheese and the garlic. Bring to a simmer. Reduce heat to low; whisk occasionally.
2. Meanwhile, rub meat with olive oil; sprinkle with salt and pepper. Grill the steaks, covered, on a greased rack over high direct heat 4-6 minutes on each side until meat reaches desired doneness (for medium-rare, a thermometer should read 135°; medium, 140°; medium-well, 145°). Remove from grill; let stand for 10 minutes while sauce finishes cooking.
3. When sauce is reduced by half, pour over steaks; top with the remaining 2 tsp. blue cheese.
½ STEAK WITH 3 TBSP. SAUCE: 547 cal., 39g fat (17g sat. fat), 138mg chol., 1088mg sod., 3g carb. (2g sugars, 0 fiber), 34g pro.

JALAPENO POPPER STUFFED CHICKEN BREASTS

GRILLED RIBEYE WITH
GARLIC BLUE CHEESE
MUSTARD SAUCE

HONEY-MUSTARD
GLAZED SALMON

HONEY-MUSTARD GLAZED SALMON

You won't need to fish for compliments from your dinner guests when you serve this spectacular salmon!
—Taste of Home *Test Kitchen*

Takes: 20 min. • **Makes:** 10 servings

- 10 salmon fillets (5 oz. each)
- 2/3 cup packed brown sugar
- 2 Tbsp. Dijon mustard
- 2 Tbsp. honey
- 1/2 tsp. salt

1. Place fillets, skin side down, on a greased baking sheet. In a small bowl, combine brown sugar, mustard, honey and salt; spoon over salmon.
2. Broil 3-4 in. from the heat until fish just begins to flake easily with a fork, 8-12 minutes.

1 FILLET: 292 cal., 13g fat (3g sat. fat), 71mg chol., 265mg sod., 18g carb. (18g sugars, 0 fiber), 24g pro.

Test Kitchen Tips

- How can you tell when salmon is done? Cooked salmon should be opaque and a little firm and should flake easily with a fork. Still not sure? Use a thermometer to make sure the salmon has reached an internal temperature of 145°.

- If you'd like to add a little heat to this recipe, stir 1 tsp. chili-garlic sauce into your glaze—a generous pinch of red pepper flakes or cayenne will do the trick too! For extra flavor, try adding minced garlic or smoked paprika.

HABANERO RASPBERRY RIBS
(PICTURED ON PAGE 159)

Roasting these tender, tangy ribs in the oven means you can enjoy them any time of year—no waiting for grilling season. The heat from the habanero and the sweetness of the jam complement each other perfectly.
—*Yvonne Roat, Linden, MI*

- -

Prep: 10 min. • **Bake:** 3 hours 10 min.
Makes: 5 servings

- 2 racks pork baby back ribs (about 4½ lbs.)
- 2½ cups barbecue sauce, divided
- 2 cups seedless raspberry jam
- 1 habanero pepper, finely chopped
  Additional barbecue sauce, optional

1. Preheat oven to 325°. Place each rack of ribs on a double thickness of heavy-duty foil (about 28x18 in.). Combine 2 cups barbecue sauce, the jam and habanero; pour over ribs. Wrap foil tightly around ribs.
2. Place in a shallow roasting pan. Bake until meat is tender, about 3 hours.
3. Carefully unwrap ribs. Place on baking sheets. Brush with the remaining ½ cup barbecue sauce. Broil 4 in. from the heat until bubbly, 8-10 minutes. If desired, serve with additional barbecue sauce.
NOTE: Wear disposable gloves when cutting hot peppers; the oils can burn skin. Avoid touching your face.
1 SERVING: 1067 cal., 38g fat (14g sat. fat), 147mg chol., 1562mg sod., 139g carb. (122g sugars, 1g fiber), 41g pro.

AIR-FRYER BEEF TURNOVERS

My mom's recipe for these flavorful pockets called for dough made from scratch, but I streamlined it by using refrigerated crescent rolls and an air fryer. My children love the turnovers plain or dipped in ketchup, and they're also great with mustard.
—*Claudia Bodeker, Ash Flat, AR*

- -

Takes: 30 min. • **Makes:** 1 dozen

- 1 lb. ground beef
- 1 medium onion, chopped
- 1 jar (16 oz.) sauerkraut, rinsed, drained and chopped
- 1 cup shredded Swiss cheese
- 3 tubes (8 oz. each) refrigerated crescent rolls

1. In a large skillet, cook beef and onion over medium heat until meat is no longer pink, crumbling meat, 5-7 minutes; drain. Add sauerkraut and cheese.
2. Preheat air fryer to 350°. Unroll the crescent roll dough and separate into rectangles; pinch seams to seal. Place ½ cup beef mixture in the center of each rectangle. Bring corners to the center and pinch to seal. In batches, place the turnovers in a single layer on greased tray in air-fryer basket. Cook until golden brown, 12-15 minutes.
2 TURNOVERS: 634 cal., 35g fat (7g sat. fat), 63mg chol., 1426mg sod., 54g carb. (14g sugars, 2g fiber), 27g pro.

AIR-FRYER BEEF TURNOVERS

CHICKEN WITH SHALLOT SAUCE

OLD-FASHIONED POOR MAN'S STEAK

These tasty steaks fit into everybody's budget. A special friend shared the recipe with me, and I think of her each time I make it.
—*Susan Wright, Mineral Wells, WV*

Prep: 25 min. + chilling • **Cook:** 4 hours
Makes: 9 servings

- 1 cup crushed saltine crackers (about 30 crackers)
- ⅓ cup water
  Salt and pepper to taste
- 2 lbs. ground beef
- ¼ cup all-purpose flour
- 2 Tbsp. canola oil
- 2 cans (10¾ oz. each) condensed cream of mushroom soup, undiluted
  Hot mashed potatoes or noodles
  Minced fresh parsley, optional

1. In a large bowl, combine the cracker crumbs, water, salt and pepper. Crumble beef over the mixture and mix lightly but thoroughly. Press into an ungreased 9-in. square pan. Cover and refrigerate for at least 3 hours.
2. Cut into 3-in. squares; dredge in flour. In a large skillet, heat oil over medium heat; add beef and cook until browned on both sides, 2-3 minutes on each side.
3. Transfer to a 3-qt. slow cooker with a slotted spatula or spoon. Add soup.
4. Cover and cook on high until meat is no longer pink, about 4 hours. Serve with mashed potatoes or noodles. If desired, top with minced parsley.
1 SERVING: 292 cal., 18g fat (6g sat. fat), 68mg chol., 372mg sod., 10g carb. (1g sugars, 1g fiber), 22g pro.

CHICKEN WITH SHALLOT SAUCE

Even though it doesn't take long to put together, this flavorful chicken tastes as if it simmered all day. It's wonderful with mashed potatoes and a green vegetable.
—*Kathy Anderson, Rockford, IL*

Prep: 10 min. • **Cook:** 50 min.
Makes: 6 servings

- 6 bacon strips, chopped
- 1 broiler/fryer chicken (3 to 4 lbs.), cut up
- ½ tsp. salt
- ½ tsp. pepper
- 10 shallots, thinly sliced
- 1 cup water
- 1 whole garlic bulb, cloves separated and peeled
- ½ cup balsamic vinegar

1. In a large skillet, cook bacon over medium heat until crisp. Remove to paper towels with a slotted spoon; drain, reserving 2 Tbsp. drippings in pan.
2. Sprinkle chicken with salt and pepper; brown in the drippings. Remove from pan and keep warm.
3. Add shallots to pan; cook and stir until tender. Stir in water and garlic. Return chicken to pan. Bring to a boil. Reduce heat; cover and simmer 30-35 minutes or until a thermometer inserted in a thigh reads 170°-175°.
4. Remove chicken to a serving platter; keep warm. Skim fat from the cooking juices. Mash garlic; add vinegar. Bring the liquid to a boil; cook until slightly thickened. Spoon sauce over chicken; sprinkle with the bacon.
7 OZ. COOKED CHICKEN WITH ¼ CUP SAUCE: 456 cal., 24g fat (7g sat. fat), 117mg chol., 448mg sod., 20g carb. (8g sugars, 1g fiber), 38g pro.

OLD-FASHIONED
POOR MAN'S STEAK

Scrub 1 large **baking potato**; pierce several times with a fork. Bake at 400° until tender, 50-75 minutes. Cut an "X" in the potato; fluff the pulp with a fork and season with **salt** and **pepper**. Top with 2 slices **Canadian bacon** and 1 poached **egg**, then drizzle with 2 Tbsp. **prepared hollandaise** and sprinkle with **minced parsley**.

- Eggs Benedict Baked Potatoes -

This baked potato dish would be eggs-cellent for a breakfast-for-dinner evening! Whip it up as a quick meal for one or make multiples to feed the whole family.

⏱ 5️
SPAGHETTI WITH EGGS & BACON

Most people are surprised to see this combination of ingredients. Then they taste it—and it's gone in a flash!
—*Gail Jenner, Etna, CA*

- -

Takes: 25 min. • **Makes:** 4 servings

- 8   oz. uncooked spaghetti
- 4   large eggs
- ¾   cup half-and-half cream
- ½   cup grated Parmesan cheese
- ½   lb. bacon strips, cooked and crumbled

1. In a 6-qt. stockpot, cook spaghetti according to package directions. In a small saucepan, whisk eggs and cream until blended. Cook over low heat until a thermometer reads 160°, stirring constantly (do not allow to simmer). Remove from the heat; stir in the Parmesan cheese.
2. Drain spaghetti; return to stockpot. Add sauce and bacon; toss to combine. Serve immediately. If desired, sprinkle with additional Parmesan cheese.
1 SERVING : 486 cal., 21g fat (9g sat. fat), 238mg chol., 611mg sod., 45g carb. (3g sugars, 2g fiber), 26g pro.

⏱ 5️ 🍎
CAESAR SALMON WITH ROASTED TOMATOES & ARTICHOKES

This is my go-to recipe for quick dinners, either for family or guests. This dish is colorful, healthy, easy to prepare and absolutely delicious.
—*Mary Hawkes, Prescott, AZ*

- -

Takes: 25 min. • **Makes:** 4 servings

- 4   salmon fillets (5 oz. each)
- 5   Tbsp. reduced-fat Caesar vinaigrette, divided
- ¼   tsp. pepper, divided
- 2   cups grape tomatoes
- 1   can (14 oz.) water-packed artichoke hearts, drained and quartered
- 1   medium sweet orange or yellow pepper, cut into 1-in. pieces

1. Preheat oven to 425°. Place salmon on half of a 15x10x1-in. baking pan coated with cooking spray. Brush with 2 Tbsp. vinaigrette; sprinkle with ⅛ tsp. pepper.
2. In a large bowl, combine the tomatoes, artichoke hearts and sweet pepper. Add the remaining 3 Tbsp. vinaigrette and ⅛ tsp. pepper; toss to coat. Place tomato mixture on the remaining half of the pan. Roast until fish just begins to flake easily with a fork and vegetables are tender, 12-15 minutes.
1 FILLET WITH ¾ CUP TOMATO MIXTURE: 318 cal., 16g fat (3g sat. fat), 73mg chol., 674mg sod., 12g carb. (4g sugars, 2g fiber), 28g pro. **DIABETIC EXCHANGES:** 4 lean meat, 1 vegetable, 1 fat.

CAESAR SALMON WITH ROASTED TOMATOES & ARTICHOKES

BBQ MEAT LOAF MINIS

Kids can have fun helping to prepare these mini meat loaves in muffin cups. If we're in the mood for extra spice, we add 2 teaspoons chili powder and 1 cup of salsa to the meat mixture.
—*Linda Call, Falun, KS*

Takes: 30 min. • **Makes:** 6 servings

1 pkg. (6 oz.) stuffing mix
1 cup water
2 Tbsp. hickory smoke-flavored barbecue sauce
1 lb. ground beef
1 cup shredded cheddar cheese
Additional hickory smoke-flavored barbecue sauce, optional

1. Preheat oven to 375°. In a large bowl, combine stuffing mix, water and 2 Tbsp. barbecue sauce. Add beef; mix lightly but thoroughly. Press ⅓ cup mixture into each of 12 ungreased muffin cups.
2. Bake, uncovered, until a thermometer reads 160°, 18-22 minutes. Sprinkle tops with cheese; bake until the cheese is melted, 2-4 minutes longer. If desired, serve with additional barbecue sauce.
FREEZE OPTION: Securely wrap and freeze cooled meat loaves in foil. To use, partially thaw in refrigerator overnight. Place meat loaves on a greased shallow baking pan. Bake in a preheated 350° oven until heated through. Top with cheese as directed.
2 MINI MEAT LOAVES: 330 cal., 17g fat (7g sat. fat), 67mg chol., 668mg sod., 21g carb. (4g sugars, 1g fiber), 21g pro.

CARIBBEAN CHICKEN STIR-FRY

Fruit in stir-fry? You might be surprised by how good this dish is. It's a promising go-to option when time's tight.
—*Jeanne Holt, St. Paul, MN*

Takes: 25 min. • **Makes:** 4 servings

2 tsp. cornstarch
¼ cup water
1 lb. boneless skinless chicken breasts, cut into ½-in. strips
2 tsp. Caribbean jerk seasoning
1 can (15 oz.) mixed tropical fruit, drained and coarsely chopped
2 pkg. (8.8 oz. each) ready-to-serve brown rice

1. In a small bowl, mix cornstarch and water until smooth; set aside.
2. Heat a large skillet coated with cooking spray over medium-high heat. Add chicken; sprinkle with jerk seasoning. Stir-fry until no longer pink, 3-5 minutes. Stir cornstarch mixture and add to pan. Add fruit. Bring to a boil; cook and stir until sauce is thickened, 1-2 minutes.
3. Meanwhile, heat rice according to package directions. Serve with chicken.
¾ CUP STIR-FRY WITH 1 CUP RICE: 419 cal., 5g fat (1g sat. fat), 63mg chol., 208mg sod., 54g carb. (17g sugars, 3g fiber), 27g pro.

BBQ MEAT LOAF MINIS

CARIBBEAN CHICKEN
STIR-FRY

COD & ASPARAGUS BAKE

COD & ASPARAGUS BAKE

The lemon pulls this flavorful and healthy dish together. If you prefer, use grated Parmesan cheese instead of Romano.
—*Thomas Faglon, Somerset, NJ*

Takes: 30 min. • **Makes:** 4 servings

- 4 cod fillets (4 oz. each)
- 1 lb. fresh thin asparagus, trimmed
- 1 pint cherry tomatoes, halved
- 2 Tbsp. lemon juice
- 1½ tsp. grated lemon zest
- ¼ cup grated Romano cheese

1. Preheat oven to 375°. Place the cod and asparagus in a 15x10x1-in. baking pan brushed with oil. Add tomatoes, cut sides down. Brush fish with lemon juice; sprinkle with lemon zest. Sprinkle fish and vegetables with Romano cheese. Bake until the fish just begins to flake easily with a fork, about 12 minutes.
2. Remove pan from the oven; preheat broiler. Broil mixture 3-4 in. from heat until vegetables are lightly browned, 2-3 minutes.
1 SERVING: 141 cal., 3g fat (2g sat. fat), 45mg chol., 184mg sod., 6g carb. (3g sugars, 2g fiber), 23g pro. **DIABETIC EXCHANGES:** 3 lean meat, 1 vegetable.

Test Kitchen Tips

- If asparagus isn't in season, fresh green beans make a fine substitute and will cook in about the same amount of time.
- We tested cod fillets that were about ¾ in. thick. You'll need to adjust the bake time up or down if your fillets are thicker or thinner.

RANCH PORK ROAST

RANCH PORK ROAST

This simple pork roast with a mild rub is perfect for new cooks. The leftover meat is tender and flavorful, and can be used in countless recipes calling for cooked pork.
—*Taste of Home Test Kitchen*

Prep: 10 min. • **Bake:** 50 min. + standing
Makes: 8 servings

- 1 boneless pork loin roast (2½ lbs.)
- 2 Tbsp. olive oil
- 1 Tbsp. ranch salad dressing mix
- 2 tsp. Dijon mustard
- 1 garlic clove, minced
- ½ tsp. pepper

1. Preheat oven to 350°. If desired, tie pork with kitchen string at 2-in. intervals to help the roast hold its shape. Combine the next 5 ingredients; rub over roast. Place on a rack in a shallow roasting pan. Pour 1 cup water into pan.
2. Bake, uncovered, until a thermometer reads 145°, 50-55 minutes. Let stand for 10-15 minutes before slicing.
FREEZE OPTION: Freeze the cooled sliced pork in freezer containers. To use, partially thaw in refrigerator overnight. Heat through in a covered saucepan, gently stirring; add broth or water if necessary.
4 OZ. COOKED PORK: 212 cal., 10g fat (3g sat. fat), 70mg chol., 248mg sod., 2g carb. (0 sugars, 0 fiber), 27g pro. **DIABETIC EXCHANGES:** 4 lean meat, ½ fat.

LEMON CHICKEN
WITH BASIL

CHICKEN PROVOLONE

Though this is one of my simplest dishes, it's one of my husband's favorites. It is easy to prepare and looks fancy served on a dark plate with a garnish of fresh parsley or basil. Add some buttered noodles for an easy side dish.
—Dawn Bryant, Thedford, NE

Takes: 25 min. • **Makes:** 4 servings

- 4 boneless skinless chicken breast halves (4 oz. each)
- ¼ tsp. pepper
- 8 fresh basil leaves
- 4 thin slices prosciutto or deli ham
- 4 slices provolone cheese

1. Sprinkle chicken with pepper. In a large skillet coated with cooking spray, cook the chicken over medium heat until a thermometer reads 165°, 4-5 minutes on each side.
2. Transfer chicken to an ungreased baking sheet; top with the basil, prosciutto and cheese. Broil 6-8 in. from the heat until cheese is melted, 1-2 minutes.

1 CHICKEN BREAST HALF: 236 cal., 11g fat (6g sat. fat), 89mg chol., 435mg sod., 1g carb. (0 sugars, 0 fiber), 33g pro. **DIABETIC EXCHANGES:** 4 lean meat.

LEMON CHICKEN WITH BASIL

No matter when I eat it, this tangy slow-cooked chicken reminds me of summer meals with friends and family.
—Deborah Posey, Virginia Beach, VA

Prep: 5 min. • **Cook:** 3 hours
Makes: 4 servings

- 4 boneless skinless chicken breast halves (6 oz. each)
- 2 medium lemons
- 1 bunch fresh basil leaves (¾ oz.)
- 2 cups chicken stock
  Optional: Additional grated lemon zest and chopped basil

1. Place chicken breasts in a 3-qt. slow cooker. Finely grate enough zest from lemons to measure 4 tsp.; cut lemons in half and squeeze juice. Add zest and juice to the slow cooker.

2. Tear basil leaves directly into the slow cooker. Add chicken stock. Cook, covered, on low until the meat is tender, 3-4 hours. When cool enough to handle, shred meat with 2 forks. If desired, stir in additional lemon zest and chopped basil.
FREEZE OPTION: Freeze the cooled chicken mixture in freezer containers. To use, partially thaw in the refrigerator overnight. Heat through in a saucepan, stirring occasionally; add broth or water if necessary.
5 OZ. COOKED CHICKEN: 200 cal., 4g fat (1g sat. fat), 94mg chol., 337mg sod., 3g carb. (1g sugars, 0 fiber), 37g pro. **DIABETIC EXCHANGES:** 5 lean meat.

Test Kitchen Tip

For a sweet and savory treat, layer chicken, butter lettuce leaves and apple slices on toasted raisin bread.

PANCETTA & MUSHROOM-STUFFED
CHICKEN BREAST

SPICY CHICKEN NUGGETS

We devour these golden brown chicken nuggets at least once a week. If you want to tone down the heat, skip the chipotle pepper.
—*Cheryl Cook, Palmyra, VA*

Takes: 30 min. • **Makes:** 6 servings

    1½ cups panko bread crumbs
    1½ cups grated Parmesan cheese
    ½   tsp. ground chipotle pepper, optional
    ¼   cup butter, melted
    1½ lbs. boneless skinless chicken
        thighs, cut into 1½-in. pieces

1. Preheat oven to 400°. In a shallow bowl, mix bread crumbs, cheese and, if desired, chipotle pepper. Place butter in a separate shallow bowl. Dip chicken pieces in butter, then in crumb mixture, patting to help coating adhere.
2. Place chicken in a greased 15x10x1-in. baking pan; sprinkle with the remaining crumb mixture. Bake until no longer pink, 20-25 minutes.
1 SERVING: 371 cal., 22g fat (10g sat. fat), 113mg chol., 527mg sod., 13g carb. (1g sugars, 1g fiber), 29g pro.

PANCETTA & MUSHROOM-STUFFED CHICKEN BREAST

I was inspired by a stuffed chicken Marsala dish I had at a restaurant, and wanted to come up with my own version using a different flavor profile.
—*Ashley Laymon, Lititz, PA*

Prep: 15 min. • **Bake:** 30 min.
Makes: 4 servings

    4   slices pancetta
    1   Tbsp. olive oil
    1   shallot, finely chopped
    ¾   cup chopped fresh mushrooms
    ¼   tsp. salt, divided
    ¼   tsp. pepper, divided
    4   boneless skinless chicken breast
        halves (6 oz. each)
    ½   cup prepared pesto

1. Preheat oven to 350°. In a large skillet, cook pancetta over medium heat until partially cooked but not crisp; drain on paper towels.
2. In the same skillet, heat the oil over medium-high heat. Add shallot; cook and stir for 1-2 minutes or until lightly browned. Stir in the mushrooms; cook until tender, 1-2 minutes. Add ⅛ tsp. salt and ⅛ tsp. pepper.
3. Pound chicken breasts with a meat mallet to ¼-in. thickness. Spread each with 2 Tbsp. pesto; layer with 1 slice pancetta and a fourth of the mushroom mixture. Fold chicken in half, enclosing filling; secure with toothpicks. Sprinkle with remaining salt and pepper.
4. Transfer to a greased 13x9-in. baking dish. Bake until a thermometer inserted in the chicken reads 165°, 30-35 minutes. Discard toothpicks before serving.
1 STUFFED CHICKEN BREAST HALF:
420 cal., 25g fat (6g sat. fat), 112mg chol., 1013mg sod., 5g carb. (2g sugars, 1g fiber), 41g pro.

Test Kitchen Tip

For those who don't like mushrooms, substitute 1 cup baby spinach and saute it with the shallots.

MOM'S
ROAST CHICKEN

MOM'S ROAST CHICKEN

This is the best way to cook a whole chicken; it roasts up super juicy with crisp, golden skin. Although it's simply seasoned, it packs in so much flavor.
—*James Schend, Pleasant Prairie, WI*

Prep: 15 min. + chilling
Bake: 35 min. + standing
Makes: 6 servings

- 1 broiler/fryer chicken (4 to 5 lbs.)
- 2 tsp. kosher salt
- 1 tsp. coarsely ground pepper
- 2 tsp. olive oil
  Optional: Minced fresh thyme or rosemary

1. Rub outside of chicken with salt and pepper. Transfer the chicken to a rack on a rimmed baking sheet. Refrigerate, uncovered, overnight.
2. Preheat oven to 450°. Remove chicken from refrigerator while oven heats. Heat a 12-in. cast-iron or ovenproof skillet in the oven for 15 minutes.
3. Place chicken on a work surface, neck side down. Cut through skin where legs connect to body. Press thighs down so joints pop and legs lie flat.
4. Carefully place chicken, breast side up, in hot skillet; press legs down so they lie flat on bottom of pan. Brush with oil. Roast until a thermometer inserted in thickest part of thigh reads 170°-175°, 35-40 minutes.
5. Remove chicken from oven; let stand for 10 minutes before carving. If desired, top with herbs before serving.

5 OZ. COOKED CHICKEN: 405 cal., 24g fat (6g sat. fat), 139mg chol., 760mg sod., 0 carb. (0 sugars, 0 fiber), 44g pro.

ROSEMARY-APRICOT PORK TENDERLOIN

You'll be surprised at how quickly this dish comes together for an easy weeknight meal. And with very little effort, you'll have tender and juicy meat that begs to be added to a salad or sandwich the next day.
—*Marie Rizzio, Interlochen, MI*

Prep: 15 min. • **Bake:** 25 min.
Makes: 8 servings

- 3 Tbsp. minced fresh rosemary or 1 Tbsp. dried rosemary, crushed
- 3 Tbsp. olive oil, divided
- 4 garlic cloves, minced
- 1 tsp. salt
- ½ tsp. pepper
- 2 pork tenderloins (1 lb. each)

GLAZE

- 1 cup apricot preserves
- 3 Tbsp. lemon juice
- 2 garlic cloves, minced

1. Preheat oven to 425°. In a small bowl, combine rosemary, 1 Tbsp. oil, garlic, salt and pepper; brush over pork.
2. In a large cast-iron or other ovenproof skillet, brown pork in remaining 2 Tbsp. oil on all sides. Bake for 15 minutes.
3. In a small bowl, combine the glaze ingredients; brush over pork. Bake until a thermometer reads 145°, 10-15 minutes longer, basting occasionally with the pan juices. Let stand for 5 minutes before slicing.

3 OZ. COOKED PORK: 280 cal., 9g fat (2g sat. fat), 63mg chol., 357mg sod., 27g carb. (15g sugars, 0 fiber), 23g pro.

ROSEMARY-APRICOT PORK TENDERLOIN

SLOW-COOKED CHERRY PORK CHOPS

I mixed and matched several recipes to come up with this one. I'm always happy to adapt recipes for my slow cooker. It's so easy to prepare a meal that way.
—*Mildred Sherrer, Fort Worth, TX*

- -

Prep: 10 min. • **Cook:** 3 hours
Makes: 6 servings

- 6 bone-in pork loin chops (8 oz. each)
- ⅛ tsp. salt
  Dash pepper
- 1 cup canned cherry pie filling
- 2 tsp. lemon juice
- ½ tsp. chicken bouillon granules
- ⅛ tsp. ground mace
  Additional cherry pie filling, warmed, optional

1. In a large skillet coated with cooking spray, brown pork chops over medium heat on both sides. Season with salt and pepper.

2. In a 3-qt. slow cooker, combine pie filling, lemon juice, bouillon and mace. Add the pork chops. Cook, covered, on low until the meat is no longer pink, 3-4 hours. Serve with additional pie filling if desired.

1 SERVING: 366 cal., 18g fat (7g sat. fat), 111mg chol., 204mg sod., 11g carb. (9 sugars, 1 fiber), 36g pro.

SWEET & SPICY CHIPOTLE CHICKEN

My husband and I have created many wonderful memories by sharing this meal with our friends. In the winter, we bake it indoors; in the summer, it works well on the grill too! Either way, the chicken pretty much cooks itself, leaving you plenty of time to visit with friends and family.
—*Ashlie Delshad, West Lafayette, IN*

- -

Prep: 15 min. + marinating
Bake: 1 hour 50 min. + standing
Makes: 8 servings

- 2 chipotle peppers in adobo sauce plus 3 Tbsp. adobo sauce
- ¼ cup tomato paste
- 3 Tbsp. honey
- 2 Tbsp. olive oil
- 1 tsp. sea salt
- 1 roasting chicken (6 to 7 lbs.)

1. Pulse chipotle peppers, adobo sauce, tomato paste, honey, olive oil and sea salt in a food processor or blender until smooth. Spread mixture evenly over chicken. Refrigerate, covered, at least 1 hour or overnight.

2. Preheat oven to 400°. Place chicken on a rack in a shallow roasting pan, breast side up. Tuck wings under the chicken; tie drumsticks together.

3. Roast chicken for 20 minutes. Reduce oven setting to 350°. Roast 1½-1¾ hours longer or until a thermometer inserted in the thickest part of thigh reads 170°-175°. (Cover loosely with foil if chicken browns too quickly.)

4. Remove chicken from oven; tent with foil. Let stand 15 minutes before carving. If desired, skim fat and thicken the pan drippings for gravy. Serve with chicken.

6 OZ. COOKED CHICKEN: 462 cal., 27g fat (7g sat. fat), 134mg chol., 437mg sod., 9g carb. (8g sugars, 1g fiber), 43g pro.

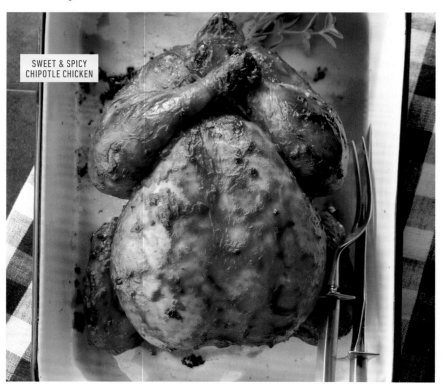

SWEET & SPICY CHIPOTLE CHICKEN

AIR-FRYER BACON-WRAPPED SCALLOPS WITH PINEAPPLE QUINOA

Bacon-wrapped scallops seem so decadent and fancy that I often forget how easy they are to prepare. Paired with pineapple quinoa, this elegant entree can be ready in under 30 minutes.
—*Laura Greenberg, Lake Balboa, CA*

Takes: 30 min. • **Makes:** 4 servings

- 1   can (14½ oz.) vegetable broth
- 1   cup quinoa, rinsed
- ¼   tsp. salt
- ⅛   tsp. plus ¼ tsp. pepper, divided
- 10 bacon strips
- 16 sea scallops (about 2 lbs.), side muscles removed
- 1   cup drained canned pineapple tidbits

1. In a small saucepan, bring broth to a boil. Add quinoa, salt and ⅛ tsp. pepper. Reduce heat; simmer, covered, until the liquid is absorbed, 12-15 minutes.

2. Meanwhile, preheat air fryer to 400°. Arrange 8 strips of bacon in a single layer on tray in air-fryer basket. Cook for 3 minutes or until partially cooked but not crisp. Remove and set aside. Add remaining 2 bacon strips; cook until crisp, 5-6 minutes. Finely chop the crisp bacon strips. Cut the partially cooked bacon strips lengthwise in half.

3. Wrap a halved bacon strip around each scallop; secure with a toothpick. Sprinkle with remaining ¼ tsp. pepper.

4. Arrange scallops in a single layer on greased tray in air-fryer basket. Cook until firm and opaque, 8-10 minutes.

5. Remove quinoa from heat; fluff with a fork. Stir in pineapple and chopped bacon. Serve with scallops.

4 SCALLOPS WITH ¾ CUP QUINOA:
455 cal., 12g fat (3g sat. fat), 75mg chol., 1717mg sod., 45g carb. (10g sugars, 3g fiber), 41g pro.

AIR-FRYER
BACON-WRAPPED SCALLOPS
WITH PINEAPPLE QUINOA

ROAST LEG OF LAMB
WITH ROSEMARY

ROAST LEG OF LAMB WITH ROSEMARY

Rubbing rosemary, garlic and onion onto this delectable roast lamb takes it to a whole new level of deliciousness!
—*Suzy Horvath, Milwaukie, OR*

Prep: 10 min. • **Bake:** 2 hours + standing
Makes: 8 servings

⅓ cup olive oil
¼ cup minced fresh rosemary
¼ cup finely chopped onion
4 garlic cloves, minced
½ tsp. salt
¼ tsp. pepper
1 bone-in leg of lamb (5 to 6 lbs.), trimmed

1. Preheat oven to 325°. Combine the oil, rosemary, onion, garlic, salt and pepper; rub over lamb. Place fat side up on a rack in a shallow roasting pan.
2. Bake, uncovered, for 2-2½ hours or until meat reaches desired doneness (for medium-rare, a thermometer should read 135°; medium, 140°; medium-well, 145°), basting occasionally with the pan juices. Let stand for 15 minutes before slicing.
5 OZ. COOKED LAMB: 316 cal., 18g fat (5g sat. fat), 128mg chol., 206mg sod., 1g carb. (0 sugars, 0 fiber), 36g pro.

Test Kitchen Tips

- Although we prefer cooking with fresh herbs whenever possible, you can use dried rosemary instead of fresh in this recipe. Instead of ¼ cup fresh rosemary leaves, use 4 tsp. dried leaves. To release the flavor, rub them between your hands before combining with the other ingredients.

- This leg of lamb can be marinated ahead of time. In fact, the longer it marinates (up to 24 hours), the more flavorful it will be!

SPINACH-ARTICHOKE RIGATONI

SPINACH-ARTICHOKE RIGATONI

I love pasta, and so does my family. However, they are not so keen on their veggies. This one-pot meal gets us all eating our spinach.
—*Yvonne Starlin, Westmoreland, TN*

Takes: 30 min. • **Makes:** 4 servings

3 cups uncooked rigatoni or large tube pasta
1 pkg. (10 oz.) frozen creamed spinach
1 can (14 oz.) water-packed artichoke hearts, rinsed, drained and quartered
2 cups shredded part-skim mozzarella cheese, divided
¼ cup grated Parmesan cheese
½ tsp. salt
¼ tsp. pepper

1. Preheat broiler. Prepare rigatoni and spinach according to package directions.
2. Drain pasta, reserving ½ cup pasta water; return pasta to the pot. Add the artichoke hearts, ½ cup mozzarella cheese, Parmesan cheese, salt, pepper and creamed spinach; toss to combine, adding the reserved pasta water to thin as desired.
3. Transfer to a greased 2-qt. broiler-safe baking dish; sprinkle with the remaining 1½ cups mozzarella cheese. Broil 4-6 in. from heat until the cheese is melted, 2-3 minutes.
1½ CUPS: 448 cal., 14g fat (8g sat. fat), 37mg chol., 1224mg sod., 54g carb. (6g sugars, 3g fiber), 28g pro.

SPINACH RAVIOLI BAKE

This entree is unbelievably simple to prepare yet tastes delicious. Because you use frozen ravioli—straight from the bag without cooking it first—you save so much time.
—*Susan Kehl, Pembroke Pines, FL*

Prep: 5 min. • **Bake:** 40 min.
Makes: 6 servings

- 2 cups spaghetti sauce
- 1 pkg. (25 oz.) frozen sausage ravioli or ravioli of your choice
- 2 cups shredded part-skim mozzarella cheese
- 1 pkg. (10 oz.) frozen chopped spinach, thawed and squeezed dry
- ¼ cup grated Parmesan cheese

1. Preheat oven to 350°. Place 1 cup spaghetti sauce in a greased shallow 2-qt. baking dish. Top with half each of ravioli, mozzarella cheese, spinach and Parmesan cheese. Repeat layers.
2. Bake, uncovered, until heated through and cheese is melted, 40-45 minutes.
1 CUP: 470 cal., 17g fat (7g sat. fat), 67mg chol., 1441mg sod., 54g carb. (7g sugars, 7g fiber), 27g pro.

MOM'S SLOPPY TACOS

No matter how hectic the weeknight, there's always time to serve your family a healthy meal with recipes this easy and delicious!
—*Kami Jones, Avondale, AZ*

Takes: 30 min. • **Makes:** 6 servings

- 1½ lbs. extra-lean ground beef (95% lean)
- 1 can (15 oz.) tomato sauce
- ¾ tsp. garlic powder
- ½ tsp. salt
- ¼ tsp. pepper
- ¼ tsp. cayenne pepper
- 12 taco shells, warmed
  Optional: Shredded lettuce, shredded cheese, chopped tomatoes, avocado and olives

1. In a large skillet, cook beef over medium heat until no longer pink, 6-8 minutes, crumbling beef. Stir in the tomato sauce, garlic powder, salt, pepper and cayenne. Bring to a boil. Reduce the heat; simmer, uncovered, for 10 minutes.
2. Fill each taco shell with ¼ cup beef mixture and toppings of your choice.
2 TACOS: 264 cal., 10g fat (4g sat. fat), 65mg chol., 669mg sod., 17g carb. (1g sugars, 1g fiber), 25g pro. **DIABETIC EXCHANGES:** 3 lean meat, 1 starch, 1 fat.

SPINACH RAVIOLI BAKE

TASTY ONION CHICKEN

TASTY ONION CHICKEN

French-fried onions are the secret to a yummy, crunchy coating that keeps the chicken juicy and tender. This entree is perfect with green beans and buttermilk biscuits.
—*Jennifer Hoeft, Thorndale, TX*

Takes: 30 min. • **Makes:** 4 servings

- ½ cup butter, melted
- 1 Tbsp. Worcestershire sauce
- 1 tsp. ground mustard
- 1 can (2.8 oz.) French-fried onions, crushed
- 4 boneless skinless chicken breast halves (4 oz. each)

1. In a shallow bowl, combine butter, Worcestershire sauce and mustard. Place the onions in another shallow bowl. Dip chicken in butter mixture; coat with onions.
2. Place the chicken in a greased 11x7-in. baking dish; drizzle with the remaining butter mixture. Bake, uncovered, at 400° for 20-25 minutes or until a thermometer reads 165°.

1 CHICKEN BREAST HALF: 460 cal., 36g fat (18g sat. fat), 124mg chol., 449mg sod., 10g carb. (0 sugars, 0 fiber), 23g pro.

SUPER QUICK CHICKEN FRIED RICE

After my first child was born, I needed meals that were satisfying and fast. This delicious fried rice is now part of our routine dinners.
—*Alicia Gower, Auburn, NY*

Takes: 30 min. • **Makes:** 6 servings

- 1 pkg. (12 oz.) frozen mixed vegetables
- 2 Tbsp. olive oil, divided
- 2 large eggs, lightly beaten
- 4 Tbsp. sesame oil, divided
- 3 pkg. (8.8 oz. each) ready-to-serve garden vegetable rice
- 1 rotisserie chicken, skin removed, shredded
- ¼ tsp. salt
- ¼ tsp. pepper

1. Prepare frozen vegetables according to package directions. Meanwhile, in a large skillet, heat 1 Tbsp. olive oil over medium-high heat. Pour in eggs; cook and stir until eggs are thickened and no liquid egg remains. Remove from pan.
2. In same skillet, heat 2 Tbsp. sesame oil and the remaining 1 Tbsp. olive oil over medium-high heat. Add rice; cook and stir until the rice begins to brown, 10-12 minutes.
3. Stir in chicken, salt and pepper. Add the eggs and vegetables; heat through, breaking eggs into small pieces and stirring to combine. Drizzle with the remaining 2 Tbsp. sesame oil.

1½ CUPS: 548 cal., 25g fat (5g sat. fat), 163mg chol., 934mg sod., 43g carb. (3g sugars, 3g fiber), 38g pro.

SUPER QUICK CHICKEN FRIED RICE

7

Instant Pot® & Air Fryer

What would we do without our kitchen gadgets? Today's tools make creating homemade meals easier than ever. These recipes take advantage of two of the most popular kitchen devices to make healthy, delicious recipes, from appetizers to desserts and everything in between.

PRESSURE-COOKER SALSA
LONDON BROIL P. 217

PRESSURE-COOKER HERBED
CHICKEN & SHRIMP

PRESSURE-COOKER HERBED CHICKEN & SHRIMP

Tender chicken and shrimp make a flavorful combination that's easy to prepare, yet elegant enough to serve at a dinner party. I serve it over hot cooked rice with crusty bread and a green salad.
—*Diana Knight, Reno, NV*

- -

Prep: 15 min. • **Cook:** 30 min. + releasing
Makes: 4 servings

- 1 tsp. salt
- 1 tsp. pepper
- 1 broiler/fryer chicken (3 to 4 lbs.), cut up and skin removed
- 1 Tbsp. canola oil
- 1 large onion, chopped
- 1 can (8 oz.) tomato sauce
- ½ cup white wine or chicken broth
- 1 garlic clove, minced
- 1 tsp. dried basil
- ¼ cup butter, softened
- 1 lb. uncooked shrimp (31-40 per lb.), peeled and deveined
   Hot cooked pasta, optional

1. Combine salt and pepper; rub over the chicken pieces. Select saute setting on a 6-qt. electric pressure cooker. Adjust for medium heat; add oil. When oil is hot, working in batches, brown chicken on all sides. Press cancel.
2. Combine the next 5 ingredients; pour over chicken. Dot with butter. Lock lid; close pressure-release valve. Adjust to pressure-cook on high for 15 minutes. Let pressure release naturally for 10 minutes; quick-release any remaining pressure. A thermometer inserted in chicken should read at least 165°.
3. Select saute setting; adjust for medium heat. Stir in shrimp. Cook until shrimp turn pink, about 5 minutes. Serve over pasta, if desired.
1 SERVING: 606 cal., 34g fat (13g sat. fat), 330mg chol., 1275mg sod., 7g carb. (3g sugars, 1g fiber), 61g pro.

PRESSURE-COOKER SPICY LIME CHICKEN

PRESSURE-COOKER SPICY LIME CHICKEN

This tender chicken with light lime flavor is a natural filling for tacos, but my son Austin also loves it spooned over cooked rice and sprinkled with his favorite taco toppings.
—*Christine Hair, Odessa, FL*

- -

Prep: 10 min. • **Cook:** 10 min.
Makes: 6 servings

- 4 boneless skinless chicken breast halves (6 oz. each)
- 2 cups chicken broth
- 3 Tbsp. lime juice
- 1 Tbsp. chili powder
- 1 tsp. grated lime zest
   Fresh cilantro leaves, optional

1. Place chicken in a 6-qt. electric pressure cooker. Combine broth, lime juice and chili powder; pour over chicken. Lock lid; close pressure-release valve. Adjust to pressure-cook on high for 6 minutes. Quick-release the pressure. A thermometer inserted in chicken should read at least 165°.
2. Remove chicken. When cool enough to handle, shred meat with 2 forks; return to pressure cooker. Stir in lime zest. If desired, serve with cilantro.
FREEZE OPTION: Freeze cooled meat mixture in freezer containers. To use, partially thaw in refrigerator overnight. Microwave, covered, on high until heated through, stirring occasionally; add broth or water if necessary.
1 SERVING: 132 cal., 3g fat (1g sat. fat), 64mg chol., 420mg sod., 2g carb. (1g sugars, 1g fiber), 23g pro. **DIABETIC EXCHANGES:** 3 lean meat.

onions, oregano and bay leaf. Lock lid; close pressure-release valve. Adjust to pressure-cook on high for 2 minutes. Quick-release pressure.

2. Discard bay leaf and any unopened mussels. Sprinkle with parsley, salt and pepper. If desired, serve with baguette slices.

NOTE: Wear disposable gloves when cutting hot peppers; the oils can burn skin. Avoid touching your face.

12 MUSSELS: 293 cal., 12g fat (2g sat. fat), 65mg chol., 931mg sod., 12g carb. (1g sugars, 1g fiber), 28g pro.

AIR-FRYER OKRA WITH SMOKED PAPRIKA

When you want to cook okra without frying it, roast it with lemon juice for a lighter version—you can use an air fryer or a traditional oven. Smoked paprika gives the dish even more roasty oomph.
—*Lee Evans, Queen Creek, AZ*

- -

Takes: 20 min. • **Makes:** 4 servings

- 1   lb. fresh okra pods
- 1   Tbsp. olive oil
- 1   Tbsp. lemon juice
- ½ tsp. smoked paprika
- ¼ tsp. salt
- ⅛ tsp. garlic powder
- ⅛ tsp. pepper

Preheat air fryer to 375°. Toss together all ingredients. Place okra on greased tray in air-fryer basket. Cook until tender and lightly browned, 15-20 minutes, stirring occasionally.

⅔ CUP: 57 cal., 4g fat (1g sat. fat), 0 chol., 155mg sod., 6g carb. (3g sugars, 3g fiber), 2g pro. **DIABETIC EXCHANGES:** 1 vegetable, 1 fat.

PRESSURE-COOKER STEAMED MUSSELS WITH PEPPERS

Here's a worthy way to use your one-pot cooker. Serve French bread along with the mussels to soak up the deliciously seasoned broth. If you like your food spicy, add the jalapeno's seeds.
—*Taste of Home Test Kitchen*

- -

Prep: 30 min. • **Cook:** 5 min.
Makes: 4 servings

- 2   lbs. fresh mussels, scrubbed and beards removed
- 2   Tbsp. olive oil
- 1   jalapeno pepper, seeded and chopped
- 3   garlic cloves, minced
- 1   bottle (8 oz.) clam juice
- ½ cup white wine or additional clam juice
- ⅓ cup chopped sweet red pepper
- 3   green onions, sliced
- ½ tsp. dried oregano
- 1   bay leaf
- 2   Tbsp. minced fresh parsley
- ¼ tsp. salt
- ¼ tsp. pepper
     French bread baguette, sliced, optional

1. Tap mussels; discard any that do not close. Select saute setting on a 6-qt. electric pressure cooker. Adjust for medium heat; add oil. When oil is hot, cook and stir jalapeno until crisp-tender, 2-3 minutes. Add garlic; cook 1 minute longer. Press cancel. Stir in mussels, clam juice, wine, red pepper, green

PRESSURE-COOKER STEAMED MUSSELS WITH PEPPERS

AIR-FRYER SOUTHWESTERN CHICKEN ENCHILADAS

These quick and easy enchiladas are a perfect dinner for Taco Tuesday or any day of the week. Use rotisserie chicken for a quick source of cooked chicken.
—*Joan Hallford, North Richland Hills, TX*

Prep: 20 min. • **Cook:** 10 min./batch
Makes: 6 servings

- 2 cups shredded cooked chicken
- 1¼ cups shredded Monterey Jack cheese or pepper jack cheese, divided
- 1¼ cups shredded sharp cheddar cheese, divided
- ½ cup hominy or whole kernel corn, rinsed and drained
- ½ cup canned black beans, rinsed and drained
- 1 can (4 oz.) chopped green chiles
- 1 Tbsp. chili seasoning mix
- ¼ tsp. salt
- ¼ tsp. pepper
- 12 flour tortillas (6 in.), warmed
- 1 cup enchilada sauce
  Optional: Sour cream, guacamole, salsa and limes

1. Do not preheat air fryer. In a large bowl, combine chicken, ½ cup Monterey Jack cheese, ½ cup cheddar cheese, hominy, beans, chiles and seasonings. Line air fryer basket with foil, letting ends extend up side; grease foil. Place ¼ cup chicken mixture off center on each tortilla; roll up. In 2 batches, place in air fryer, seam side down. Top with half the enchilada sauce; sprinkle with half the remaining Monterey Jack and cheddar cheeses.
2. Cook until heated through and cheeses are melted, 10-12 minutes. Repeat with remaining ingredients. Serve with the toppings of your choice.
2 ENCHILADAS: 525 cal., 24g fat (12g sat. fat), 86mg chol., 1564mg sod., 43g carb. (3g sugars, 3g fiber), 33g pro.

AIR-FRYER
SOUTHWESTERN
CHICKEN ENCHILADAS

AIR-FRYER
STEAK FAJITAS

AIR-FRYER STEAK FAJITAS
Zesty salsa and tender strips of flank steak make these traditional fajitas extra special.
—*Rebecca Baird, Salt Lake City, UT*

- -

Takes: 30 min. • **Makes:** 6 servings

- 2 large tomatoes, seeded and chopped
- ½ cup diced red onion
- ¼ cup lime juice
- 1 pepper, seeded and minced
- 3 Tbsp. minced fresh cilantro
- 2 tsp. ground cumin, divided
- ¾ tsp. salt, divided
- 1 beef flank steak (about 1½ lbs.)
- 1 large onion, halved and sliced
- 6 whole wheat tortillas (8 in.), warmed
  Optional: Sliced avocado and lime wedges

1. For salsa, place first 5 ingredients in a small bowl; stir in 1 tsp. cumin and ¼ tsp. salt. Let stand until serving.
2. Preheat air fryer to 400°. Sprinkle steak with the remaining 1 tsp. cumin and ½ tsp. salt. Place on greased tray in air-fryer basket. Cook until meat reaches desired doneness (for medium-rare, a thermometer should read 135°; medium, 140°; medium-well, 145°), 6-8 minutes per side. Remove from basket and let stand 5 minutes.
3. Meanwhile, place onion on tray in air-fryer basket. Cook until crisp-tender, 2-3 minutes, stirring once. Slice steak thinly across the grain; serve in tortillas with onion and salsa. If desired, serve with avocado and lime wedges.
1 FAJITA: 309 cal., 9g fat (4g sat. fat), 54mg chol., 498mg sod., 29g carb. (3g sugars, 5g fiber), 27g pro. **DIABETIC EXCHANGES:** 4 lean meat, 2 starch.

PRESSURE-COOKER SMOKED SAUSAGE & WHITE BEANS
My husband grew up in the South, where sausage and beans were on the menu weekly. I quickly became a fan. The pressure cooker eliminates the lengthy process of soaking the beans overnight and then slow-cooking them. Serve this dish over white rice and use crusty bread to soak up the broth. I used a gourmet smoked sausage flavored with Gouda and pear for this dish, but you can use any smoked sausage you'd like.
—*Debbie Glasscock, Conway, AR*

- -

Prep: 20 min. • **Cook:** 25 min.
Makes: 8 servings

- 10 cups water
- 1 lb. dried great northern beans
- 1 lb. smoked sausage, sliced
- 1 smoked ham hock (about ½ lb.)
- 1 large onion, chopped
- 5 garlic cloves, minced
- 1 tsp. kosher salt
- 1 tsp. sugar
- 1 tsp. each dried parsley flakes, oregano and basil
- ¼ tsp. pepper
  Hot cooked rice and minced fresh parsley
  Sriracha chili sauce, optional

1. Place water, beans, sausage, ham hock, onion, garlic, salt, sugar and seasonings in a 6-qt. electric pressure cooker. Lock lid; close pressure-release valve. Adjust to pressure-cook on high for 22 minutes.
2. Quick-release pressure. Remove the ham hock. Serve bean mixture with rice, parsley and desired amount of cooking liquid. If desired, serve with chili sauce.
1¼ CUPS BEAN MIXTURE: 382 cal., 16g fat (7g sat. fat), 38mg chol., 909mg sod., 40g carb. (4g sugars, 12g fiber), 21g pro.

PRESSURE-COOKER
SMOKED SAUSAGE &
WHITE BEANS

PRESSURE-COOKER
RED BEANS & RICE

PRESSURE-COOKER RED BEANS & RICE

My family loves New Orleans–style cooking, so I make this dish often. I appreciate how simple it is, and the smoky ham flavor is scrumptious.
—*Celinda Dahlgren, Napa, CA*

- -

Prep: 20 min. • **Cook:** 45 min. + releasing
Makes: 6 servings

    3   cups water
    2   smoked ham hocks (about 1 lb.)
    1   cup dried red beans
    1   medium onion, chopped
 1½   tsp. minced garlic
    1   tsp. ground cumin
    1   medium tomato, chopped
    1   medium green pepper, chopped
    1   tsp. salt
    4   cups hot cooked rice

1. Place the first 6 ingredients in a 6-qt. electric pressure cooker. Lock lid; close pressure-release valve. Adjust to pressure-cook on high for 35 minutes. Let pressure release naturally.
2. Remove ham hocks; let cool slightly. Remove meat from bones. Finely chop meat and return to pressure cooker; discard bones. Stir in tomato, green pepper and salt. Select saute setting and adjust for low heat. Simmer, stirring constantly, until the chopped pepper is tender, 8-10 minutes. Serve with rice.
FREEZE OPTION: Freeze cooled bean mixture in freezer containers. To use, partially thaw in refrigerator overnight. Microwave, covered, on high in a microwave-safe dish until heated through, gently stirring; add water if necessary.
⅓ CUP BEAN MIXTURE WITH ⅔ CUP RICE: 216 cal., 2g fat (0 sat. fat), 9mg chol., 671mg sod., 49g carb. (3g sugars, 12g fiber), 12g pro.

AIR-FRYER LIME & GIN COCONUT MACAROONS

AIR-FRYER LIME & GIN COCONUT MACAROONS

I took these macaroons to our annual cookie exchange, where we always name a queen. I won the crown!
—*Milissa Kirkpatrick, Palestine, TX*

- -

Prep: 20 min. • **Cook:** 5 min./batch
Makes: about 2½ dozen

    4   large egg whites, room temperature
  ⅔   cup sugar
    3   Tbsp. gin
 1½   tsp. grated lime zest
  ¼   tsp. salt
  ¼   tsp. almond extract
    1   pkg. (14 oz.) sweetened shredded coconut
  ½   cup all-purpose flour
    8   oz. white baking chocolate, melted

1. Preheat air fryer to 350°. Whisk the first 6 ingredients until blended. In another bowl, toss coconut with flour; stir in the egg white mixture.
2. In batches, place by tablespoonfuls 1 in. apart on greased tray in air-fryer basket. Cook until browned, 4-5 minutes. Remove to wire racks to cool.
3. Dip bottoms of macaroons into melted chocolate, allowing excess to drip off. Place on waxed paper; let stand until set. Store in an airtight container.
1 COOKIE: 133 cal., 7g fat (6g sat. fat), 0 chol., 67mg sod., 17g carb. (15g sugars, 1g fiber), 2g pro.

Test Kitchen Tip

If you don't have an air fryer, you can make this recipe in an oven instead. These are also great dipped in melted dark chocolate!

AIR-FRYER
ROSEMARY-LEMON
CHICKEN THIGHS

AIR-FRYER ROSEMARY-LEMON CHICKEN THIGHS

These chicken thighs always remind me of Sunday dinner. The lemon-and-herb butter really makes the chicken flavorful and juicy! If you don't have an air fryer, the chicken can be baked in the oven at 400° for about 45 minutes.
—*Alyssa Lang, North Scituate, RI*

Prep: 10 min. • **Cook:** 25 min.
Makes: 4 servings

- ¼ cup butter, softened
- 3 garlic cloves, minced
- 2 tsp. minced fresh rosemary or
  ½ tsp. dried rosemary, crushed
- 1 tsp. minced fresh thyme or
  ¼ tsp. dried thyme
- 1 tsp. grated lemon zest
- 1 Tbsp. lemon juice
- 4 bone-in chicken thighs
  (about 1½ lbs.)
- ⅛ tsp. salt
- ⅛ tsp. pepper

1. Preheat air fryer to 400°. In a small bowl, combine butter, garlic, rosemary, thyme, lemon zest and lemon juice. Spread 1 tsp. butter mixture under the skin of each chicken thigh. Spread remaining butter over the skin of each thigh. Sprinkle with salt and pepper.
2. Place the chicken, skin side up, on greased tray in air-fryer basket. Cook for 20 minutes, turning once. Turn chicken again (skin side up) and cook until a thermometer reads 170°-175°, about 5 minutes longer.
1 CHICKEN THIGH: 329 cal., 26g fat (11g sat. fat), 111mg chol., 234mg sod., 1g carb. (0 sugars, 0 fiber), 23g pro.

PRESSURE-COOKER
CRANBERRY STUFFED APPLES

PRESSURE-COOKER CRANBERRY STUFFED APPLES

Cinnamon, nutmeg and walnuts add a homey autumn flavor to these stuffed apples. What a lovely old-fashioned treat!
—*Grace Sandvigen, Rochester, NY*

Prep: 10min. • **Cook:** 5 min.
Makes: 5 servings

- 5 medium apples
- ⅓ cup fresh or frozen cranberries, thawed and chopped
- ¼ cup packed brown sugar
- 2 Tbsp. chopped walnuts
- ¼ tsp. ground cinnamon
- ⅛ tsp. ground nutmeg
  Optional: Whipped cream or vanilla ice cream

1. Core apples, leaving bottoms intact. Peel the top third of each apple. Place trivet insert and 1 cup water in a 6-qt. electric pressure cooker. Combine cranberries, brown sugar, walnuts, cinnamon and nutmeg; spoon into apples. Place apples on trivet.
2. Lock lid; close pressure-release valve. Adjust to pressure-cook on high for 3 minutes. Quick-release pressure. If desired, serve with whipped cream or ice cream.
1 STUFFED APPLE: 142 cal., 2g fat (0 sat. fat), 0 chol., 5mg sod., 33g carb. (27g sugars, 4g fiber), 1g pro. **DIABETIC EXCHANGES:** 1 starch, 1 fruit.

AIR-FRYER
NACHO DOGS

1. Cut a slit down the length of each hot dog without cutting through; insert a halved cheese stick into the slit. Set aside.

2. Preheat air fryer to 350°. In a large bowl, stir together flour, yogurt, salsa, chili powder, jalapenos and ¼ cup crushed tortilla chips to form a soft dough. Place dough on a lightly floured surface; divide into 6 pieces. Roll a piece of dough into a 15-in. long strip; wrap strip in a spiral around a cheese-stuffed hot dog. Repeat with remaining dough and hot dogs. Spray wrapped dogs with cooking spray and gently roll in remaining crushed chips. Spray air fryer basket with cooking spray; place hot dogs in basket not touching each other, leaving room to expand.

3. In batches, cook until the dough is slightly browned and the cheese starts to melt, 8-10 minutes. If desired, serve with additional salsa, guacamole and sour cream.

NOTE: Wear disposable gloves when cutting hot peppers; the oils can burn skin. Avoid touching your face.

1 NACHO DOG: 216 cal., 9g fat (5g sat. fat), 23mg chol., 513mg sod., 26g carb. (3g sugars, 1g fiber), 9g pro.

AIR-FRYER NACHO DOGS

Adults and kids alike will love these yummy southwest-inspired hot dogs. This dish is not only budget-friendly, but it's hot, cheesy and delicious too.
—*Joan Hallford, North Richland Hills, TX*

- -

Prep: 25 min. • **Cook:** 10 min./batch.
Makes: 6 servings

6 hot dogs
3 cheddar cheese sticks, halved lengthwise
1¼ cups self-rising flour
1 cup plain Greek yogurt
¼ cup salsa
¼ tsp. chili powder
3 Tbsp. chopped seeded jalapeno pepper
1 cup crushed nacho-flavored tortilla chips, divided
Optional: Guacamole and sour cream

AIR-FRYER GARLIC & WINE LAMB CHOPS

This recipe is special to me because the flavor reminds me of my mother's lamb roast that cooks all day. It's a special meal that doesn't take much time or effort, so you can have it all year.
—*Dorice Winston, Concord, NC*

Prep: 15 min. + marinating
Cook: 10 min./batch
Makes: 4 servings

1 cup dry white wine or chicken broth
⅓ cup olive oil
5 garlic cloves, crushed
1 fresh rosemary sprig or 1 Tbsp. dried rosemary, crushed
1 fresh thyme sprig or 1 Tbsp. dried thyme
1 Tbsp. herbes de Provence
1 Tbsp. Worcestershire sauce
1 tsp. salt
1 tsp. dried minced onion
1 tsp. pepper
8 lamb rib chops (about 1 in. thick and 3 oz. each)

1. In a large bowl or shallow dish, combine all ingredients but lamb. Add lamb; turn to coat. Refrigerate 6 hours or overnight.
2. Drain lamb, discarding marinade. Preheat air fryer to 390°. In batches, arrange chops in greased air fryer. Cook until meat reaches desired doneness (for medium-rare, a thermometer should read 135°; medium, 140°; medium-well, 145°), 4-5 minutes on each side. Let stand for 5 minutes before serving.
2 LAMB CHOPS: 228 cal., 13g fat (3g sat. fat), 68mg chol., 272mg sod., 2g carb. (0 sugars, 0 fiber), 22g pro. **DIABETIC EXCHANGES:** 3 lean meat, 1 fat.

AIR-FRYER GARLIC & WINE LAMB CHOPS

PRESSURE-COOKER
CLAM SAUCE

PRESSURE-COOKER SPICY PORK & SQUASH RAGU

This recipe is a marvelously spicy combo perfect for cooler fall weather—so satisfying after a day spent outdoors.
—*Monica Osterhaus, Paducah, KY*

Prep: 20 min. • **Cook:** 15 min. + releasing
Makes: 10 servings

- 2 cans (14½ oz. each) stewed tomatoes, undrained
- 1 pkg. (12 oz.) frozen cooked winter squash, thawed
- 1 large sweet onion, cut into ½-in. pieces
- 1 medium sweet red pepper, cut into ½-in. pieces
- ¾ cup reduced-sodium chicken broth
- 1½ tsp. crushed red pepper flakes
- 2 lbs. boneless country-style pork ribs
- 1 tsp. salt
- ¼ tsp. garlic powder
- ¼ tsp. pepper
     Hot cooked pasta
     Shaved Parmesan cheese, optional

1. Combine the first 6 ingredients in a 6-qt. electric pressure cooker. Sprinkle ribs with salt, garlic powder and pepper; place in pressure cooker. Lock lid; close the pressure-release valve. Adjust to pressure-cook on high for 15 minutes. Let pressure release naturally for 10 minutes; quick-release remaining pressure.
2. Remove cover; stir to break pork into smaller pieces. Serve with pasta. If desired, top with Parmesan cheese.
FREEZE OPTION: Freeze cooled ragu in freezer containers. To use, partially thaw in refrigerator overnight. Heat through in a saucepan, stirring occasionally.
1 CUP RAGU: 196 cal., 8g fat (3g sat. fat), 52mg chol., 469mg sod., 13g carb. (6g sugars, 2g fiber), 18g pro. **DIABETIC EXCHANGES:** 2 lean meat, 1 starch.

PRESSURE-COOKER CLAM SAUCE

I serve this bright and fresh clam sauce often, usually with pasta. But it's also delectable as a hot dip for special get-togethers.
—*Frances Pietsch, Flower Mound, TX*

Prep: 10 min. • **Cooks:** 5 minutes
Makes: 4 cups

- 4 Tbsp. butter
- 2 Tbsp. olive oil
- ½ cup finely chopped onion
- 8 oz. fresh mushrooms, chopped
- 2 garlic cloves, minced
- 2 cans (10 oz. each) whole baby clams
- ½ cup water
- ¼ cup sherry
- 2 tsp. lemon juice
- 1 bay leaf
- ¾ tsp. dried oregano
- ½ tsp. garlic salt
- ¼ tsp. white pepper
- ¼ tsp. Italian seasoning
- ¼ tsp. pepper
- 2 Tbsp. chopped fresh parsley
     Hot cooked pasta
     Grated Parmesan cheese, optional

1. Select saute setting on a 6-qt. electric pressure cooker. Adjust for medium heat; add butter and oil. When hot, add onion; cook and stir 2 minutes. Add mushrooms and garlic; cook 1 minute longer. Press cancel.
2. Drain clams, reserving liquid; coarsely chop. Add clams, reserved clam juice and the next 9 ingredients to pressure cooker. Lock lid; close pressure-release valve. Adjust to pressure-cook on high 2 minutes. Quick-release pressure.
3. Discard bay leaf; stir in parsley. Serve with pasta. If desired, serve with grated Parmesan cheese and additional lemon juice and parsley.
½ CUP: 138 cal., 10g fat (4g sat. fat), 40mg chol., 580mg sod., 5g carb. (1g sugars, 0 fiber), 7g pro.

PRESSURE-COOKER SPICY
PORK & SQUASH RAGU

PRESSURE-COOKER
BALSAMIC PORK TENDERLOIN

PRESSURE-COOKER BALSAMIC PORK TENDERLOIN

This pork tenderloin with a sweet brown sugar and balsamic glaze will become a go-to dinner your whole family will love. It's perfect for busy weeknights, but also special enough for company.
—*Karen Kelly, Germantown, MD*

Prep: 10 min. • **Cook:** 20 min. + releasing
Makes: 8 servings

- ¼ cup packed brown sugar
- ¼ cup plus 2 Tbsp. water, divided
- ¼ cup balsamic vinegar
- 1 Tbsp. minced fresh rosemary
- 3 garlic cloves, minced
- 1 Tbsp. soy sauce
- 2 pork tenderloins (1 lb. each), halved widthwise
- 1 Tbsp. olive oil
- 1 Tbsp. cornstarch

1. In a small bowl, whisk brown sugar, ¼ cup water, vinegar, rosemary, garlic and soy sauce; set aside.
2. Select saute or browning setting on a 6-qt. electric pressure cooker. Adjust for medium heat; add oil. When oil is hot, brown the pork in batches. Press cancel. Return all pork and the vinegar mixture to pressure cooker.
3. Lock lid; close pressure-release valve. Adjust to pressure-cook on high for 20 minutes. Let pressure release naturally. Remove pork to a serving platter. Whisk cornstarch and remaining 2 Tbsp. water until smooth; stir into pressure cooker. Select saute setting and adjust for low heat. Simmer, stirring constantly, until thickened, 3-5 minutes. Drizzle over pork. If desired, sprinkle with additional rosemary.
1 SERVING: 188 cal., 6g fat (2g sat. fat), 64mg chol., 162mg sod., 10g carb. (9g sugars, 0 fiber), 23g pro.

AIR-FRYER SPINACH FETA TURNOVERS

AIR-FRYER SPINACH FETA TURNOVERS

These quick and easy turnovers are one of my wife's favorite entrees. The refrigerated pizza dough makes preparation a snap!
—*David Baruch, Weston, FL*

Takes: 30 min. • **Makes:** 4 servings

- 2 large eggs
- 1 pkg. (10 oz.) frozen spinach, thawed, squeezed dry and chopped
- ¾ cup crumbled feta cheese
- 2 garlic cloves, minced
- ¼ tsp. pepper
- 1 tube (13.8 oz.) refrigerated pizza crust
  Refrigerated tzatziki sauce, optional

1. Preheat air fryer to 425°. In a bowl, whisk eggs; set aside 1 Tbsp. of eggs. Combine the spinach, feta cheese, garlic, pepper and remaining beaten eggs.
2. Unroll pizza crust; roll into a 12-in. square. Cut into four 6-in. squares. Top each square with about ⅓ cup of the spinach mixture. Fold into a triangle and pinch edges to seal. Cut slits in top; brush with reserved egg.
3. Working in batches if necessary, place triangles in a single layer on greased tray in air-fryer basket. Cook until golden brown, 10-12 minutes. If desired, serve with tzatziki sauce.
1 TURNOVER: 361 cal., 9g fat (4g sat. fat), 104mg chol., 936mg sod., 51g carb. (7g sugars, 4g fiber), 17g pro.

AIR-FRYER
PRETZEL-CRUSTED CATFISH

AIR-FRYER PRETZEL-CRUSTED CATFISH

I love the flavor of this catfish recipe. I'm not a big fish lover, so any concoction that has me loving fish is a keeper in my book. It's wonderful served with classic southern sides like corn muffins, greens, herbed rice pilaf or mac and cheese.
—*Kelly Williams, Forked River, NJ*

- -

Prep: 15 min. • **Cook:** 10 min./batch
Makes: 4 servings

- 4   catfish fillets (6 oz. each)
- ½   tsp. salt
- ½   tsp. pepper
- 2   large eggs
- ⅓   cup Dijon mustard
- 2   Tbsp. 2% milk
- ½   cup all-purpose flour
- 4   cups honey mustard miniature pretzels, coarsely crushed
     Cooking spray
     Lemon slices, optional

1. Preheat air fryer to 325°. Sprinkle catfish with salt and pepper. Whisk eggs, mustard and milk in a shallow bowl. Place the flour and pretzels in separate shallow bowls. Coat fillets with flour, then dip in the egg mixture and coat with crushed pretzels.
2. In batches, place fillets in a single layer on greased tray in air-fryer basket; spritz with cooking spray. Cook until the fish flakes easily with a fork, 10-12 minutes. If desired, serve with lemon slices.
1 FILLET: 466 cal., 14g fat (3g sat. fat), 164mg chol., 1580mg sod., 45g carb. (2g sugars, 2g fiber), 33g pro.

> ### Test Kitchen Tip
> If you don't have an air fryer, you can make this recipe in a deep fryer, an electric skillet or on the stovetop.

PRESSURE-COOKER LAVA CAKE

PRESSURE-COOKER LAVA CAKE

Because I love chocolate, this decadent cake has long been a favorite. It's even great cold the next day—assuming you have any leftovers!
—*Elizabeth Farrell, Hamilton, MT*

- -

Prep: 15 min. • **Cook:** 20 min. + standing
Makes: 8 servings

- 1   cup all-purpose flour
- 1   cup packed brown sugar, divided
- 5   Tbsp. baking cocoa, divided
- 2   tsp. baking powder
- ¼   tsp. salt
- ½   cup 2% milk
- 2   Tbsp. canola oil
- ½   tsp. vanilla extract
- ⅛   tsp. ground cinnamon
- 1¼ cups hot water
     Optional: Fresh raspberries and vanilla ice cream

1. Whisk flour, ½ cup brown sugar, 3 Tbsp. cocoa, baking powder and salt. In another bowl, whisk milk, oil and vanilla until blended. Add to flour mixture; stir just until moistened.
2. Spread into a 1½-qt. baking dish coated with cooking spray. Mix cinnamon and the remaining ½ cup brown sugar and 2 Tbsp. cocoa; stir in hot water. Pour over batter (do not stir).
3. Place trivet insert and 1 cup water in a 6-qt. electric pressure cooker. Cover baking dish with foil. Fold an 18x12-in. piece of foil lengthwise into thirds, making a sling. Use the sling to lower the dish onto the trivet. Lock lid; close pressure-release valve. Adjust to pressure-cook on high for 20 minutes. Quick-release pressure.
4. Using foil sling, carefully remove baking dish. Let stand for 15 minutes. A toothpick inserted in cake portion should come out clean. If desired, serve with raspberries and ice cream.
1 SERVING: 208 cal., 4g fat (0 sat. fat), 0 chol., 208mg sod., 42g carb. (28g sugars, 1g fiber), 3g pro.

AIR-FRYER TURKEY
CLUB ROULADES

AIR-FRYER TURKEY
CLUB ROULADES

Weeknights turn elegant when these
quick-prep roulades are on the menu.
Not a fan of turkey? Substitute lightly
pounded chicken breasts.
—Taste of Home *Test Kitchen*

Prep: 20 min. • **Cook:** 10 min./batch
Makes: 8 servings

- ¾ lb. fresh asparagus, trimmed
- 8 turkey breast cutlets (about 1 lb.)
- 1½ tsp. Dijon mustard
- 1½ tsp. mayonnaise
- 8 slices deli ham
- 8 slices provolone cheese
- ½ tsp. poultry seasoning
- ½ tsp. pepper
- 8 bacon strips

SAUCE
- ⅓ cup Dijon mustard
- ⅓ cup mayonnaise
- 4 tsp. 2% milk
- ¼ tsp. poultry seasoning

1. Preheat air fryer to 375°. Place
the asparagus on greased tray in
air-fryer basket. Cook until crisp-tender,
4-5 minutes, tossing halfway through
cooking time. Set aside.
2. Mix together 1½ tsp. each mustard
and mayonnaise; spread over the turkey
cutlets. Layer with ham, cheese and
asparagus. Sprinkle with poultry
seasoning and pepper. Roll up tightly
and wrap with bacon.
3. In batches, arrange roulades in a
single layer on greased tray in air-fryer
basket. Cook until bacon is crisp and
turkey is no longer pink, 8-10 minutes,
turning occasionally.
4. For sauce, combine all the sauce
ingredients; serve with roulades.
1 ROULADE WITH 1 TBSP. SAUCE: 224 cal.,
11g fat (5g sat. fat), 64mg chol., 1075mg
sod., 2g carb. (1g sugars, 0 fiber), 25g pro.

PRESSURE-COOKER
PINEAPPLE CHICKEN

We love Hawaiian-style chicken made in
a slow cooker, but sometimes we need
something that comes together fast! We
tweaked our favorite recipe to work in a
pressure cooker for a quick and easy
weeknight dinner. Add a side salad for
a complete meal.
—Courtney Stultz, Weir, KS

Prep: 10 min. • **Cook:** 20 min. + releasing
Makes: 6 servings

- 1½ lbs. boneless skinless chicken
  breasts
- 1 can (20 oz.) unsweetened
  pineapple chunks, undrained
- ¼ cup barbecue sauce
- 1 cup chicken broth
- 1 cup uncooked long grain brown rice
- ½ tsp. salt
  Optional: Minced fresh cilantro
  and sliced green onions

1. Combine the first 6 ingredients in a
6-qt. electric pressure cooker. Lock lid;
close pressure-release valve. Adjust to
pressure-cook on high for 20 minutes.
2. Let pressure release naturally.
Remove chicken to a cutting board
and shred with 2 forks. Add shredded
chicken back to pot and stir until
combined. If desired, sprinkle with
cilantro and green onions.
1 CUP: 313 cal., 4g fat (1g sat. fat), 63mg
chol., 536mg sod., 41g carb. (16g sugars,
3g fiber), 27g pro. **DIABETIC EXCHANGES:**
3 lean meat, 2½ starch.

> *"The flavor was great, and
> the leftovers were even
> better the next day."*
> —SHANNONDOBOS126, TASTEOFHOME.COM

PRESSURE-COOKER
PINEAPPLE CHICKEN

PRESSURE-COOKER
MEAT LOAF

up around sides of loaf, but do not cover top of loaf.

2. Place trivet insert and 1 cup water in a 6-qt. electric pressure cooker. Place foil-wrapped loaf on trivet. Lock lid; close pressure-release valve. Adjust to pressure-cook on high for 45 minutes.

3. Let pressure release naturally for 10 minutes; quick-release any remaining pressure. A thermometer inserted in meat loaf should read at least 160°. Remove meat loaf from pressure cooker and top with barbecue sauce. Let stand 10 minutes before removing from foil and slicing.

1 PIECE: 315 cal., 21g fat (7g sat. fat), 131mg chol., 678mg sod., 6g carb. (2g sugars, 0 fiber), 25g pro.

Test Kitchen Tip

Because this recipe cooks the ground beef quickly, it's best to work with a higher-fat blend of beef. This will keep your meat loaf from drying out. Ask your butcher for a 60 / 40 or 70 / 30 blend (this is the ratio of lean meat to fat).

PRESSURE-COOKER MEAT LOAF

I used to make this recipe a lot when my kids were growing up and I was working. It's easy to make and a family favorite. You can make several loaves ahead and freeze them. Thaw a loaf in the refrigerator overnight, and it's ready to cook.

—*Kallee Krong-McCreery, Escondido, CA*

Prep: 15 min. + standing
Cook: 45 min. + releasing
Makes: 8 servings

- 1 cup soft bread crumbs
- 2 large eggs, lightly beaten
- ⅓ cup 2% milk
- ¼ cup finely chopped onion
- 2 Tbsp. ketchup
- 1 tsp. seasoned salt
- 1 tsp. dried parsley flakes
- 1½ lbs. lean ground beef (90% lean)
- 1 lb. bulk pork sausage
- ¼ cup barbecue sauce

1. In a large bowl, combine the first 7 ingredients. Add beef and pork; mix lightly but thoroughly. On a 12x8 piece of foil, shape into a 8x5-in. loaf. Bring foil

- Easy Boiled Eggs -

Eat them straight or use them in salads, sandwiches and many more recipes. Modern gadgets make it a snap to always have some boiled eggs ready and waiting in the fridge!

For air fryer:
Preheat air fryer to 275°. Place eggs in a single layer on tray in air fryer. Cook 15 minutes. Remove eggs; rinse in cold water and then place in ice water until completely cooled. Drain and refrigerate.

For pressure cooker:
Pressure-cook the eggs on high for 5 minutes, wait 5 minutes before releasing pressure and then plunge the eggs into an ice water bath for 5 minutes. For extra large or jumbo eggs, increase the cooking time to 7 or 8 minutes, respectively.

AIR-FRYER
BLACK BEAN
CHIMICHANGAS

AIR-FRYER BUFFALO CHICKEN WINGS

Cayenne, red sauce and spices keep these tangy wings good and hot, just like the originals. And the air fryer keeps them a bit healthier than a fried version.
—*Nancy Chapman, Center Harbor, NH*

Prep: 10 min. • **Cook:** 25 min./batch
Makes: about 4 dozen

- 25 whole chicken wings (about 5 lbs.)
- 1 cup butter, cubed
- ¼ cup Louisiana-style hot sauce
- ¾ tsp. cayenne pepper
- ¾ tsp. celery salt
- ½ tsp. onion powder
- ½ tsp. garlic powder
  Optional: Celery ribs, crumbled blue cheese and ranch salad dressing

1. Preheat air fryer to 300°. Cut chicken wings into 3 sections; discard wing tip sections. In batches, arrange wings in a single layer on greased tray in air-fryer basket. Cook 10 minutes. Increase temperature to 400°; cook until chicken juices run clear and wings are golden brown, 15-20 minutes longer.
2. Meanwhile, in a small saucepan, melt butter. Stir in hot sauce and spices. Place chicken in a large bowl; add sauce and toss to coat. Remove to a serving plate with a slotted spoon. Serve with celery, crumbled blue cheese and ranch dressing if desired.
1 PIECE: 83 cal., 7g fat (3g sat. fat), 24mg chol., 106mg sod., 0 carb. (0 sugars, 0 fiber), 5g pro.

AIR-FRYER BLACK BEAN CHIMICHANGAS

These chimichangas get a little love from the air fryer, so they're healthier than their deep-fried counterparts. Black beans provide protein, and the recipe is a smart way to use up leftover rice.
—*Kimberly Hammond, Kingwood, TX*

Prep: 20 min. • **Cook:** 5 min./batch
Makes: 6 servings

- 2 cans (15 oz. each) black beans, rinsed and drained
- 1 pkg. (8.8 oz.) ready-to-serve brown rice
- ⅔ cup frozen corn
- ⅔ cup minced fresh cilantro
- ⅔ cup chopped green onions
- ½ tsp. salt
- 6 whole wheat tortillas (8 in.), warmed if necessary
- 4 tsp. olive oil
  Optional: Guacamole and salsa

1. Preheat air fryer to 400°. In a large microwave-safe bowl, mix beans, rice and corn; microwave, covered, until heated through, 4-5 minutes, stirring halfway. Stir in cilantro, green onions and salt.
2. To assemble, spoon ¾ cup bean mixture across the center of each tortilla. Fold the bottom and sides of tortilla over filling and roll up. Brush with olive oil.
3. In batches, place chimichangas seam side down on greased tray in air-fryer basket. Cook until golden brown and crispy, 2-3 minutes. If desired, serve with guacamole and salsa.
1 CHIMICHANGA: 337 cal., 5g fat (0 sat. fat), 0 chol., 602mg sod., 58g carb. (2g sugars, 10g fiber), 13g pro.

AIR-FRYER
BUFFALO
CHICKEN WINGS

PRESSURE-COOKER
SALSA LONDON BROIL

PRESSURE-COOKER SALSA LONDON BROIL

I love using my pressure cooker for this recipe because it comes together so quickly but still has that long, slow-cooked flavor. The veggies semi-melt into the sauce to give it an added savory taste.

—*Ann Sheehy, Lawrence, MA*

Prep: 15 min. • **Cook:** 10 min. + releasing
Makes: 4 servings

- 1 to 1½ lbs. beef top round steak
- 1 jar (16 oz.) salsa
- 1 medium sweet potato, peeled and chopped
- 1 large carrot, thinly sliced
- 1 garlic clove, minced
  Lime wedges
  Chopped fresh cilantro, optional

1. Cut steak into thirds; place in a 6-qt. electric pressure cooker. Add the salsa, sweet potato, carrot and garlic. Lock lid; close pressure-release valve. Adjust to pressure-cook on high for 10 minutes. Let pressure release naturally.
2. Slice steak. Serve with vegetables. Garnish with lime wedges and, if desired, chopped cilantro.
1 SERVING: 239 cal., 4g fat (1g sat. fat), 63mg chol., 503mg sod., 23g carb. (10g sugars, 2g fiber), 27g pro. **DIABETIC EXCHANGES:** 4 lean meat, 1½ starch.

Test Kitchen Tip

To make in a stovetop pressure cooker, close cover according to manufacturer's directions; place pressure regulator on vent pipe. Bring cooker to full pressure over high heat. Reduce to medium-high; cook 10 minutes. (Regulator should maintain a slow steady rocking motion or release of steam; adjust heat if needed.) Remove from heat. Allow pressure to drop on its own.

AIR-FRYER PARMESAN BREADED SQUASH

AIR-FRYER PARMESAN BREADED SQUASH

This yellow squash is beautifully crisp. You don't have to turn the pieces, but do keep an eye on them. If you don't have an air fryer, you can make this recipe in the oven.

—*Debi Mitchell, Flower Mound, TX*

Prep: 15 min. • **Cook:** 10 min./batch
Makes: 4 servings

- 4 cups thinly sliced yellow summer squash (3 medium)
- 3 Tbsp. olive oil
- ½ tsp. salt
- ½ tsp. pepper
- ⅛ tsp. cayenne pepper
- ¾ cup panko bread crumbs
- ¾ cup grated Parmesan cheese

1. Preheat air fryer to 350°. Place the squash in a large bowl. Add oil and seasonings; toss to coat.
2. In a shallow bowl, mix bread crumbs and cheese. Dip squash in the crumb mixture to coat both sides, patting to help the coating adhere. In batches, arrange the squash in a single layer on tray in air-fryer basket. Cook until squash is tender and coating is golden brown, about 10 minutes.
½ CUP: 203 cal., 14g fat (3g sat. fat), 11mg chol., 554mg sod., 13g carb. (4g sugars, 2g fiber), 6g pro. **DIABETIC EXCHANGES:** 3 fat, 1 vegetable, ½ starch.

**PRESSURE-COOKER
GERMAN GOULASH**

PRESSURE-COOKER AUTUMN APPLE CHICKEN

Fill the whole house with the aroma of chicken with apples and barbecue sauce. This is a meal you won't want to wait to dig into.
—*Caitlyn Hauser, Brookline, NH*

- -

Prep: 25 min. • **Cook:** 20 min.
Makes: 4 servings

- 4 bone-in chicken thighs (about 1½ lbs.), skin removed
- ¼ tsp. salt
- ¼ tsp. pepper
- 1 Tbsp. canola oil
- ½ cup apple cider or juice
- 1 medium onion, chopped
- ⅓ cup barbecue sauce
- 1 Tbsp. honey
- 1 garlic clove, minced
- 2 medium Fuji or Gala apples, coarsely chopped

1. Sprinkle chicken with salt and pepper. Select saute or browning setting on a 6-qt. electric pressure cooker. Adjust for medium heat; add oil. When oil is hot, brown chicken; remove and keep warm.
2. Add cider, stirring to loosen browned bits from pan. Stir in onion, barbecue sauce, honey, garlic and chicken. Press cancel. Lock lid; close pressure-release valve. Adjust to pressure-cook on high for 10 minutes. Let pressure release naturally for 5 minutes; quick-release any remaining pressure. A thermometer inserted in chicken thighs should read at least 170°.
3. Remove chicken; keep warm. Select saute setting and adjust for low heat. Add apples; simmer, stirring constantly, until apples are tender, about 10 minutes. Serve with chicken.
1 CHICKEN THIGH WITH ½ CUP APPLE MIXTURE: 340 cal., 13g fat (3g sat. fat), 87mg chol., 458mg sod., 31g carb. (24g sugars, 3g fiber), 25g pro. **DIABETIC EXCHANGES:** 4 lean meat, 1½ starch, ½ fruit.

PRESSURE-COOKER GERMAN GOULASH

When my father was stationed in Germany, we had a friend who didn't speak English, but she would bring us traditional dishes to try. This was one of my favorites. I'm sure she cooked it in the oven or on the stovetop for hours, but with a pressure cooker, it's ready in less than an hour.
—*Johnna Johnson, Scottsdale, AZ*

- -

Prep: 25 min. • **Cook:** 50 min. + releasing
Makes: 8 servings

- 3 Tbsp. olive oil
- 1 boneless chuck roast (2½ lbs.) cut into 2-in. cubes
- 4 small onions, thinly sliced
- 1 cup beer or beef broth
- ½ cup dry red wine or beef broth
- 3 Tbsp. tomato paste
- 2 Tbsp. sweet Hungarian paprika
- 1 Tbsp. beef base
- 1 tsp. caraway seeds
- 1 tsp. dried marjoram
- ½ tsp. salt
- ¼ tsp. pepper
- 2 bay leaves
- Hot cooked pasta

1. Select saute or browning setting on a 6-qt. electric pressure cooker. Adjust for medium heat; add oil. When the oil is hot, brown meat in batches. Remove and keep warm. Cook onions in drippings until tender, 4-5 minutes. Press cancel. Combine the next 10 ingredients; add to cooker. Return beef to cooker.
2. Lock lid; close pressure-release valve. Adjust to pressure-cook on high for 25 minutes. Let pressure release naturally for 10 minutes; quick-release any remaining pressure.
3. Select saute setting and adjust for medium heat; bring liquid to a boil. Cook until sauce reaches desired thickness, about 20 minutes. Remove bay leaves. Serve with pasta.
½ CUP: 203 cal., 14g fat (3g sat. fat), 11mg chol., 554mg sod., 13g carb. (4g sugars, 2g fiber), 6g pro. **DIABETIC EXCHANGES:** 3 fat, 1 vegetable, ½ starch.

AIR-FRYER FISH TACOS

These crispy tacos are good enough to challenge the best food truck. I love that the fish is deliciously guilt-free because it's air-fried instead of deep-fried.
—*Lena Lim, Seattle, WA*

- -

Prep: 30 min. • **Cook:** 10 min./batch
Makes: 8 servings

- ¾ cup reduced-fat sour cream
- 1 can (4 oz.) chopped green chiles
- 1 Tbsp. fresh cilantro leaves
- 1 Tbsp. lime juice
- 4 tilapia fillets (4 oz. each)
- ½ cup all-purpose flour
- 1 large egg white, beaten
- ½ cup panko bread crumbs
  Cooking spray
- ½ tsp. salt
- ½ tsp. each white pepper, cayenne pepper and paprika
- 8 corn tortillas (6 in.), warmed
- 1 large tomato, finely chopped

1. Place sour cream, chiles, cilantro and lime juice in a food processor; cover and process until blended. Set aside.
2. Cut each tilapia fillet lengthwise into 2 portions. Place the flour, egg white and bread crumbs in separate shallow bowls. Dip tilapia in the flour, then the egg white, then the crumbs.
3. Preheat air fryer to 400°. In batches, arrange fillets in a single layer on greased tray in air-fryer basket; spritz with cooking spray. Cook until the fish flakes easily with a fork, 10-12 minutes, turning once.
4. Combine seasonings; sprinkle over fish. Place a portion of fish on each tortilla; top with about 2 Tbsp. sour cream mixture. Sprinkle with tomato. If desired, top with additional cilantro.
1 TACO: 178 cal., 3g fat (1g sat. fat), 30mg chol., 269mg sod., 22g carb. (2g sugars, 2g fiber), 16g pro. **DIABETIC EXCHANGES:** 2 lean meat, 1½ starch, ½ fat.

AIR-FRYER
FISH TACOS

8

Make-Ahead Marvels

With today's busy schedules, it helps to work ahead. All these recipes
let you get a jump on your meals—whether it's a slow-cooked dish,
a freezer-friendly recipe, or a meal that's assembled ahead of
time and popped in the oven when you're ready.

EASY EGG ROLLS
P. 248

FREEZER MASHED
POTATOES

FREEZER MASHED POTATOES

Can you freeze mashed potatoes? You bet you can! I always make these tasty potatoes for my kids when they go away to school. All they have to do is keep them in a freezer until it's mashed potato time!
—*Jessie Fortune, Pocahontas, AR*

Prep: 30 min. + freezing • **Bake:** 30 min.
Makes: 14 servings

- 5 lbs. potatoes (about 9 large), peeled and cut into chunks
- 2 Tbsp. butter, softened
- 1 cup sour cream
- 6 oz. cream cheese, cubed
- ½ tsp. onion powder
- ½ tsp. salt
- ¼ tsp. pepper

1. Place potatoes in a large saucepan and cover with water. Bring to a boil. Reduce the heat; cover and cook for 10-15 minutes or until tender. Drain.
2. In a large bowl, mash the potatoes with butter. Beat in the sour cream, cream cheese, onion powder, salt and pepper. Transfer to a greased 13x9-in. baking dish. Bake, uncovered, at 350° until heated through, 30-35 minutes. Or, transfer 1½-cup portions to greased 2-cup baking dishes. Cover and freeze up to 6 months.
NOTE: To use frozen potatoes, thaw in the refrigerator overnight. Bake at 350° until heated through, 30-35 minutes.
¾ CUP: 195 cal., 6g fat (4g sat. fat), 19mg chol., 173mg sod., 31g carb. (4g sugars, 3g fiber), 6g pro.

Test Kitchen Tip

These mashed potatoes can last up to 2 months in an airtight container in the freezer. Ideally, you should allow them to thaw overnight in the refrigerator before baking. However, if you're in a pinch, you can thaw them on the stovetop over low heat; stir occasionally so they don't scorch.

CHICKEN & RICE CASSEROLE

CHICKEN & RICE CASSEROLE

Everyone loves this casserole because it's a tasty combination of hearty and crunchy ingredients in a creamy sauce. You can assemble the casserole ahead of time and keep it in the fridge; just wait to add the chips until you're ready to bake it.
—*Myrtle Matthews, Marietta, GA*

Prep: 15 min. • **Bake:** 1 hour
Makes: 12 servings

- 4 cups cooked white rice or a combination of wild and white rice
- 4 cups diced cooked chicken
- ½ cup slivered almonds
- 1 small onion, chopped
- 1 can (8 oz.) sliced water chestnuts, drained
- 1 pkg. (10 oz.) frozen peas, thawed
- ¾ cup chopped celery
- 1 can (10¾ oz.) condensed cream of celery soup, undiluted
- 1 can (10¾ oz.) condensed cream of chicken soup, undiluted
- 1 cup mayonnaise
- 2 tsp. lemon juice
- 1 tsp. salt
- 2 cups crushed potato chips
  Paprika

1. Preheat oven to 350°. In a greased 13x9-in. baking dish, combine the first 7 ingredients. In a large bowl, combine soups, mayonnaise, lemon juice and salt. Pour over the chicken mixture and toss to coat.
2. Sprinkle with potato chips and paprika. Bake until heated through, about 1 hour.
1 CUP: 439 cal., 26g fat (5g sat. fat), 51mg chol., 804mg sod., 31g carb. (3g sugars, 3g fiber), 19g pro.

ALMOND
BROCCOLI SALAD

BARBECUED MEATBALLS

Grape jelly and chili sauce are the secret ingredients that make this dish taste so fantastic. I prepare the meatballs and sauce in advance if I'm hosting a party, and reheat them before guests arrive.
—Irma Schnuelle, Manitowoc, WI

Prep: 20 min. • **Cook:** 15 min.
Makes: about 3 dozen

- ½ cup dry bread crumbs
- ⅓ cup finely chopped onion
- ¼ cup 2% milk
- 1 large egg, lightly beaten
- 1 Tbsp. minced fresh parsley
- 1 tsp. salt
- 1 tsp. Worcestershire sauce
- ½ tsp. pepper
- 1 lb. lean ground beef (90% lean)
- ¼ cup canola oil
- 1 bottle (12 oz.) chili sauce
- 1 jar (10 oz.) grape jelly

1. In a large bowl, combine the first 8 ingredients. Crumble beef over the bread crumb mixture and mix lightly but thoroughly. Shape into 1-in. balls. In a large skillet, brown meatballs in oil on all sides.
2. Remove meatballs and drain. In the same skillet, combine chili sauce and jelly; cook and stir over medium heat until jelly has melted. Return meatballs to pan; heat through.
1 MEATBALL: 71 cal., 3g fat (1g sat. fat), 13mg chol., 215mg sod., 9g carb. (7g sugars, 0 fiber), 3g pro.

ALMOND BROCCOLI SALAD

This colorful salad is easy to make, and I like that it can be prepared ahead of time. Add the almonds and bacon just before serving so they stay crunchy.
—Margaret Garbade, Tulsa, OK

Takes: 25 min. • **Makes:** 12 servings

- 1 bunch broccoli (about 1½ lbs.)
- 1 cup mayonnaise
- ¼ cup red wine vinegar
- 2 Tbsp. sugar
- ¼ tsp. salt
- ½ tsp. freshly ground pepper
- 1 pkg. (7 oz.) mixed dried fruit
- ¼ cup finely chopped red onion
- 1 pkg. (2¼ oz.) slivered almonds, toasted
- 4 bacon strips, cooked and crumbled

1. Cut florets from broccoli, reserving stalks; cut florets into 1-in. pieces. Using a paring knife, remove peel from thick stalks; cut stalks into ½-in. pieces.
2. In a small bowl, mix the mayonnaise, vinegar, sugar, salt and pepper. In a large bowl, combine broccoli, dried fruit and onion. Add the mayonnaise mixture; toss to coat. Refrigerate until serving.
3. Just before serving, sprinkle with almonds and bacon.
¾ CUP: 236 cal., 17g fat (3g sat. fat), 1mg chol., 180mg sod., 21g carb. (15g sugars, 3g fiber), 3g pro.

BARBECUED MEATBALLS

OPEN-FACED PIZZA BURGERS

I'm not sure where I first saw this recipe, but I'm glad I did! My family requests these burgers often. A dash of oregano livens up canned pizza sauce.
—*Sharon Schwartz, Burlington, WI*

Takes: 30 min. • **Makes:** 12 servings

- 1½ lbs. ground beef
- ¼ cup chopped onion
- 1 can (15 oz.) pizza sauce
- 1 can (4 oz.) mushroom stems and pieces, drained
- 1 Tbsp. sugar
- ½ tsp. dried oregano
- 6 hamburger buns, split and toasted
- 1½ cups shredded part-skim mozzarella cheese

1. In a large cast-iron or other heavy skillet, cook beef and onion over medium heat until the meat is no longer pink, 3-5 minutes, breaking the beef into crumbles. Drain. Stir in pizza sauce, mushrooms, sugar and oregano; mix well. Spoon onto buns; sprinkle with mozzarella cheese.
2. Place on ungreased baking sheets. Broil 4 in. from the heat until the cheese is melted, about 2 minutes.
FREEZE OPTION: Place the split and toasted buns on a baking sheet. Spoon the meat mixture onto buns; freeze for 1 hour. Transfer to freezer-safe airtight containers. To use, thaw completely in the refrigerator. Sprinkle with cheese. Broil 4 in. from the heat until heated through and the cheese is melted, about 2 minutes.
1 PIZZA BURGER: 205 cal., 8g fat (4g sat. fat), 36mg chol., 357mg sod., 15g carb. (4g sugars, 1g fiber), 16g pro.

EGGPLANT
CASSEROLE

breaking meat into crumbles; drain. Add tomatoes, salt and pepper. Cook and stir until the tomatoes are tender, about 5 minutes. Remove from the heat. Stir in milk, egg and eggplant; mix well.
3. Transfer to a greased 13x9-in. baking dish. In a small bowl, combine the bread crumbs and butter; sprinkle over the top. Bake, uncovered, until heated through, 30-35 minutes.

1⅓ CUPS: 342 cal., 19g fat (8g sat. fat), 113mg chol., 186mg sod., 18g carb. (7g sugars, 4g fiber), 25g pro.

Test Kitchen Tips

- Because the eggplant and beef are precooked, this casserole can be frozen before or after baking. If you plan to bake it to save for a later date, skip the topping—it won't hold up well in the freezer.

- While it's fine to leave the skin on eggplant in some dishes, the texture and flavor won't work well here, so this recipe calls for peeled eggplant.

EGGPLANT CASSEROLE

With lots of vegetables, this good-for-you dish is low in calories but full of flavor. I make it often in summer when fresh produce is abundant.
—*Marelyn Baugher, Holdrege, NE*

Prep: 20 min. • **Bake:** 30 min.
Makes: 6 servings

- 1   medium eggplant, peeled and cubed
- 1½ lbs. ground beef
- 1   medium onion, chopped
- 1   medium green pepper, chopped
- 3   medium tomatoes, chopped
       Salt and pepper to taste
- ½   cup 2% milk
- 1   large egg, beaten
- ½   cup dry bread crumbs
- 2   Tbsp. butter, melted

1. Preheat oven to 375°. In a saucepan, bring 4 cups water to a boil; add the eggplant. Boil until tender, 5-8 minutes. Drain and set aside.
2. In a large skillet, cook beef, onion and green pepper over medium heat until beef is no longer pink, 6-8 minutes,

SO-TENDER SWISS STEAK

serve steak and gravy with noodles
or mashed potatoes.
FREEZE OPTION: Freeze cooled beef
mixture in freezer containers. To use,
partially thaw in refrigerator overnight.
Heat through in a covered saucepan,
stirring occasionally; if necessary
add broth or water.
4 OZ. COOKED BEEF: 213 cal., 7g fat (2g sat.
fat), 64mg chol., 424mg sod., 9g carb. (1g
sugars, 1g fiber), 27g pro.

AVOCADO SALSA

I first made this recipe for a party, and
it was an absolute success. People love
the combination of flavors. Scoop it up
with chips, spoon it over chicken or steak,
or eat it on its own!
—*Susan Vandermeer, Ogden, UT*

- -

Prep: 20 min. + chilling
Makes: about 7 cups

  1⅔ cups (about 8¼ oz.) frozen corn,
       thawed
   2 cans (2¼ oz. each) sliced ripe olives,
       drained
   1 medium sweet red pepper, chopped
   1 small onion, chopped
   5 garlic cloves, minced
  ⅓ cup olive oil
  ¼ cup lemon juice
   3 Tbsp. cider vinegar
   1 tsp. dried oregano
  ½ tsp. salt
  ½ tsp. pepper
   4 medium ripe avocados, peeled
       Tortilla chips

1. Combine corn, olives, red pepper
and onion. In another bowl, mix the
next 7 ingredients. Pour over corn
mixture; toss to coat. Refrigerate,
covered, overnight.
2. Just before serving, chop avocados
and stir into the salsa. Serve with the
tortilla chips.
¼ CUP: 82 cal., 7g fat (1g sat. fat), 0 chol.,
85mg sod., 5g carb. (1g sugars, 2g fiber),
1g pro. **DIABETIC EXCHANGES:** 1½ fat.

SO-TENDER SWISS STEAK

When I was little, my mother's Swiss
steak was the dinner I requested the
most. Now it's a favorite in my house too.
—*Linda McGinty, Parma, OH*

- -

Prep: 30 min. • **Bake:** 2 hours
Makes: 8 servings

  ¼ cup all-purpose flour
  ½ tsp. salt
  ¼ tsp. pepper
   2 lbs. beef top round steak, cut into
       serving-size pieces
   2 Tbsp. canola oil
   1 medium onion, thinly sliced
   2 cups water
   2 Tbsp. Worcestershire sauce
  GRAVY
  ¼ cup all-purpose flour
  ¼ tsp. salt
  ⅛ tsp. pepper
  1¼ cups beef broth or water
       Optional: Hot cooked noodles or
       mashed potatoes

1. Preheat the oven to 325°. In a large
shallow dish, combine flour, salt and
pepper. Pound steak with a mallet to
tenderize. Add meat, a few pieces at
a time, and toss to coat.
2. In an ovenproof Dutch oven, brown
steak in oil on both sides. Arrange the
onion slices between layers of meat.
Add water and Worcestershire sauce.
3. Bake, covered, until the meat is very
tender, 2-2½ hours. Remove meat to a
serving platter and keep warm.
4. For gravy, in a small bowl, combine
flour, salt, pepper and broth until smooth;
stir into the pan juices. Bring to a boil
over medium heat; cook and stir until
thickened, about 2 minutes. If desired,

AVOCADO
SALSA

- No-Fry Fried Ice Cream -

This scrumptious dessert has a crispy cinnamon coating just like the fried ice cream served in your favorite Mexican restaurant, but with less oil. Make it ahead of time and freeze it until serving.

Using a ½-cup ice cream scoop, place 8 scoops **ice cream** on a baking sheet. Freeze until firm, about 1 hour. Meanwhile, combine ¼ cup **brown sugar**, 1 Tbsp. melted **butter** and 1 tsp. **cinnamon**. Stir in 2 cups crushed **cornflakes**. Transfer mixture to an ungreased 15x10x1-in. baking pan. Bake at 350° until lightly browned, 4-6 minutes. Cool completely. Roll ice cream balls in crumb mixture. Cover and freeze until firm, at least 1 hour. Serve with **whipped cream** and **caramel ice cream** topping.

BEEF OSSO
BUCCO

1. In a large resealable container, combine flour, ½ tsp. salt and pepper. Add beef, a few pieces at a time, and shake to coat.
2. In a large skillet, brown beef in butter and oil. Transfer meat and drippings to a 6-qt. slow cooker. Add wine to skillet, stirring to loosen browned bits from pan; pour over meat. Add the tomatoes, broth, carrots, onion, celery, thyme, oregano, bay leaves and the remaining ¼ tsp. salt.
3. Cook, covered, on low until meat is tender, 7-9 hours. Discard bay leaves.
4. Skim fat from cooking juices; transfer juices to a large saucepan. Bring to a boil. Combine the cornstarch and water until smooth; gradually stir into the pan. Bring to a boil; cook and stir until sauce is thickened, about 2 minutes.
5. Combine next 4 ingredients. Serve the beef with sauce and gremolata. If desired, serve over polenta.

1 SHANK WITH 1 CUP SAUCE AND 4 TSP. GREMOLATA: 398 cal., 15g fat (6g sat. fat), 112mg chol., 640mg sod., 17g carb. (5g sugars, 4g fiber), 47g pro

Test Kitchen Tip
If you're not a fan of polenta, pair this dish with any starchy side that will soak up the rich juices—French bread, mashed potatoes or pasta. The dish reheats well, so you can make it ahead of time and keep it in the fridge.

BEEF OSSO BUCCO
Our osso bucco boasts a thick, savory sauce complemented by the addition of gremolata, a chopped herb condiment made with lemon zest, garlic and parsley.
—Taste of Home *Test Kitchen*

Prep: 30 min. • **Cook:** 7 hours
Makes: 6 servings

½ cup all-purpose flour
¾ tsp. salt, divided
½ tsp. pepper
6 beef shanks (14 oz. each)
2 Tbsp. butter
1 Tbsp. olive oil
½ cup white wine or beef broth
1 can (14½ oz.) diced tomatoes, undrained
1½ cups beef broth
2 medium carrots, chopped
1 medium onion, chopped
1 celery rib, sliced
1 Tbsp. dried thyme
1 Tbsp. dried oregano
2 bay leaves
3 Tbsp. cornstarch
¼ cup cold water
GREMOLATA
⅓ cup minced fresh parsley
1 Tbsp. grated lemon zest
1 Tbsp. grated orange zest
2 garlic cloves, minced
 Polenta, optional

CHICKEN CHILES
RELLENOS STRATA

OVERNIGHT YEAST WAFFLES

PM

CHICKEN CHILES RELLENOS STRATA

This versatile bake can be made as an entree, a brunch option or a potluck dish. It's one of the easiest meals to assemble on a busy weeknight.
—*Kallee Krong-McCreery, Escondido, CA*

Prep: 20 min. + chilling
Bake: 35 min. + standing
Makes: 10 servings

- 6 cups cubed French bread (about 6 oz.)
- 2 cans (4 oz. each) chopped green chiles
- 2 cups shredded Monterey Jack cheese
- 2 cups shredded cooked chicken
- 12 large eggs
- 1½ cups 2% milk
- 2 tsp. baking powder
- 1 tsp. garlic salt
- 1 cup shredded cheddar cheese
  Salsa

1. In a greased 13x9-in. baking dish, layer half each of the bread cubes, chiles, Monterey Jack cheese and chicken. Repeat layers.
2. In a large bowl, whisk eggs, milk, baking powder and garlic salt until blended. Pour over layers. Sprinkle with cheddar cheese. Refrigerate, covered, overnight.
3. Preheat oven to 350°. Remove strata from refrigerator while the oven heats. Bake, uncovered, until puffed and golden at edges, 35-40 minutes. Let the strata stand 10 minutes before serving. Serve with salsa.
1 PIECE: 338 cal., 20g fat (9g sat. fat), 282mg chol., 820mg sod., 13g carb. (3g sugars, 1g fiber), 27g pro.

PM

OVERNIGHT YEAST WAFFLES

You might not think you'd have time to cook up waffles for breakfast, but this batter is made the night before so it's ready to go when you get up. These easy, fluffy waffles are so good, I freeze them to have some handy for busy mornings.
—*Mary Balcomb, Florence, OR*

Prep: 15 min. + chilling
Cook: 5 min./batch • **Makes:** 10 servings

- 1 pkg. (¼ oz.) active dry yeast
- ½ cup warm water (110° to 115°)
- 1 tsp. sugar
- 2 cups warm 2% milk (110° to 115°)
- ½ cup butter, melted
- 2 large eggs, room temperature, lightly beaten
- 2¾ cups all-purpose flour
- 1 tsp. salt
- ½ tsp. baking soda

1. In a large bowl, dissolve yeast in warm water. Add sugar; let stand for 5 minutes. Add the milk, butter and eggs; mix well. Combine flour and salt; stir into the milk mixture. Cover and refrigerate overnight.
2. Stir batter; sift in baking soda and stir well. Bake waffles in a preheated waffle maker according to the manufacturer's directions until golden brown.
2 WAFFLES: 220 cal., 12g fat (7g sat. fat), 74mg chol., 366mg sod., 22g carb. (3g sugars, 1g fiber), 6g pro.

> *"My very picky 7-year-old ate five, and told me not to lose the recipe!"*
> —DJ-SPOI, TASTEOFHOME.COM

FALAFEL

2. In a food processor, pulse cilantro and mint until finely chopped. Add chickpeas, garlic, coriander, chili powder, salt and, if desired, pepper. Pulse until mixture is blended and the texture of coarse meal. Transfer to a large bowl. Cover; refrigerate for at least 1 hour.

3. Stir in the sesame seeds and baking powder. Shape into sixteen 2-in. balls. In an electric skillet or a deep-fat fryer, heat oil to 375°. Fry chickpea balls, a few at a time, until golden brown, about 2 minutes, turning occasionally. Drain on paper towels.

4 PIECES: 224 cal., 13g fat (1g sat. fat), 0 chol., 760mg sod., 32g carb. (1g sugars, 16g fiber), 9g pro.

Test Kitchen Tip

Chilling the falafel mixture makes it easier to shape it into balls, so make sure you don't skip that step! You can chill it for longer to make in advance, but don't add the baking powder until you're ready to shape and cook the falafel mixture.

FALAFEL

A common street food in the Middle East, falafel are gluten free, crunchy on the outside and tender on the inside. They are full of flavor from the cilantro, mint, coriander and nutty sesame seeds. The classic version is deep-fried, but they can also be pan-fried, baked or cooked in an air fryer. Serve in or alongside pita bread with cucumbers, tomatoes, olives and tahini sauce.
—*Nithya Narasimhan, Chennai, India*

- -

Prep: 10 min. + standing • **Cook:** 15 min.
Makes: 16 pieces

1 cup dried chickpeas
½ tsp. baking soda
1 cup fresh cilantro leaves
½ cup fresh mint leaves
5 garlic cloves
1 tsp. ground coriander
1 tsp. chili powder
1 tsp. salt
½ tsp. pepper, optional
1 tsp. sesame seeds
1 tsp. baking powder
  Oil for deep-fat frying

1. Cover chickpeas with water. Stir in baking soda. Cover; let stand overnight. Drain; rinse and pat dry.

CANDIED BACON PALMIERS

You need only three ingredients to make this beautiful and delicious appetizer! I also like to serve them as a breakfast pastry when I make a brunch buffet. They are special and just a little different from what's usually served.
—*Jolene Martinelli, Fremont, NH*

Prep: 20 min. + chilling • **Bake:** 15 min.
Makes: 3 dozen

- 6 bacon strips
- 1 pkg. (17.3 oz.) frozen puff pastry, thawed
- ¾ cup packed light brown sugar

1. In a large skillet, cook bacon over medium heat until crisp. Remove to paper towels to drain; crumble. Unfold 1 sheet of puff pastry. Sprinkle with half the brown sugar and half the bacon.
2. Roll up the left and right sides toward the center, jelly-roll style, until the rolls meet in the middle. Repeat with the remaining pastry sheet and ingredients. Refrigerate until firm enough to slice, about 30 minutes.
3. Preheat oven to 400°. Cut each roll crosswise into ½-in. slices. Place slices 2 in. apart on parchment-lined baking sheets. Bake until golden and crisp, 15-20 minutes. Cool on pans 2 minutes. Remove to wire racks to cool.
FREEZE OPTION: Cover and freeze sliced, unbaked palmiers on waxed paper-lined baking sheets until firm. Transfer to freezer containers; close tightly and return to freezer. To use, thaw and bake palmiers as directed.
1 PALMIER: 91 cal., 4g fat (1g sat. fat), 1mg chol., 70mg sod., 12g carb. (4g sugars, 1g fiber), 1g pro.

CANDIED BACON PALMIERS

LEMON
OLIVE OIL CAKE

LEMON OLIVE OIL CAKE

Olive oil cakes stay tender and moist longer than butter-based cakes, so they are wonderful if you need to make dessert ahead of time. Serve with your favorite seasonal berries.
—Nicole Gackowski, Antioch, CA

Prep: 15 min. • **Bake:** 30 min. + cooling
Makes: 8 servings

```
 2   large eggs
⅔   cup sugar
½   cup extra virgin olive oil
⅓   cup 2% milk
 1   Tbsp. grated lemon zest
 3   Tbsp. lemon juice
 1   cup all-purpose flour
 1   tsp. baking powder
¼   tsp. salt
     Confectioners' sugar
```

1. Preheat oven to 350°. Line a greased 8-in. round baking pan with parchment. Beat eggs on high speed for 3 minutes. Gradually add sugar, beating until thickened. Gradually beat in oil. Beat in milk, lemon zest and lemon juice.
2. In another bowl, whisk flour, baking powder and salt; fold into egg mixture. Transfer batter to the prepared pan, spreading evenly.
3. Bake until a toothpick inserted in the center comes out clean, 30-35 minutes. Cool in the pan for 15 minutes before removing to a wire rack; remove the parchment. Let cool completely. Dust with confectioners' sugar.

1 PIECE: 266 cal., 15g fat (2g sat. fat), 47mg chol., 157mg sod., 30g carb. (18g sugars, 1g fiber), 4g pro.

Test Kitchen Tip

This cake keeps amazingly well for up to a week in an airtight container. It does not need to be refrigerated and is actually better the day after it's baked—perfect to prepare ahead for a party or potluck.

PORTOBELLO MUSHROOM & CREAM CHEESE TAQUITOS

PORTOBELLO MUSHROOM & CREAM CHEESE TAQUITOS

This party appetizer was inspired by a dish I saw on *Top Chef*. I simplified it a little and tweaked the flavors a bit. The taquitos can be made ahead and reheated in a 250° oven for 10 minutes.
—Lily Julow, Lawrenceville, GA

Prep: 30 min. • **Cook:** 15 min.
Makes: 10 servings

```
 2   Tbsp. extra virgin olive oil
 8   oz. large portobello mushrooms,
     gills discarded, finely chopped
 1   tsp. dried oregano
 1   tsp. dried thyme
½   tsp. crushed red pepper flakes
¼   tsp. salt
 1   pkg. (8 oz.) cream cheese, softened
 4   oz. whole-milk ricotta cheese
10   flour tortillas (8 in.)
     Oil for deep-fat frying
     Major Grey's chutney
```

1. In a cast-iron or other heavy skillet, heat olive oil to 350°. Add mushrooms; saute 4 minutes. Add oregano, thyme, pepper flakes and salt; saute until mushrooms are browned, 4-6 minutes. Cool. Wipe out skillet.
2. Combine cheeses; fold in mushrooms, mixing well. Spread 3 Tbsp. mushroom mixture on bottom half of each tortilla. Roll up tightly, making sure filling isn't seeping from either end. Secure rolls with toothpicks.
3. In same skillet, heat oil to 375°. Fry taquitos, a few at a time, until golden brown, 2-4 minutes. Drain on paper towels. When taquitos are cool enough to handle, discard toothpicks. Serve with chutney.

1 TAQUITO: 375 cal., 25g fat (7g sat. fat), 27mg chol., 380mg sod., 30g carb. (2g sugars, 2g fiber), 8g pro.

MUSHROOM & OLIVE BRUSCHETTA

I tried this delicious bruschetta toast at a party, and knew I had to make it myself. I couldn't find the person who brought the dish, so I began trying to duplicate it on my own. The original was made on an English muffin, but party rye or baguette slices work as well.
—*Lynne German, Buford, GA*

- -

Prep: 15 min. • **Bake:** 10 min.
Makes: 4 dozen

- 1½ cups finely shredded cheddar cheese
- ½ cup canned mushroom stems and pieces, drained and chopped
- ½ cup chopped green onions
- ½ cup chopped pitted green olives
- ½ cup chopped ripe olives
- ½ cup mayonnaise
- ¼ tsp. curry powder
- 2 French bread baguettes (10½ oz. each)
  Julienned green onions, optional

1. Preheat oven to 400°. Combine the first 7 ingredients. Cut each baguette into 24 slices; place on ungreased baking sheets. Bake until lightly toasted, about 5 minutes.
2. Top baguette slices with the cheese mixture. Bake until the cheese is melted, 4-5 minutes. If desired, top with julienned green onions.
FREEZE OPTION: Cover and freeze the toasted, topped and unbaked baguette slices on a parchment-lined baking sheet until firm. Transfer to a freezer container; return to freezer. To use, bake baguette slices on ungreased baking sheets in a preheated 400° oven until heated through, 8-10 minutes.
1 PIECE: 66 cal., 3g fat (1g sat. fat), 4mg chol., 161mg sod., 7g carb. (0 sugars, 0 fiber), 2g pro.

FETA CHICKEN BURGERS

My friends always request these tasty grilled chicken burgers. I sometimes add olives to punch up the flavor. The mayo topping is too good to skip.
—*Angela Robinson, Findlay, OH*

- -

Takes: 30 min. • **Makes:** 6 servings

- ¼ cup finely chopped cucumber
- ¼ cup reduced-fat mayonnaise
  BURGERS
- ½ cup chopped roasted sweet red pepper
- 1 tsp. garlic powder
- ½ tsp. Greek seasoning
- ¼ tsp. pepper
- 1½ lbs. lean ground chicken
- 1 cup crumbled feta cheese
- 6 whole wheat hamburger buns, split and toasted
  Optional: Lettuce leaves and tomato slices

1. Preheat the broiler. In a bowl, mix cucumber and mayonnaise.
2. In a separate bowl, mix roasted red pepper and seasonings. Add ground chicken and feta cheese; mix lightly but thoroughly (mixture will be sticky). Shape into six ½-in.-thick patties.
3. Broil burgers 4 in. from heat until a thermometer reads 165°, 3-4 minutes per side. Serve on buns with cucumber sauce. If desired, top burgers with lettuce and tomato.
FREEZE OPTION: Place uncooked patties on a waxed paper–lined baking sheet; cover and freeze until firm. Remove from pan and transfer to an airtight freezer container; return to freezer. To use, broil frozen patties as directed, increasing time as necessary.
1 BURGER WITH 1 TBSP. SAUCE: 356 cal., 14g fat (5g sat. fat), 95mg chol., 703mg sod., 25g carb. (5g sugars, 4g fiber), 31g pro. **DIABETIC EXCHANGES:** 5 lean meat, 2 starch, ½ fat.

MUSHROOM & OLIVE
BRUSCHETTA

FLAKY CHICKEN WELLINGTON

This cozy and flavorful entree takes a classic recipe and makes it super easy! I cook the chicken a day or so ahead of time to make it even simpler to throw together on busy nights.
—*Kerry Dingwall, Wilmington, NC*

Prep: 30 min. • **Bake:** 15 min.
Makes: 2 pastries (3 servings each)

2 cups cubed cooked chicken
1 pkg. (10 oz.) frozen chopped spinach, thawed and squeezed dry
3 hard-boiled large eggs, chopped
½ cup finely chopped dill pickles
⅓ cup finely chopped celery
2 tubes (8 oz. each) refrigerated crescent rolls
2 tsp. prepared mustard, divided
1 cup sour cream
2 Tbsp. dill pickle juice

1. Preheat oven to 350°. In a large bowl, combine the first 5 ingredients. Unroll 1 tube of crescent dough into 1 long rectangle; press perforations to seal.
2. Spread half the mustard over dough; top with half the chicken mixture to within ¼ in. of edges. Roll up jelly-roll style, starting with a long side; pinch seam to seal. Place seam side down on a parchment-lined baking sheet. Cut slits in top. Repeat with remaining crescent dough, mustard and chicken mixture.
3. Bake for 15-20 minutes or until golden brown. Meanwhile, combine sour cream and pickle juice; serve with pastries.
FREEZE OPTION: Freeze the unbaked pastries, covered, on a parchment-lined baking sheet until firm. Transfer to a freezer container; return to the freezer. Bake on a parchment-lined baking sheet in a 350° oven for 30-35 minutes or until golden brown. Prepare sauce as directed.
⅓ PASTRY WITH ABOUT 3 TBSP. SAUCE: 495 cal., 28g fat (6g sat. fat), 144mg chol., 830mg sod., 37g carb. (10g sugars, 2g fiber), 25g pro.

VEGGIE DILL DIP

I like to keep this good-for-you dip and a variety of cut-up veggies on hand for an easy snack.
—*Hazel Baber, Yuma, AZ*

Prep: 10 min. + chilling • **Makes:** 2½ cups

2 cups 1% cottage cheese
3 Tbsp. fat-free milk
¾ cup fat-free mayonnaise
1 Tbsp. dried minced onion
1 Tbsp. dried parsley flakes
1 tsp. dill weed
1 tsp. seasoned salt
¼ tsp. garlic powder

In a blender, blend cottage cheese and milk until smooth. Stir in the remaining ingredients and mix well. Chill overnight. Serve with raw vegetables.
2 TBSP.: 37 cal., 0 fat (0 sat. fat), 2mg chol., 303mg sod., 3g carb. (2g sugars, 0 fiber), 5g pro.

VEGGIE DILL DIP

BANANA CRUMB PUDDING

gentle boil; cook and stir for 2 minutes. Remove from heat. Stir in the butter, vanilla and salt. Cool for 15 minutes, stirring occasionally.

3. Reserve 1 cup whole wafers and 1 banana for topping. Crush 2 cups wafers and set aside. In a 13x9-in. baking dish, place a single layer of whole wafers, filling gaps with crushed wafers. Layer with a third each of the bananas and pudding. Repeat layers twice. Press waxed paper onto surface of pudding. Refrigerate, covered, overnight.

4. In a bowl, beat heavy cream until it begins to thicken. Add sugar; beat until soft peaks form (do not overmix). Just before serving, remove the paper and spread whipped cream over pudding; top with the reserved sliced banana and whole wafers.

¾ CUP: 535 cal., 27g fat (13g sat. fat), 121mg chol., 370mg sod., 70g carb. (46g sugars, 1g fiber), 7g pro.

Test Kitchen Tip

Want to change things up? Add 2 Tbsp. spiced rum at the same time as the vanilla extract for an additional rich flavor note.

BANANA CRUMB PUDDING

Friends and family ask me to make my thick and creamy banana pudding for all occasions. They can't get enough of the flavor combination of the bananas and vanilla wafer crumbs. You can top this with meringue instead of whipped cream.
—*Yvonnia Butner, Pinnacle, NC*

Prep: 15 min. • **Cook:** 20 min. + chilling
Makes: 15 servings

- 1   cup sugar
- ½   cup cornstarch
- 6   cups 2% milk
- 5   large egg yolks
- ¼   cup butter, cubed
- 2   tsp. vanilla extract
- 1   tsp. kosher salt
- 2   pkg. (11 oz. each) vanilla wafers
- 7   medium bananas, sliced

TOPPING

- 2   cups heavy whipping cream
- 6   Tbsp. sugar

1. In a large heavy saucepan, mix sugar and cornstarch. Whisk in milk. Cook and stir over medium heat until thickened and bubbly. Reduce heat to low; cook and stir 2 minutes longer. Remove from heat.

2. In a bowl, whisk a small amount of the hot mixture into the egg yolks; return all to pan, whisking constantly. Bring to a

LISA'S ALL-DAY
SUGAR & SALT PORK ROAST

LEMONY CHICKEN & RICE

I couldn't say who loves this recipe best, because it gets raves every time I serve it! Occasionally I even get a phone call or an email from a friend requesting the recipe. It's certainly a favorite for my grown children and 15 grandchildren.
—*Maryalice Wood, Langley, BC*

Prep: 15 min. + marinating • **Bake:** 55 min.
Makes: 2 casseroles (4 servings each)

- 2   cups water
- ½   cup reduced-sodium soy sauce
- ¼   cup lemon juice
- ¼   cup olive oil
- 2   garlic cloves, minced
- 2   tsp. ground ginger
- 2   tsp. pepper
- 16 bone-in chicken thighs, skin removed (about 6 lbs.)
- 2   cups uncooked long grain rice
- 4   Tbsp. grated lemon zest, divided
- 2   medium lemons, sliced

1. In a large shallow dish, combine the first 7 ingredients. Add chicken; turn to coat and cover. Refrigerate 4 hours or overnight.
2. Preheat oven to 325°. Spread 1 cup rice into each of 2 greased 13x9-in. baking dishes. Top each with 1 Tbsp. lemon zest, 8 chicken thighs and half the marinade. Top with sliced lemons.
3. Bake, covered, 40 minutes. Uncover, and continue baking until a thermometer inserted in chicken reads 170°-175°, 15-20 minutes longer. Sprinkle with the remaining lemon zest.

2 CHICKEN THIGHS WITH ¾ CUP RICE MIXTURE: 624 cal., 26g fat (6g sat. fat), 173mg chol., 754mg sod., 41g carb. (1g sugars, 1g fiber), 53g pro.

LISA'S ALL-DAY
SUGAR & SALT PORK ROAST

My family loves this tender and juicy roast, so we eat it a lot. The sweet and salty crust is so delicious mixed into the pulled pork.
—*Lisa Allen, Joppa, AL*

Prep: 15 min. + chilling
Cook: 6¼ hours • **Makes:** 12 servings

- 1   cup plus 1 Tbsp. sea salt, divided
- 1   cup sugar
- 1   bone-in pork shoulder butt roast (6 to 8 lbs.)
- ¼   cup barbecue seasoning
- ½   tsp. pepper
- ½   cup packed brown sugar
- 12 hamburger buns or kaiser rolls, split

1. Combine 1 cup sea salt and sugar; rub onto all sides of the roast. Place roast in a shallow dish; refrigerate, covered, overnight.

2. Preheat oven to 300°. Using a kitchen knife, scrape salt and sugar coating from roast; discard any accumulated juices. Transfer pork to a large shallow roasting pan. Rub with the barbecue seasoning; sprinkle with pepper. Roast until tender, 6-8 hours.
3. Increase oven temperature to 500°. Combine brown sugar and remaining 1 Tbsp. sea salt; sprinkle over cooked pork. Return pork to oven and roast until a crisp crust forms, 10-15 minutes. Remove; when cool enough to handle, shred meat with 2 forks. Serve warm on buns or rolls.
FREEZE OPTION: Freeze cooled meat with some of the juices in freezer containers. To use, partially thaw in the refrigerator overnight. Heat through in a saucepan, stirring occasionally; add some water if necessary.
1 SANDWICH: 534 cal., 24g fat (9g sat. fat), 135mg chol., 2240mg sod., 33g carb. (14g sugars, 1g fiber), 43g pro.

LEMONY CHICKEN & RICE

CORN PUDDING
WITH BACON & CHEDDAR

CORN PUDDING WITH BACON & CHEDDAR

This cheddar-corn pudding can be made ahead and refrigerated overnight. Just remove from the refrigerator 30 minutes before baking.
—Lynn Albright, Fremont, NE

Prep: 25 min. • **Bake:** 40 min. + standing
Makes: 6 servings

- 1 Tbsp. olive oil
- ¾ cup chopped sweet onion
- ¾ cup chopped sweet red pepper
- 4 large eggs
- 1 cup heavy whipping cream
- 1 tsp. baking soda
- 1 tsp. hot pepper sauce
- ½ tsp. salt
- 2 cups fresh or frozen corn
- 2 cups crushed cornbread stuffing
- ½ lb. bacon strips, cooked and crumbled
- 1½ cups shredded sharp cheddar cheese, divided

1. Preheat the oven to 350°. In a 10-in. cast-iron or other ovenproof skillet, heat oil over medium heat. Add onion and red pepper; cook and stir until crisp-tender, 6-8 minutes. Remove from skillet; set aside.
2. Whisk eggs, cream, baking soda, hot pepper sauce and salt. Stir in corn, stuffing, bacon, 1 cup cheese and the onion mixture. Transfer to skillet.
3. Bake, uncovered, 35 minutes. Sprinkle with the remaining ½ cup cheese; bake the pudding until puffed and golden brown, 5-10 minutes longer. Let stand 10 minutes before serving.
¾ CUP: 516 cal., 36g fat (18g sat. fat), 211mg chol., 1117mg sod., 29g carb. (7g sugars, 3g fiber), 20g pro.

BANG BANG
SHRIMP CAKE SLIDERS

1. Place shrimp in a food processor; pulse until chopped. In a large bowl, combine egg, red pepper, 4 green onions, ginger and salt. Add shrimp and bread crumbs; mix lightly but thoroughly. Shape into twelve ½-in.-thick patties. Refrigerate 20 minutes.
2. Meanwhile, in a large bowl, combine mayonnaise and the chili sauces; stir in cabbage and remaining 2 green onions. Place buns on a baking sheet, cut sides up. Broil 3-4 in. from heat until golden brown, 2-3 minutes.
3. In a large cast-iron or other heavy skillet, heat the oil over medium heat. Add shrimp cakes in batches; cook until golden brown on both sides, 4-5 minutes per side. Serve on toasted buns with slaw. If desired, secure each slider with a toothpick. Serve with additional Sriracha chili sauce if desired.

1 SLIDER: 210 cal., 10g fat (1g sat. fat), 63mg chol., 321mg sod., 20g carb. (3g sugars, 1g fiber), 11g pro.

BANG BANG
SHRIMP CAKE SLIDERS

My family loves these shrimp sliders. The bang bang slaw dressing and shrimp cake patties can be made ahead. When you're ready to serve, toss the cabbage slaw and sear the shrimp cakes, then assemble and enjoy.
—Kim Banick, Turner, OR

- -

Prep: 30 min. + chilling
Cook: 10 min./batch • **Makes:** 12 sliders

1 lb. uncooked shrimp (41-50 per lb.), peeled and deveined
1 large egg, lightly beaten
½ cup finely chopped sweet red pepper
6 green onions, divided and chopped
1 Tbsp. minced fresh gingerroot
¼ tsp. salt
1 cup panko bread crumbs
¼ cup mayonnaise
1 Tbsp. Sriracha chili sauce
1 Tbsp. sweet chili sauce
5 cups shredded Chinese or Napa cabbage
12 mini buns or dinner rolls
3 Tbsp. canola oil

THAI CHICKEN
THIGHS

THAI CHICKEN THIGHS

With the slow cooker, a traditional Thai dish with peanut butter, jalapeno peppers and chili sauce becomes incredibly easy to make. To crank up the spice, just use more jalapeno peppers.
—Taste of Home *Test Kitchen*

Prep: 25 min. • **Cook:** 5 hours
Makes: 8 servings

- 8   bone-in chicken thighs (about 3 lbs.), skin removed
- ½   cup salsa
- ¼   cup creamy peanut butter
- 2   Tbsp. lemon juice
- 2   Tbsp. reduced-sodium soy sauce
- 1   Tbsp. chopped seeded jalapeno pepper
- 2   tsp. Thai chili sauce
- 1   garlic clove, minced
- 1   tsp. minced fresh gingerroot
- 2   green onions, sliced
- 2   Tbsp. sesame seeds, toasted
     Hot cooked basmati rice, optional

1. Place chicken in a 3-qt. slow cooker. Combine salsa, peanut butter, lemon juice, soy sauce, jalapeno, Thai chili sauce, garlic and ginger; pour over chicken. Cook, covered, on low until chicken is tender, 5-6 hours.
2. Sprinkle with the green onions and sesame seeds. Serve with rice if desired.
NOTE: Wear disposable gloves when cutting hot peppers; the oils can burn skin. Avoid touching your face.
1 CHICKEN THIGH WITH ¼ CUP SAUCE: 261 cal., 15g fat (4g sat. fat), 87mg chol., 350mg sod., 5g carb. (2g sugars, 1g fiber), 27g pro. **DIABETIC EXCHANGES:** 4 lean meat, 1 fat, ½ starch.

FIESTA TURKEY TORTILLA SOUP

FIESTA TURKEY TORTILLA SOUP

I'm always amazed that I can pull together such a delicious soup in less than half an hour!
—Amy McFadden, Chelsea, AL

Takes: 25 min. • **Makes:** 8 servings

- 4   cans (14½ oz. each) chicken broth
- 3   cups shredded cooked turkey or rotisserie chicken
- 1   can (15 oz.) black beans, rinsed and drained
- 1   can (15¼ oz.) whole-kernel corn, drained
- ½   cup medium salsa
- 5   corn tortillas (6 in.), cut into ¼-in. strips
- ¼   cup chopped fresh cilantro

1. In a Dutch oven, combine the first 5 ingredients; bring to a boil. Reduce heat; simmer for 10 minutes, stirring occasionally.
2. Meanwhile, spread tortilla strips in a single layer on a baking sheet. Bake at 400° until golden brown and crisp, 4-6 minutes.
3. Stir cilantro into soup. Top individual servings with tortilla strips. If desired, serve with additional salsa.
FREEZE OPTION: Freeze cooled soup in freezer containers. To use, partially thaw in refrigerator overnight. Heat through in a saucepan, stirring occasionally; add broth or water if necessary. Meanwhile, bake tortillas as directed and sprinkle over each serving. Serve with additional salsa if desired.
1⅓ CUPS: 203 cal., 3g fat (1g sat. fat), 58mg chol., 1264mg sod., 21g carb. (5g sugars, 4g fiber), 20g pro.

OLD-TIME CAKE DOUGHNUTS

EASY EGG ROLLS

I always loved egg rolls, but every recipe I saw was too complicated. So I start with a packaged coleslaw mix. Now I can make these treats at a moment's notice.
—Samantha Dunn, Leesville, LA

Prep: 30 min. • **Cook:** 30 min.
Makes: 28 servings

- 1 lb. ground beef
- 1 pkg. (14 oz.) coleslaw mix
- 2 Tbsp. soy sauce
- ½ tsp. garlic powder
- ¼ tsp. ground ginger
- ⅛ tsp. onion powder
- 1 Tbsp. all-purpose flour
- 28 egg roll wrappers
   Vegetable oil for frying

1. In a large skillet, cook beef over medium heat until no longer pink, 5-7 minutes, breaking into crumbles; drain and cool slightly. In a bowl, combine beef, coleslaw mix, soy sauce, garlic powder, ginger and onion powder. In a small bowl, combine the flour and enough water to make a paste.
2. With 1 corner of an egg roll wrapper facing you, place ¼ cup filling just below center of wrapper. (Cover the remaining wrappers with a damp paper towel until ready to use.) Fold bottom corner over filling; moisten remaining wrapper edges with flour paste. Fold the side corners toward center over filling. Roll up tightly, pressing at tip to seal. Repeat.
3. In an electric skillet or deep-fat fryer, heat oil to 375°. Fry egg rolls, a few at a time, until golden brown, 3-4 minutes; turn occasionally. Drain on paper towels.
1 EGG ROLL: 185 cal., 9g fat (1g sat. fat), 13mg chol., 261mg sod., 20g carb. (1g sugars, 1g fiber), 6g pro.

Test Kitchen Tip

To make ahead of time, refrigerate fried egg rolls in a single layer on a paper towel-lined tray. Reheat in a low oven for 10 minutes on each side.

OLD-TIME CAKE DOUGHNUTS

This tender cake doughnut is a little piece of heaven at breakfast. For a variation, add a little rum extract or 1 tablespoon of dark rum.
—Alissa Stehr, Gau-Odernheim, Germany

Prep: 30 min. + chilling
Cook: 5 min./batch
Makes: about 2 dozen

- 2 Tbsp. unsalted butter, softened
- 1½ cups sugar, divided
- 3 large eggs, room temperature
- 4 cups all-purpose flour
- 1 Tbsp. baking powder
- 3 tsp. ground cinnamon, divided
- ½ tsp. salt
- ⅛ tsp. ground nutmeg
- ¾ cup 2% milk
   Oil for deep-fat frying

1. In a large bowl, beat butter and 1 cup sugar until crumbly, about 2 minutes. Add eggs, 1 at a time, beating well after each addition.
2. Combine flour, baking powder, 1 tsp. cinnamon, salt and nutmeg; add to butter mixture alternately with milk, beating well after each addition. Cover and refrigerate for 2 hours.
3. Turn dough onto a heavily floured surface; pat to ¼-in. thickness. Cut with a floured 2½-in. doughnut cutter. In an electric skillet or deep fryer, heat oil to 375°.
4. Fry doughnuts, a few at a time, for 2 minutes per side or until golden brown on both sides. Drain on paper towels.
5. Combine remaining ½ cup sugar and 2 tsp. cinnamon; roll warm doughnuts in mixture.
FREEZE OPTION: After frying, wrap the doughnuts in foil; transfer to a resealable freezer container. May be frozen for up to 3 months. To use, remove foil. Thaw doughnuts at room temperature. Warm if desired. Combine ½ cup sugar and 2 tsp. cinnamon; roll warm doughnuts in mixture.
1 DOUGHNUT: 198 cal., 8g fat (1g sat. fat), 30mg chol., 112mg sod., 29g carb. (13g sugars, 1g fiber), 3g pro.
GLAZED CAKE DOUGHNUTS: Omit the cinnamon-sugar mixture. Combine 2 cups confectioners' sugar, 1-2 Tbsp. orange juice and 1 tsp. grated orange zest. Spread over cooled doughnuts.

EASY EGG ROLLS

9

One-Dish Recipes

Easy, efficient prep and ultra-fast cleanup—all that and hearty, delicious flavor too! Sheet pans, Dutch ovens, slow cookers, cast-iron skillets and casserole dishes all get their turn to produce these one-dish wonders your family will adore.

ONE-DISH TURKEY
DINNER P. 264

SAUSAGE, PEAR
& SWEET POTATO
SHEET-PAN DINNER

SAUSAGE, PEAR & SWEET POTATO SHEET-PAN DINNER

This foolproof weeknight dinner is naturally gluten free, and is on your table in no time! It's easily adaptable to use seasonal fruits or veggies.
—*Melissa Erdelac, Valparaiso, IN*

Prep: 15 min. • **Bake:** 45 min.
Makes: 5 servings

- 2   large sweet potatoes, peeled and cut into ½-in. cubes
- 1   large sweet onion, cut into wedges
- 2   Tbsp. olive oil
- 1   Tbsp. brown sugar
- ½   tsp. salt
- ½   tsp. ground allspice
- ¼   tsp. ground cinnamon
- ⅛   tsp. pepper
- 3   small pears, quartered
- 1   pkg. (19 oz.) Italian sausage links

1. Preheat oven to 425°. Place the sweet potatoes and onion in a 15x10x1-in. baking pan; drizzle with oil. Sprinkle with brown sugar and seasonings; toss to coat. Bake for 15 minutes.
2. Gently stir in pears; top with sausages. Bake 20 minutes longer, stirring once.
3. Increase oven temperature to 450°. Bake until sausages are golden brown and a thermometer inserted in sausage reads at least 160°, 8-10 minutes longer, turning once.
1 SERVING: 533 cal., 29g fat (8g sat. fat), 58mg chol., 912mg sod., 56g carb. (28g sugars, 8g fiber), 15g pro.

Test Kitchen Tip

If you like to get creative, this is the perfect recipe for you. The easiest thing to swap is the sausage—try using Polish sausage, bratwurst or other link sausages. Substitute peeled butternut squash for sweet potatoes. Another easy swap is using apples instead of pears.

VEG JAMBALAYA

VEG JAMBALAYA

If vegetarian fare often leaves you hungry, look no further. This flavorful vegetarian entree uses convenient— and satisfying—beans in place of meat.
—*Crystal Jo Bruns, Iliff, CO*

Prep: 10 min. • **Cook:** 30 min.
Makes: 6 servings

- 1   Tbsp. canola oil
- 1   medium green pepper, chopped
- 1   medium onion, chopped
- 1   celery rib, chopped
- 3   garlic cloves, minced
- 2   cups water
- 1   can (14½ oz.) diced tomatoes, undrained
- 1   can (8 oz.) tomato sauce
- ½   tsp. Italian seasoning
- ¼   tsp. salt
- ¼   tsp. crushed red pepper flakes
- ⅛   tsp. fennel seed, crushed
- 1   cup uncooked long grain rice
- 1   can (16 oz.) butter beans, rinsed and drained
- 1   can (16 oz.) red beans, rinsed and drained

1. In a Dutch oven, heat oil over medium-high heat. Add green pepper, onion and celery; cook and stir until tender. Add garlic; cook 1 minute longer.
2. Add water, tomatoes, tomato sauce and seasonings. Bring to a boil; stir in rice. Reduce heat; cover and simmer until liquid is absorbed and the rice is tender, 15-18 minutes. Stir in the beans; heat through.
1⅓ CUPS: 281 cal., 3g fat (0 sat. fat), 0 chol., 796mg sod., 56g carb. (6g sugars, 9g fiber), 11g pro.

SUNSHINE CHICKEN

SUNSHINE CHICKEN

This recipe is ideal when you're serving large groups because it takes little time or effort to prepare, and can easily be doubled. Even my husband, who doesn't enjoy cooking, likes to make this dish.
—*Karen Gardiner, Eutaw, AL*

Prep: 15 min. • **Cook:** 20 min.
Makes: 6 servings

2 to 3 tsp. curry powder
1¼ tsp. salt, divided
¼ tsp. pepper
6 boneless skinless chicken breast halves (5 oz. each)
1½ cups orange juice
1 cup uncooked long grain rice
¾ cup water
1 Tbsp. brown sugar
1 tsp. ground mustard
Chopped fresh parsley

1. Combine curry powder, ½ tsp. salt and pepper; rub over both sides of chicken. In a skillet, combine orange juice, rice, water, brown sugar, mustard and the remaining ¾ tsp. salt. Add the chicken; bring to a boil. Reduce heat; cover and simmer until chicken juices run clear, 20-25 minutes.
2. Remove from the heat and let stand, covered, until all liquid is absorbed, about 5 minutes. Sprinkle with parsley.
1 SERVING: 317 cal., 4g fat (1g sat. fat), 78mg chol., 562mg sod., 36g carb. (8g sugars, 1g fiber), 32g pro. **DIABETIC EXCHANGES:** 4 lean meat, 2 starch.

NORTH AFRICAN
CHICKEN & RICE

½ to 1 cup chopped pitted green olives
1 medium lemon, sliced
2 garlic cloves, minced
½ cup chicken broth or water
4 cups hot cooked brown rice

In a 3- or 4-qt. slow cooker, combine onion and oil. Place chicken on top of onion; sprinkle with next 7 ingredients. Top with the raisins, olives, lemon and garlic. Add broth. Cook, covered, on low until chicken is tender, 4-5 hours. Serve with hot cooked rice.

1 SERVING: 386 cal., 13g fat (3g sat. fat), 76mg chol., 556mg sod., 44g carb. (12g sugars, 3g fiber), 25g pro.

Test Kitchen Tip

This heavily spiced dish with a mixture of interesting ingredients is from North Africa and may be a bit unfamiliar. But we know you'll fall in love with its delicious combination of flavors. If olives aren't your favorite, don't leave them out entirely, but go with ½ cup instead. They add a nice underlying flavor as well as a little saltiness to the dish.

NORTH AFRICAN CHICKEN & RICE

I'm always looking to try recipes from different cultures, and this one is a huge favorite. We love the spice combinations. This version is for a slow cooker but it cooks equally well in a pressure cooker.
—*Courtney Stultz, Weir, KS*

Prep: 10 min. • **Cook:** 4 hours
Makes: 8 servings

1 medium onion, diced
1 Tbsp. olive oil
8 boneless skinless chicken thighs (about 2 lbs.)
1 Tbsp. minced fresh cilantro
1 tsp. ground turmeric
1 tsp. paprika
1 tsp. sea salt
½ tsp. pepper
½ tsp. ground cinnamon
½ tsp. chili powder
1 cup golden raisins

White Bean, Sweet Potato & Pepper Ragout

Hearty and healthy, this rich and flavorful comfort food is the perfect option for meatless Monday—or any other night of the week!

Cut 1 **red pepper** and 1 **green pepper** into 1-in. pieces. In a Dutch oven over medium, cook the peppers in 1 Tbsp. **olive oil** until tender. Add 1 peeled, quartered and sliced **large sweet potato** and ½ tsp. minced **fresh rosemary**; cook for 4-5 minutes. Add 3 minced **garlic cloves**; cook 1 minute longer. Stir in ½ cup water and ¼ tsp. **pepper**. Bring to a boil. Reduce the heat; cover and simmer until the sweet potato is tender, 5-7 minutes. Stir in 2 rinsed and drained 15-oz. cans **cannellini beans**, one 14½-oz. can **diced tomatoes** and ¼ tsp. **salt**; heat through.

🖐 🍎

HEARTY BEANS & RICE

Filling and fast, this dish has become a favorite in my family. It can be served as a side or main dish.
—*Barbara Musgrove, Fort Atkinson, WI*

Prep: 10 min. • **Cook:** 25 min.
Makes: 5 servings

- 1 lb. lean ground beef (90% lean)
- 1 can (15 oz.) black beans, rinsed and drained
- 1 can (14½ oz.) diced tomatoes with mild green chiles, undrained
- 1⅓ cups frozen corn, thawed
- 1 cup water
- ¼ tsp. salt
- 1½ cups instant brown rice

In a large saucepan, cook beef over medium heat until no longer pink, breaking into crumbles, 6-8 minutes; drain. Stir in the beans, tomatoes, corn, water and salt. Bring to a boil. Stir in rice; return to a boil. Reduce heat; cover and simmer for 5 minutes. Remove from the heat; let stand, covered, for 5 minutes.
1¼ CUPS: 376 cal., 9g fat (3g sat. fat), 56mg chol., 647mg sod., 47g carb. (6g sugars, 7g fiber), 26g pro. **DIABETIC EXCHANGES:** 3 starch, 3 lean meat, 1 vegetable.

> *"I added some kick with a few drops of hot sauce and tomato paste. The husband ate some right out of the pan!"*
> **—LIPPERTB5, TASTEOFHOME.COM**

CAROLINA CRAB BOIL

This is a fun way to feed a crowd for a tailgate or other outside party. You can serve it two ways: Drain the cooking liquid and pour out the pot on a paper-lined table so folks can dig in, or serve it as a stew in its liquid over hot rice.
—*Melissa Pelkey Hass, Waleska, GA*

Prep: 15 min. • **Cook:** 35 min.
Makes: 4 servings

- 2 tsp. canola oil
- 1 pkg. (14 oz.) smoked turkey sausage, cut into ½-in. slices
- 2 cartons (32 oz. each) reduced-sodium chicken broth
- 4 cups water
- 1 bottle (12 oz.) light beer or 1½ cups additional reduced-sodium chicken broth
- ¼ cup seafood seasoning
- 5 bay leaves
- 4 medium ears sweet corn, cut into 2-in. pieces
- 1 lb. fingerling potatoes
- 1 medium red onion, quartered
- 2 lbs. cooked snow crab legs
  Pepper to taste

1. In a stockpot, heat oil over medium-high heat; brown sausage. Stir in broth, water, beer, seafood seasoning and bay leaves. Add corn, potatoes and onion; bring to a boil. Reduce heat; simmer, uncovered, until potatoes are tender, 20-25 minutes.
2. Add crab; heat through. Drain; remove bay leaves. Transfer to a serving bowl; season with pepper.
1 SERVING: 420 cal., 12g fat (3g sat. fat), 143mg chol., 2206mg sod., 37g carb. (7g sugars, 5g fiber), 40g pro.

CAROLINA CRAB BOIL

ONE-POT
CHILI MAC

SOUTHWESTERN RICE

I created this colorful side dish after eating something similar at a restaurant. It wonderfully complements any Tex-Mex meal. I like to add cubes of grilled chicken breast to the rice to make it a whole meal in itself.
—Michelle Dennis, Clarks Hill, IN

Takes: 30 min. • **Makes:** 8 servings

- 1 Tbsp. olive oil
- 1 medium green pepper, diced
- 1 medium onion, chopped
- 2 garlic cloves, minced
- 1 cup uncooked long grain rice
- ½ tsp. ground cumin
- ⅛ tsp. ground turmeric
- 1 can (14½ oz.) reduced-sodium chicken broth
- 2 cups frozen corn (about 10 oz.), thawed
- 1 can (15 oz.) black beans, rinsed and drained
- 1 can (10 oz.) diced tomatoes and green chiles, undrained

1. In a large nonstick skillet, heat oil over medium-high heat; saute the pepper and onion 3 minutes. Add garlic; cook and stir for 1 minute.
2. Stir in rice, spices and broth; bring to a boil. Reduce the heat; simmer, covered, until rice is tender, about 15 minutes. Stir in remaining ingredients; cook, covered, until heated through.
¾ CUP: 198 cal., 3g fat (1g sat. fat), 1mg chol., 339mg sod., 37g carb. (0 sugars, 5g fiber), 7g pro.

ONE-POT CHILI MAC

This hearty entree is low in fat and full of flavor. I love that the dried pasta can be cooked right in the chili—one less pot to wash! The dish also reheats perfectly in the microwave.
—Dawn Forsberg, Country Club, MO

Prep: 25 min. • **Cook:** 15 min.
Makes: 6 servings (2 qt.)

- 1 lb. lean ground turkey
- 1 small onion, chopped
- ¼ cup chopped green pepper
- 1 tsp. olive oil
- 2 cups water
- 1 can (15 oz.) pinto beans, rinsed and drained
- 1 can (14½ oz.) reduced-sodium beef broth
- 1 can (14½ oz.) diced tomatoes with mild green chiles, undrained
- 1 can (8 oz.) no-salt-added tomato sauce
- 2 tsp. chili powder
- 1 tsp. ground cumin
- ½ tsp. dried oregano
- 2 cups uncooked multigrain penne pasta
- ¼ cup reduced-fat sour cream
- ¼ cup minced fresh cilantro

1. In a large saucepan coated with cooking spray, cook the turkey, onion and pepper in oil over medium heat, breaking turkey into crumbles, until meat is no longer pink; drain.
2. Stir in the water, beans, broth, tomatoes, tomato sauce, chili powder, cumin and oregano. Bring to a boil. Add pasta; cook until tender, 15-20 minutes, stirring occasionally. Serve with sour cream; sprinkle with cilantro.
1⅓ CUPS: 384 cal., 10g fat (2g sat. fat), 64mg chol., 598mg sod., 47g carb. (10g sugars, 8g fiber), 25g pro. **DIABETIC EXCHANGES:** 3 starch, 2 lean meat, 1 vegetable.

SOUTHWESTERN
RICE

FAVORITE COMPANY CASEROLE

Even my friends who don't eat a lot of broccoli or mushrooms admit that this casserole is a winner. It's so easy to throw together, and the leftovers are just as delicious.
—*Suzann Verdun, Lisle, IL*

Prep: 15 min. • **Bake:** 45 min.
Makes: 8 servings

- 1   pkg. (6 oz.) wild rice, cooked
- 3   cups frozen chopped broccoli, thawed
- 1½ cups cubed cooked chicken
- 1   cup cubed cooked ham
- 1   cup shredded cheddar cheese
- 1   jar (4½ oz.) sliced mushrooms, drained
- 1   cup mayonnaise
- 1   tsp. prepared mustard
- ½   to 1 tsp. curry powder
- 1   can (10¾ oz.) condensed cream of mushroom soup, undiluted
- ¼   cup grated Parmesan cheese

Preheat oven to 350°. In a greased 2-qt. baking dish, layer the first 6 ingredients in the order listed. Combine mayonnaise, mustard, curry and soup; spread over the top. Sprinkle with Parmesan cheese. Bake, uncovered, until top is light golden brown, 45-60 minutes.
1 CUP: 405 cal., 32g fat (8g sat. fat), 61mg chol., 872mg sod., 11g carb. (1g sugars, 2g fiber), 18g pro.

ROASTED CHICKEN THIGHS WITH PEPPERS & POTATOES

My family loves this easy-to-make dish! Peppers and herbs from the garden make the chicken and potatoes special.
—*Pattie Prescott, Manchester, NH*

Prep: 20 min. • **Bake:** 35 min.
Makes: 8 servings

- 2   lbs. red potatoes (about 6 medium)
- 2   large sweet red peppers
- 2   large green peppers
- 2   medium onions
- 2   Tbsp. olive oil, divided
- 4   tsp. minced fresh thyme or 1½ tsp. dried thyme, divided
- 3   tsp. minced fresh rosemary or 1 tsp. dried rosemary, crushed, divided
- 8   boneless skinless chicken thighs (about 2 lbs.)
- ½   tsp. salt
- ¼   tsp. pepper

1. Preheat oven to 450°. Cut potatoes, peppers and onions into 1-in. pieces.

Place the vegetables in a roasting pan. Drizzle with 1 Tbsp. oil and sprinkle with 2 tsp. each thyme and rosemary; toss to coat. Place chicken over the vegetables. Brush chicken with the remaining oil; sprinkle with remaining 2 tsp. thyme and 1 tsp. rosemary. Sprinkle vegetables and chicken with salt and pepper.
2. Roast until a thermometer inserted in chicken reads 170° and the vegetables are tender, 35-40 minutes.
1 CHICKEN THIGH WITH 1 CUP VEGETABLES: 308 cal., 12g fat (3g sat. fat), 76mg chol., 221mg sod., 25g carb. (5g sugars, 4g fiber), 24g pro. **DIABETIC EXCHANGES:** 3 lean meat, 1 starch, 1 vegetable, ½ fat.

Test Kitchen Tip

Common olive oil works better than virgin or extra-virgin olive oil for cooking at high heat. The higher grades have ideal flavor for cold foods, but they start to smoke at lower temperatures.

ROASTED CHICKEN THIGHS WITH PEPPERS & POTATOES

BEAN & BURGER POCKETS

This recipe started out as an alternative to baked beans—just for a change of pace. One day, I decided to add ground beef and other ingredients. Now it's a main dish we enjoy often.

—*Gwen Parsons, Boring, OR*

Prep: 5 min. • **Cook:** 65 min.
Makes: 6 servings

- 1¼ lbs. ground beef
- 1 can (14½ oz.) diced tomatoes, undrained
- 1 can (8 oz.) tomato sauce
- ½ cup chopped onion
- 1 garlic clove, minced
- 1 Tbsp. brown sugar
- 1 tsp. seasoned salt
- 1 tsp. chili powder
- ½ tsp. ground cumin
- ⅛ tsp. each dried thyme, savory, marjoram, oregano and parsley flakes
- 1 can (16 oz.) navy beans, rinsed and drained
- 1 can (16 oz.) kidney beans, rinsed and drained
- 1 can (8½ oz.) lima beans
- 12 pita pocket halves
  Shredded cheddar cheese, optional

1. In a heavy saucepan or Dutch oven, cook the beef over medium heat until no longer pink, 5-7 minutes, crumbling meat; drain.

2. Add tomatoes, tomato sauce, onion, garlic, brown sugar and seasonings. Simmer, covered, for 1 hour, stirring occasionally.

3. Stir in the beans; heat through. Spoon about ½ cup into each pita half. Top with cheese if desired.

2 FILLED PITA HALVES: 516 cal., 12g fat (4g sat. fat), 58mg chol., 1227mg sod., 68g carb. (8g sugars, 11g fiber), 34g pro.

BEAN & BURGER POCKETS

ONE-POT
SPAGHETTI DINNER

ONE-POT SPAGHETTI DINNER

You can make this meal—with a simple homemade sauce—in one pot. Although allspice adds a distinctive taste, you can use Italian seasoning instead.
—*Carol Benzel-Schmidt, Stanwood, WA*

Prep: 10 min. • **Cook:** 25 min.
Makes: 4 servings

- 1 lb. lean ground beef (90% lean)
- 1¾ cups sliced fresh mushrooms
- 3 cups tomato juice
- 1 can (14½ oz.) no-salt-added diced tomatoes, drained
- 1 can (8 oz.) no-salt-added tomato sauce
- 1 Tbsp. dried minced onion
- ½ tsp. salt
- ½ tsp. garlic powder
- ½ tsp. ground mustard
- ¼ tsp. pepper
- ⅛ tsp. ground allspice
- ⅛ tsp. ground mace, optional
- 6 oz. uncooked multigrain spaghetti, broken into pieces
  Optional: Fresh mozzarella cheese pearls or shaved Parmesan cheese

1. In a Dutch oven, cook the beef and mushrooms over medium heat until meat is no longer pink, 5-7 minutes, crumbling meat; drain. Add tomato juice, tomatoes, tomato sauce, onion and seasonings. Bring to a boil.
2. Stir in spaghetti. Simmer, covered, until spaghetti is tender, 12-15 minutes. If desired, serve with cheese.
1½ CUPS: 414 cal., 10g fat (4g sat. fat), 71mg chol., 925mg sod., 48g carb. (15g sugars, 6g fiber), 33g pro.

Test Kitchen Tip

This easy technique lets you skip the task of boiling the pasta and draining it separately. The tomato juice gives the sauce enough liquid to cook the pasta. While the ingredients simmer, stir occasionally to prevent sticking.

BACON & ASPARAGUS FRITTATA

BACON & ASPARAGUS FRITTATA

This makes a nice light meal. When I prepare it for guests, I serve it with fruit and bread. It's quick and easy, but it always wins me many compliments!
—*Gwen Clemon, Soldier, IA*

Prep: 10 min. • **Cook:** 25 min.
Makes: 6 servings

- 12 oz. bacon
- 2 cups sliced fresh asparagus (cut in ½-in. pieces)
- 1 cup chopped onion
- 2 garlic cloves, minced
- 10 large eggs, beaten
- ¼ cup minced parsley
- ½ tsp. seasoned salt
- ¼ tsp. pepper
- 1 large tomato, thinly sliced
- 1 cup shredded cheddar cheese

1. In a 9- or 10-in. ovenproof skillet, cook bacon until crisp. Drain, reserving 1 Tbsp. drippings. Heat reserved drippings on medium-high. Add asparagus, onion and garlic; saute until onion is tender. Chop bacon; set aside a third. In a large bowl, combine the remaining bacon, eggs, parsley, salt and pepper.
2. Pour egg mixture into skillet; stir. Top with tomato, cheese and reserved bacon. Cover and cook over medium-low until eggs are nearly set, 10-15 minutes.
3. Preheat broiler; place skillet 6 in. from heat. Broil until lightly browned, about 2 minutes. Serve immediately.
1 PIECE: 344 cal., 24g fat (10g sat. fat), 351mg chol., 738mg sod., 7g carb. (3g sugars, 2g fiber), 23g pro.

Test Kitchen Tip

Looking to feed a larger group? You can make this delicious meal in a 12-in. skillet by increasing each ingredient by 50% and baking the frittata for 20-25 minutes.

SLOW-COOKED
MOROCCAN CHICKEN

ONE-DISH TURKEY DINNER

This quick one-dish dinner helped keep my husband and me on track throughout the week while we were still learning to balance our busy schedules.
—*Shannon Barden, Alpharetta, GA*

Takes: 30 min. • **Makes:** 4 servings

1 lb. ground turkey
1 medium onion, chopped
1 shallot, finely chopped
3 garlic cloves, minced
¼ cup tomato paste
1 medium sweet potato, peeled and cubed
1 cup chicken broth
2 tsp. smoked paprika
½ tsp. salt
¼ tsp. pepper
3 cups chopped fresh kale
 Dash crushed red pepper flakes
1 medium ripe avocado, peeled and sliced
 Minced fresh mint, optional

1. In a large skillet, cook turkey, onion, shallot and garlic over medium heat until turkey is no longer pink and vegetables are tender, 8-10 minutes, breaking up turkey into crumbles; drain. Add tomato paste; cook and stir 1 minute longer.
2. Add the sweet potato, broth, smoked paprika, salt and pepper. Bring to a boil; reduce heat. Simmer, covered, until the sweet potato is tender, about 10 minutes, stirring occasionally. Add kale and red pepper flakes; cook and stir until kale is wilted, about 2 minutes. Serve with avocado and, if desired, mint.
FREEZE OPTION: Once cool, freeze in freezer containers. To use, partially thaw in refrigerator overnight. Heat through in a saucepan, stirring occasionally; add broth or water if necessary. Serve with avocado and, if desired, mint.
1⅓ CUPS: 318 cal., 14g fat (3g sat. fat), 76mg chol., 628mg sod., 24g carb. (8g sugars, 5g fiber), 26g pro. **DIABETIC EXCHANGES:** 3 lean meat, 2 fat, 1½ starch.

SLOW-COOKED MOROCCAN CHICKEN

Spices work their magic on plain chicken in this exciting dish. The dried fruit and couscous add an exotic touch.
—*Kathy Morgan, Ridgefield, WA*

Prep: 20 min. • **Cook:** 6 hours
Makes: 4 servings

4 medium carrots, sliced
2 large onions, halved and sliced
1 broiler/fryer chicken (3 to 4 lbs.), cut up, skin removed
½ tsp. salt
½ cup chopped dried apricots
½ cup raisins
1 can (14½ oz.) reduced-sodium chicken broth
¼ cup tomato paste
2 Tbsp. all-purpose flour
2 Tbsp. lemon juice
2 garlic cloves, minced
1½ tsp. ground ginger
1½ tsp. ground cumin
1 tsp. ground cinnamon
¾ tsp. pepper
 Hot cooked couscous

1. Place the carrots and onions in a greased 5-qt. slow cooker. Sprinkle chicken with salt; add to slow cooker. Top with apricots and raisins. In a small bowl, whisk broth, tomato paste, flour, lemon juice, garlic and seasonings until blended; add to the slow cooker.
2. Cook, covered, on low until chicken is tender, 6-7 hours. Serve with hot cooked couscous.
1 SERVING: 435 cal., 9g fat (3g sat. fat), 110mg chol., 755mg sod., 47g carb. (27g sugars, 6g fiber), 42g pro.

ONE-DISH TURKEY
DINNER

SHEET-PAN
TANDOORI CHICKEN

SHEET-PAN TANDOORI CHICKEN

This recipe is easy for weeknights, but it's also special enough for any day. The best part is there isn't much to clean up after! Put the chicken in the marinade in the morning, and everything will come together in record time for dinner!
—*Anwar Khan, Irving, TX*

Prep: 20 min. + marinating • **Bake:** 25 min.
Makes: 4 servings

- 1 cup plain Greek yogurt
- 3 Tbsp. tandoori masala seasoning
- ⅛ to ¼ tsp. crushed red pepper flakes, optional
- 8 bone-in chicken thighs (about 3 lbs.), skin removed
- 2 medium sweet potatoes, peeled and cut into ½-in. wedges
- 1 Tbsp. olive oil
- 16 cherry tomatoes
  Lemon slices
  Optional: Minced fresh cilantro and naan flatbread

1. In a large bowl, whisk yogurt, tandoori seasoning and, if desired, pepper flakes until blended. Add the chicken and turn to coat. Cover and refrigerate 6-8 hours, turning occasionally.
2. Preheat oven to 450°. Drain chicken, discarding marinade in bowl. Place the chicken in a greased 15x10x1-in. baking pan. Add sweet potatoes; drizzle with oil. Bake 15 minutes. Add the tomatoes and lemon slices. Bake until a thermometer inserted into chicken reads 170°-175°, 10-15 minutes longer.
3. Broil chicken 4-5 in. from the heat until browned, 4-5 minutes. If desired, serve with cilantro and naan.
2 CHICKEN THIGHS WITH 1 CUP SWEET POTATOES AND 4 TOMATOES: 589 cal., 27g fat (9g sat. fat), 186mg chol., 187mg sod., 29g carb. (13g sugars, 6g fiber), 52g pro.

HEIRLOOM TOMATO TART

HEIRLOOM TOMATO TART

Here's a delicious way to use the tomato bounty from your garden or the terrific buys from the local farmers market.
—*Kathryn Conrad, Milwaukee, WI*

Prep: 20 min. • **Bake:** 10 min.
Makes: 6 servings

- 2 tsp. cornmeal, divided
- 1 sheet refrigerated pie crust
  Cooking spray
- 3 Tbsp. shredded Asiago cheese
- 3 large heirloom tomatoes, cut into ¼-in. slices
- 3 small heirloom tomatoes, cut into ¼-in. slices
- 1 Tbsp. extra virgin olive oil
- ½ tsp. coarsely ground pepper
- ¼ tsp. salt
- ¼ cup crumbled goat or feta cheese
  Fresh basil leaves, optional

1. Preheat the oven to 450°. Sprinkle a large baking sheet with 1 tsp. cornmeal.
2. On a lightly floured surface, unroll crust into a 12-in. circle; transfer to prepared sheet. Spritz the crust with cooking spray. Sprinkle with remaining 1 tsp. cornmeal, pressing the cornmeal gently into crust. Prick crust thoroughly with a fork. Sprinkle with Asiago cheese.
3. Bake for 10 minutes or until lightly browned. Cool on a wire rack.
4. Layer with tomatoes. Drizzle with olive oil; sprinkle with pepper and salt. Top with goat cheese. Garnish with basil if desired. Serve immediately.
1 PIECE: 236 cal., 14g fat (6g sat. fat), 16mg chol., 270mg sod., 24g carb. (5g sugars, 2g fiber), 4g pro.

MEDITERRANEAN
ONE-DISH MEAL

🍎
EASY PEPPER STEAK

This popular beef dish is tasty as well as colorful.

—*Carolyn Butterfield, Atkinson, NE*

- -

Prep: 10 min. • **Cook:** 55 min.
Makes: 4 servings

1   lb. beef top round steak, cut into
    ¼x2-in. strips
1   Tbsp. paprika
2   Tbsp. butter
1   can (10½ oz.) beef broth
2   garlic cloves, minced
2   medium green peppers, cut into
    strips
1   cup thinly sliced onion
2   Tbsp. cornstarch
2   Tbsp. reduced-sodium soy sauce
⅓   cup cold water
2   fresh tomatoes, peeled and cut
    into wedges
    Cooked rice

1. Sprinkle meat with paprika. In a large skillet, melt butter over medium-high heat. Brown beef. Add broth and garlic. Simmer, covered, for 30 minutes.
2. Add green peppers and onion. Cover; continue to simmer for 5 minutes longer.
3. Combine cornstarch, soy sauce and water; stir into the meat mixture. Cook and stir until thickened. Gently stir in tomatoes and heat through. Serve over rice.
1 SERVING: 365 cal., 4g fat (1g sat. fat), 65mg chol., 465mg sod., 48g carb. (5g sugars, 4g fiber), 32g pro.

Test Kitchen Tip

Beef top round steak is a leaner, less tender cut of the meat. To get a more tender result, use a meat mallet prior to cooking. Starting at 1 end of the steak and gradually working toward the other, use the spiked side of the mallet to hit and flatten the meat evenly without damaging it.

🍎
MEDITERRANEAN ONE-DISH MEAL

I came up with this recipe one night while improvising with what I had on hand. I love to make simple, healthy one-dish dinners with lots of vegetables. Greek olives and feta give this meal a depth of flavor people love.

—*Donna Jesser, Everett, WA*

- -

Prep: 15 min. • **Cook:** 25 min.
Makes: 4 servings

¾   lb. Italian turkey sausage links,
    cut into 1-in. pieces
1   medium onion, chopped
2   garlic cloves, minced
1   can (14½ oz.) no-salt-added
    diced tomatoes, undrained
¼   cup Greek olives
1   tsp. dried oregano
½   cup quinoa, rinsed
3   cups fresh baby spinach
½   cup crumbled feta cheese

1. In a large saucepan coated with cooking spray, cook sausage and onion over medium heat until the sausage is browned and onion is tender. Add the garlic; cook 1 minute longer. Stir in the tomatoes, olives and oregano; bring to a boil.
2. Stir in quinoa. Top with spinach; do not stir. Reduce heat; cover and simmer for 12-15 minutes or until liquid is absorbed. Remove from the heat; fluff with a fork. Sprinkle with cheese.
1 CUP: 307 cal., 14g fat (3g sat. fat), 58mg chol., 845mg sod., 26g carb. (6g sugars, 5g fiber), 21g pro.

EASY PEPPER
STEAK

SPANISH-STYLE PAELLA

SPANISH-STYLE PAELLA

If you enjoy cooking ethnic foods, this hearty rice dish is a wonderful one. It's brimming with generous chunks of sausage, shrimp and veggies.
—*Taste of Home Test Kitchen*

- -

Prep: 10 min. • **Cook:** 35 min.
Makes: 8 servings

- ½ lb. Spanish chorizo links, sliced
- ½ lb. boneless skinless chicken breasts, cubed
- 1 Tbsp. olive oil
- 1 garlic clove, minced
- 1 cup uncooked short grain rice
- 1 cup chopped onion
- 1½ cups chicken broth
- 1 can (14½ oz.) stewed tomatoes, undrained
- ½ tsp. paprika
- ¼ tsp. ground cayenne pepper
- ¼ tsp. salt
- 10 strands saffron, crushed, or ⅛ tsp. ground saffron
- ½ lb. uncooked medium shrimp, peeled and deveined
- ½ cup sweet red pepper strips
- ½ cup green pepper strips
- ½ cup frozen peas
  Optional: Minced fresh parsley and lemon wedges

1. In a large saucepan or skillet over medium-high heat, cook sausage and chicken in oil for 5 minutes or until the sausage is lightly browned and chicken is no longer pink, stirring frequently. Add garlic; cook 1 minute longer. Drain if necessary.
2. Stir in rice and onion. Cook until onion is tender and the rice is lightly browned, stirring frequently. Add broth, tomatoes, paprika, cayenne, salt and saffron. Bring to a boil. Reduce heat to low; cover and cook for 10 minutes.
3. Stir in the shrimp, peppers and peas. Cover and cook 10 minutes longer or until the rice is tender, shrimp are pink and liquid is absorbed. Top with fresh parsley and lemon wedges if desired.

SAUCY BEEF & CABBAGE DINNER

1 CUP: 237 cal., 7g fat (2g sat. fat), 62mg chol., 543mg sod., 27g carb. (5g sugars, 2g fiber), 16g pro.

SAUCY BEEF & CABBAGE DINNER

Using cabbage is a wonderful way to bulk up a meal without adding extra fat and calories. The cabbage in this dish is tender but still has a nice crunch.
—*Marcia Doyle, Pompano, FL*

- -

Prep: 15 min. • **Cook:** 25 min.
Makes: 8 servings

- 1 lb. lean ground beef (90% lean)
- 1 large onion, chopped
- 1 cup sliced fresh mushrooms
  Optional: Fresh thyme and fresh parsley, chopped
- 1 medium head cabbage, chopped
- 1 can (46 oz.) reduced-sodium tomato juice
- 1 cup instant brown rice
- 1 can (6 oz.) tomato paste
- ¼ cup packed brown sugar
- 2 Tbsp. lemon juice
- 1 tsp. dried thyme
- 1 tsp. dried parsley flakes
- ½ tsp. pepper

1. In a Dutch oven, cook the beef, onion and mushrooms over medium heat until meat is no longer pink, breaking beef into crumbles; drain. If desired, sprinkle with thyme and parsley.
2. Add remaining ingredients. Bring to a boil. Reduce heat; cover and simmer until the cabbage and rice are tender, 15-20 minutes.
1⅓ CUPS: 253 cal., 5g fat (2g sat. fat), 35mg chol., 170mg sod., 36g carb. (19g sugars, 5g fiber), 17g pro. **DIABETIC EXCHANGES:** 2 vegetable, 2 lean meat, 1½ starch.

ONE-SKILLET PASTA

1 Tbsp. brown sugar
1 Tbsp. chili powder
8 oz. uncooked angel hair pasta
1 cup shredded cheddar cheese

1. In a large cast-iron or other heavy skillet, cook the turkey, onion and red pepper over medium heat, breaking turkey into crumbles, until meat is no longer pink; drain.
2. Add the tomatoes, broth, mushrooms, brown sugar and chili powder. Bring to a boil. Reduce heat; simmer, uncovered, for 30 minutes.
3. Add pasta; return to a boil. Reduce heat; simmer, covered, until the pasta is tender, 30-35 minutes. Sprinkle with cheese. Cover and cook until cheese is melted, 2-3 minutes longer.
1⅔ CUPS: 553 cal., 19g fat (7g sat. fat), 114mg chol., 994mg sod., 55g carb. (14g sugars, 7g fiber), 41g pro.

Test Kitchen Tip
You can use a different meat in this recipe—ground chicken or beef would work well. If you choose to use lean turkey, you don't need to drain the fat after browning.

ONE-SKILLET PASTA
This recipe was given to me 25 years ago, and it remains a family favorite. It's a simple dish that's a fabulous twist on the traditional spaghetti. Cooking it all in one pot saves time on prep and cleanup.
—*Susan Spence, Lawrenceville, VA*

Prep: 20 min. • **Cook:** 1¼ hours
Makes: 5 servings

1½ lbs. ground turkey
1 medium onion, finely chopped
1 medium sweet red pepper, finely chopped
1 can (28 oz.) diced tomatoes, undrained
1 can (14½ oz.) fire-roasted diced tomatoes, undrained
1 can (14½ oz.) reduced-sodium beef broth
1 can (4 oz.) sliced mushrooms, drained

CHICKEN BULGUR SKILLET

This recipe was given to me by a friend, and I've altered it slightly to suit our tastes. We like it with a fresh green salad.
—*Leann Hillmer, Sylvan Grove, KS*

Prep: 15 min. • **Cook:** 30 min.
Makes: 4 servings

- 1 lb. boneless skinless chicken breasts, cut into 1-in. cubes
- 2 tsp. olive oil
- 2 medium carrots, chopped
- ⅔ cup chopped onion
- 3 Tbsp. chopped walnuts
- ½ tsp. caraway seeds
- ¼ tsp. ground cumin
- 1½ cups bulgur
- 2 cups reduced-sodium chicken broth
- 2 Tbsp. raisins
- ¼ tsp. salt
- ⅛ tsp. ground cinnamon

1. In a large cast-iron or other heavy skillet, cook chicken in oil over medium-high heat until meat is no longer pink. Remove and keep warm. In the same skillet, cook and stir the carrots, onion, nuts, caraway seeds and cumin until the onion starts to brown, 3-4 minutes.
2. Stir in bulgur. Gradually add the broth; bring to a boil over medium heat. Reduce heat; add the raisins, salt, cinnamon and chicken. Cover and simmer until bulgur is tender, 12-15 minutes.

1½ CUPS: 412 cal., 8g fat (1g sat. fat), 66mg chol., 561mg sod., 51g carb. (8g sugars, 12g fiber), 36g pro.

> *"Very easy to make and yummy! Each bite had an amazing flavor. I served it in a bowl."*
> —LORETTA LIZZI, TASTEOFHOME.COM

CHICKEN BULGUR
SKILLET

TACO SKILLET PIZZA
WITH CORNBREAD CRUST

TACO SKILLET PIZZA WITH CORNBREAD CRUST

Our family loves taco pizza, and so I've made many versions of it. This recipe is like a deep-dish skillet pizza. It's a hearty meal that can be served straight out of the pan.
—*Pamela Shank, Parkersburg, WV*

Prep: 30 min. • **Bake:** 15 min.
Makes: 6 servings

- ½ lb. lean ground beef (90% lean)
- 1 cup refried beans
- ⅓ cup salsa
- 2 Tbsp. taco seasoning
- 1 pkg. (6 oz.) Mexican-style cornbread/muffin mix
- ⅓ cup tortilla chips, crushed
- 1 cup shredded cheddar cheese
  Toppings: Torn romaine, chopped tomatoes, sour cream, chopped onion, chopped cilantro and fried tortilla strips

1. Preheat the oven to 350°. In a 10-in. cast-iron or other ovenproof skillet, cook beef over medium heat until no longer pink, 6-8 minutes, crumbling beef; drain. Transfer to a small bowl. Stir in beans, salsa and taco seasoning; keep warm. Wipe pan clean.
2. Prepare the cornbread mix according to package directions; stir in the crushed tortilla chips. Pour into skillet. Bake until set, 12-15 minutes.
3. Spread ground beef mixture over the cornbread to within 1 in. of edges; sprinkle with cheese. Bake until cheese is melted and crust is golden brown, 3-5 minutes. Serve with toppings.
1 WEDGE: 329 cal., 14g fat (6g sat. fat), 75mg chol., 1052mg sod., 31g carb. (3g sugars, 3g fiber), 19g pro.

> ### Test Kitchen Tip
> If you can't find a Mexican-style mix, use a package of regular cornbread or corn muffin mix (8½ oz.) instead.

SHEET-PAN CHICKEN CURRY DINNER

SHEET-PAN CHICKEN CURRY DINNER

My husband loves anything curry and will even eat veggies when they have a curry sauce. This is a quick way to get a whole meal on the table with minimal fuss. Serve with a side of jasmine rice.
—*Trisha Kruse, Eagle, ID*

Prep: 20 min. • **Bake:** 40 min.
Makes: 6 servings

- 2 lbs. sweet potatoes, peeled and cubed
- 2 cups fresh cauliflowerets
- 1 large onion, chopped
- 3 garlic cloves, minced
- 2 Tbsp. olive oil
- 2 tsp. curry powder, divided
- 1¼ tsp. salt, divided
- 1 tsp. lemon-pepper seasoning, divided
- 6 bone-in chicken thighs (about 2¼ lbs.), skin removed
- 1 tsp. smoked paprika
- ¼ cup chicken broth

1. Preheat oven to 425°. Line a 15x10x1-in. baking pan with heavy-duty foil. Place the sweet potatoes, cauliflower, onion and garlic on prepared pan. Drizzle with oil; sprinkle with 1 tsp. curry powder, ¾ tsp. salt and ½ tsp. lemon pepper; toss to coat.
2. Arrange chicken over the vegetables. Mix paprika and remaining 1 tsp. curry powder, ½ tsp. salt and ½ tsp. lemon pepper; sprinkle over chicken. Roast until the vegetables are almost tender, 30-35 minutes. Drizzle with broth; bake until a thermometer inserted in chicken reads 170°-175° and the vegetables are tender, 7-10 minutes longer.
1 SERVING: 409 cal., 14g fat (3g sat. fat), 87mg chol., 686mg sod., 42g carb. (17g sugars, 6g fiber), 28g pro. **DIABETIC EXCHANGES:** 4 lean meat, 3 starch, 1 fat.

ONE-POT DUTCH OVEN PASTA BAKE

HOT DOG CASSEROLE

When our children were small and I was busy trying to get all those extra things done that are part of a mom's normal schedule, I would make this quick hot dish. The kids loved it!
—JoAnn Gunio, Franklin, NC

Prep: 10 min. • **Bake:** 70 min.
Makes: 8 servings

- 3 Tbsp. butter
- 2 Tbsp. all-purpose flour
- 1 to 1½ tsp. salt
- ¼ to ½ tsp. pepper
- 1½ cups 2% milk
- 5 medium red potatoes, thinly sliced
- 1 pkg. (1 lb.) hot dogs, halved lengthwise and cut into ½-in. slices
- 1 medium onion, chopped
- ⅓ cup shredded cheddar cheese
  Chopped green onions, optional

1. Preheat the oven to 350°. In a small saucepan, melt butter. Stir in flour, salt and pepper until smooth. Gradually add milk. Bring to a boil; cook and stir until thickened and bubbly, about 2 minutes.
2. In a greased 2½-qt. baking dish, layer a third of the potatoes, half the hot dogs and half the onion. Repeat layers. Top with remaining potatoes. Pour white sauce over all.
3. Bake, covered, for 1 hour. Uncover; sprinkle with cheese. Bake until potatoes are tender, 10-15 minutes longer. Garnish with green onions if desired.
1 CUP: 330 cal., 24g fat (11g sat. fat), 52mg chol., 967mg sod., 18g carb. (4g sugars, 2g fiber), 11g pro.

Test Kitchen Tip
You can store this casserole in an airtight container in the fridge for up to 4 days. We don't recommend freezing this casserole recipe, so make sure you eat it up!

ONE-POT DUTCH OVEN PASTA BAKE

I was in a hurry one night, so I went on a pantry search to see what I had on hand. I found penne pasta and decided to go Italian! We all loved this dish, and it's one of my weeknight faves now! It's a satisfying timesaver since the pasta cooks in the same pot.
—Tammy Reid, Oklahoma City, OK

Prep: 10 min. • **Cook:** 30 min.
Makes: 4 servings

- 1 lb. ground beef
- ½ medium onion, chopped
- 2 garlic cloves, minced
- 1 can (8 oz.) tomato sauce
- 3 cups uncooked penne pasta
- 1 cup beef broth
- 3 cups water
- 1 can (14 oz.) diced tomatoes
- 1 tsp. onion powder
- 1 Tbsp. Italian seasoning
- 1 pkg. (5 oz.) fresh spinach
  Shredded Parmesan cheese, optional

1. Heat a Dutch oven over medium heat; add ground beef and onion. Cook and stir until beef is no longer pink, 5-7 minutes, crumbling meat; drain.
2. Add garlic; cook 1 minute longer. Add tomato sauce, pasta, broth, water, diced tomatoes and seasonings. Stir; bring to a boil.
3. Cover, reduce heat and simmer until the pasta is tender, stirring occasionally. Top with spinach; cover just until wilted. Stir. If desired, sprinkle with Parmesan cheese before serving.
2 CUPS: 452 cal., 15g fat (5g sat. fat), 70mg chol., 773mg sod., 50g carb. (7g sugars, 5g fiber), 30g pro.

HOT DOG CASSEROLE

10

Delectable Desserts

Why not finish off your meal with a fabulous homemade dessert? If you're thinking that it takes too much time and effort to create a stupendous sweet, think again. Whether you're cooking for your family or making a treat for a party, these easy recipes are just what you need to satisfy everyone's cravings.

SLOW-COOKER PINA COLADA
BANANAS FOSTER P. 293

POSSUM PIE

POSSUM PIE

We found this recipe in a box in the cafe we own; it was used in the early 1950s by a previous owner. This pie has been on our menu since we discovered it.
—*David Heilemann, Eureka Springs, AR*

Prep: 20 min. + chilling
Makes: 8 servings

- 6   oz. cream cheese, softened
- ¾   cup confectioners' sugar
- 1   graham cracker crust (9 in.)
- ¼   cup chopped pecans
- 1¾ cups cold whole milk
- ¾   tsp. vanilla extract
- ¼   cup instant vanilla pudding mix
- ⅓   cup instant chocolate pudding mix
- ½   cup heavy whipping cream, whipped
- 12 to 16 pecan halves

1. In a small bowl, beat cream cheese and confectioners' sugar until smooth. Spoon into the crust. Sprinkle with the chopped pecans.
2. In a bowl, whisk the milk, vanilla and pudding mixes for 2 minutes. Let stand for 2 minutes or until soft-set. Spoon over the pecans.
3. Refrigerate for at least 4 hours. Top with whipped cream and pecan halves.
1 PIECE: 388 cal., 24g fat (10g sat. fat), 44mg chol., 276mg sod., 40g carb. (32g sugars, 1g fiber), 5g pro.

EASY APPLE CAKE

This old-fashioned cake is moist, dense and down-home delicious. Even better, it's quick to fix. Serve warm, with some whipped cream or frozen custard. It's been one of my family's very favorite recipes for decades.
—*Sherry Ashenfelter, Waterville, OH*

Prep: 25 min. • **Bake:** 35 min. + cooling
Makes: 20 servings

- 1¾ cups sugar
- 1   cup canola oil
- 3   large eggs
- 1   tsp. vanilla extract

- 2   cups all-purpose flour
- 1¼ tsp. baking powder
- 1   tsp. salt
- 1   tsp. ground cinnamon
- ¼   tsp. baking soda
- 2   cups finely chopped
      peeled tart apples
- 1   cup chopped walnuts
- 1¼ cups whipped topping

1. Preheat oven to 350°. In a large bowl, beat the sugar, oil, eggs and vanilla until well blended. Combine the flour, baking powder, salt, cinnamon and baking soda; gradually beat into sugar mixture until blended. Fold in apples and walnuts.
2. Transfer to a greased 13x9-in. baking dish. Bake for 35-45 minutes or until a toothpick inserted in the center comes out clean. Cool on a wire rack. Serve with whipped topping.

1 PIECE: 278 cal., 16g fat (3g sat. fat), 32mg chol., 169mg sod., 31g carb. (19g sugars, 1g fiber), 4g pro.

Test Kitchen Tips

- Granny Smith are the go-to apples for this cake recipe, but other tart varieties, such as Braeburn and Jonathan, work well too. Or, use a mix of tart and tart-sweet apples, such as Gala or Fuji.

- Grab some ice cream—especially vanilla, if you have it. Drizzle a bit of caramel syrup on top, or go with nuts and whipped cream. For a lighter take, simply dust confectioners' sugar over top.

PUMPKIN CHEESECAKE BARS

CITRUS CORNMEAL CAKE

Cornmeal adds a rustic quality to this delicate dessert flavored with citrus and almond. It's sure to be a staple in your recipe collection, and it also makes a fabulous holiday party hostess gift.
—*Roxanne Chan, Albany, CA*

- -

Prep: 25 min. • **Bake:** 25 min. + cooling
Makes: 8 servings

- ½ cup lemon yogurt
- ⅓ cup honey
- ¼ cup olive oil
- 1 large egg
- 2 large egg whites
- ¼ tsp. almond extract
- ¾ cup all-purpose flour
- ½ cup cornmeal
- 1 tsp. baking powder
- ½ tsp. grated orange zest
- 1 can (15 oz.) mandarin oranges, drained
- 3 Tbsp. sliced almonds

1. Preheat oven to 350°. In a bowl, beat yogurt, honey, oil, egg, egg whites and extract until well blended. In a second bowl, combine flour, cornmeal and baking powder; gradually beat into the yogurt mixture until blended. Stir in orange zest.
2. Coat a 9-in. fluted tart pan with a removable bottom with cooking spray; pour batter in pan. Arrange oranges over the batter; sprinkle with almonds. Bake until a toothpick inserted in the center comes out clean, 25-30 minutes. Cool on a wire rack for 10 minutes before cutting. Serve warm or room temperature.
1 PIECE: 240 cal., 9g fat (1g sat. fat), 27mg chol., 85mg sod., 36g carb. (20g sugars, 2g fiber), 5g pro.

PUMPKIN CHEESECAKE BARS

This recipe was extremely popular at the annual Christmas party sponsored by our homemakers club. The bars are a terrific dessert for fall.
—*Agnes Jasa, Malabar, FL*

- -

Prep: 15 min. • **Bake:** 45 min. + cooling
Makes: 16 bars

- 1 cup all-purpose flour
- ⅓ cup packed brown sugar
- 5 Tbsp. cold butter
- 1 cup finely chopped pecans
- 1 pkg. (8 oz.) cream cheese, softened
- ¾ cup sugar
- ½ cup canned pumpkin
- 2 large eggs, room temperature, lightly beaten
- 1 tsp. vanilla extract
- 1½ tsp. ground cinnamon
- 1 tsp. ground allspice

1. Preheat oven to 350°. Combine flour and brown sugar. Cut in the butter until crumbly. Stir in pecans; set aside ¾ cup mixture for topping.
2. Press remaining crumb mixture into a greased 8-in. square baking pan. Bake for 15 minutes or until edges are lightly browned. Cool on a wire rack.
3. In a large bowl, beat the cream cheese and sugar until smooth. Beat in pumpkin, eggs, vanilla, cinnamon and allspice. Pour over crust. Sprinkle with reserved crumb mixture.
4. Bake for 30-35 minutes or until golden brown. Cool completely on a wire rack. Cut into bars. Store in the refrigerator.
1 BAR: 228 cal., 15g fat (6g sat. fat), 52mg chol., 88mg sod., 22g carb. (15g sugars, 1g fiber), 4g pro.

CITRUS CORNMEAL
CAKE

TRADITIONAL
FUNNEL CAKES

TRADITIONAL FUNNEL CAKES

When I was in high school, I made these funnel cakes for my family every Sunday after church. They are crisp and tender, just like the kind we always ate at the state fair.

—Susan Tingley, Portland, OR

Prep: 15 min. • **Cook:** 5 min./batch
Makes: 8 servings

- 2 cups 2% milk
- 3 large eggs, room temperature
- ¼ cup sugar
- 2 cups all-purpose flour
- 2 tsp. baking powder
  Oil for deep-fat frying
  Confectioners' sugar
  Lingonberry jam or red currant jelly

1. In a bowl, combine the milk, eggs and sugar. Combine flour and baking powder; beat into the egg mixture until smooth.
2. In a cast-iron or electric skillet, heat 2 in. oil to 375°. Cover the bottom of a funnel spout with your finger; ladle ½ cup batter into funnel. Holding the funnel several inches above the skillet, release your finger; move the funnel in a spiral motion until all the batter is released. Scrape funnel with a rubber spatula if needed.
3. Fry until golden brown, about 1 minute on each side. Drain on paper towels. Repeat with remaining batter. Dust each cake with confectioners' sugar; serve warm with jam.
NOTE: To pour batter easily into hot oil, you can also use a liquid measuring cup or a turkey baster.
1 FUNNEL CAKE: 300 cal., 15g fat (2g sat. fat), 84mg chol., 157mg sod., 33g carb. (10g sugars, 1g fiber), 8g pro.

SWEETENED RICOTTA
WITH BERRIES

3. In a small bowl, combine berries and sugar; set aside. Place ricotta in a food processor. Add honey and salt; cover and process until blended. While processing, gradually add cream in a steady stream; process until creamy. Serve with berries.
⅓ CUP RICOTTA WITH ¼ CUP BERRIES : 366 cal., 25g fat (15g sat. fat), 86mg chol., 171mg sod., 27g carb. (23g sugars, 2g fiber), 10g pro.

15-MINUTE COOKIES

My mom used to pack these cookies in our school lunches. They're inexpensive and easy to prepare, so all seven of us siblings learned to make them. Now they're also a favorite with my children.
—*Kerry Bouchard, Augusta, MT*

- -

Takes: 15 min. • **Makes:** about 3 dozen

½ cup butter, cubed
½ cup 2% milk
2 cups sugar
3 cups quick-cooking oats or old-fashioned oats
5 Tbsp. baking cocoa
½ cup raisins, chopped nuts or sweetened shredded coconut

1. In a large saucepan, heat the butter, milk and sugar. Bring to a boil, stirring occasionally. Boil for 1 minute.
2. Remove from the heat. Stir in oats, cocoa, and raisins, nuts or coconut. Drop by tablespoonfuls onto waxed paper. Cool.
1 COOKIE: 101 cal., 3g fat (2g sat. fat), 7mg chol., 22mg sod., 18g carb. (13g sugars, 1g fiber), 1g pro.

SWEETENED RICOTTA WITH BERRIES

Ricotta is a lovely fast cheese that can easily be made at home from whole milk, skim milk or whey. This creamy dessert is luscious when generously topped with fresh raspberries and strawberries.
—*Matthew Lawrence, Vashon, WA*

- -

Prep: 40 min. + chilling
Makes: 7 servings

HOMEMADE RICOTTA
8 cups whole milk
1 cup heavy whipping cream
½ cup lemon juice
DESSERT
1 cup fresh blackberries
1 cup fresh raspberries
1 tsp. sugar
3 Tbsp. honey
⅛ tsp. salt
¼ cup heavy whipping cream

1. In a Dutch oven, heat milk and cream to 180° over low heat, stirring constantly. Stir in lemon juice. Remove from heat and let stand for 15 minutes (milk and whey will separate).
2. Line a large strainer with 4 layers of cheesecloth and place over a large bowl; pour in milk mixture. Strain for about 1 hour or until most of the liquid is strained. Discard the liquid. Wrap the ricotta in the cheesecloth. Refrigerate for at least 1 hour. Squeeze out any liquid; remove cheesecloth and discard liquid from bowl.

ICE CREAM BOWLS

ICE CREAM BOWLS

Once you sample these homemade waffle ice cream bowls, you'll want to serve them time and again! You can prepare them with beautiful designs in a special pizzelle cookie maker, or without designs in the oven. —Taste of Home *Test Kitchen*

Prep: 15 min. • **Bake:** 35 min.
Makes: 16 servings

- 3 large eggs, room temperature
- ¾ cup sugar
- ½ cup butter, melted
- 2 tsp. vanilla extract
- 1½ cups all-purpose flour
- 2 tsp. baking powder

1. In a small bowl, beat eggs on medium speed until blended. Gradually beat in sugar until thick and lemon colored. Add butter and vanilla. Combine flour and baking powder; gradually add to egg mixture. Invert two 6-oz. custard cups on paper towels; coat with cooking spray.
2. Prepare cookies in a preheated pizzelle cookie maker according to the manufacturer's directions, using 2 Tbsp. batter for each cookie. Immediately remove the cookies and drape over inverted custard cups. To shape the cookies into bowls, place another custard cup coated with cooking spray over each cookie. Let stand until set. Remove cookies from the custard cups and set aside. Repeat with the remaining batter. Store in an airtight container.
TO MAKE IN THE OVEN: Preheat oven to 400°. Line a baking sheet with parchment. Draw two 7-in. circles on the parchment. Spread 2 Tbsp. batter over each circle. Bake for 4-5 minutes or until edges are golden brown. Immediately remove the cookies and drape over inverted custard cups. Shape into bowls as directed above.
1 BOWL: 145 cal., 7g fat (4g sat. fat), 50mg chol., 119mg sod., 19g carb. (10g sugars, 0 fiber), 2g pro.

TURTLE ICE CREAM SAUCE

Making this rich caramel-fudge sauce is a family affair at our house—the kids love to unwrap the caramels! The sauce can be made ahead and frozen.
—*Marci Cullen, Milton, WI*

- -

Prep: 10 min. • **Cook:** 15 min. + cooling
Makes: 9 cups

   2 cups butter, cubed
   2 cans (12 oz. each) evaporated milk
   2 cups sugar
   ⅓ cup dark corn syrup
   ⅛ tsp. salt
   2 cups semisweet chocolate chips
   1 pkg. (14 oz.) caramels
   1 tsp. vanilla extract

1. In a Dutch oven, combine the first 7 ingredients. Cook, stirring constantly, over medium-low heat until caramels are melted and mixture is smooth (do not boil). Reduce heat to low.
2. With an electric hand mixer on medium speed, beat in the vanilla; continue beating for 5 minutes. Beat on high for 2 minutes. Remove from the heat and cool for 30 minutes (sauce will thicken as it cools). Pour into food storage containers; refrigerate. Serve warm or cold.
2 TBSP.: 83 cal., 3g fat (1g sat. fat), 4mg chol., 30mg sod., 15g carb. (14g sugars, 0 fiber), 1g pro.

CREAM CHEESE ICE CREAM

This is hands-down the best homemade ice cream I've ever eaten. It tastes like rich cheesecake with a hint of lemon.
—*Johnnie McLeod, Bastrop, LA*

- -

Prep: 20 min. + chilling
Process: 20 min./batch + freezing
Makes: 12 servings

   2½ cups half-and-half cream
   1   cup whole milk
   1¼ cups sugar
   2   large eggs, lightly beaten
   12 oz. cream cheese, cubed
   1   Tbsp. lemon juice
   1   tsp. vanilla extract

1. In a large saucepan, heat cream and milk to 175°; stir in sugar until dissolved. Whisk a small amount of the hot mixture into the eggs. Return all to pan, whisking constantly. Cook and stir over low heat until mixture reaches at least 160° and coats the back of a metal spoon.
2. Remove from heat. Whisk in cream cheese until smooth. Cool quickly by placing pan in a bowl of ice water; stir for 2 minutes. Stir in lemon juice and vanilla. Press foil or waxed paper onto surface of the custard. Refrigerate for several hours or overnight.
3. Fill cylinder of an ice cream maker two-thirds full; freeze according to the manufacturer's directions. Refrigerate remaining mixture until ready to freeze. Transfer to a freezer container; freeze for 2-4 hours before serving.
½ CUP: 273 cal., 16g fat (10g sat. fat), 87mg chol., 135mg sod., 25g carb. (25g sugars, 0 fiber), 5g pro.

CREAM CHEESE ICE CREAM

- Lemon Ice -

This cool and refreshing recipe transforms the simplest ingredients into a light and elegant dessert—the perfect end to a summer meal.

In a saucepan over low heat, cook and stir 2 cups **sugar** and 1 cup **water** until **sugar** is dissolved. Remove from the heat; stir in 2 cups **lemon juice**. Pour into a freezer container. Freeze until slushy, 8 hours or overnight. If desired, garnish with **lemon slices** and **mint**.

RICOTTA CHEESECAKE

When I was a nurse, my co-workers and I regularly swapped recipes during lunch breaks. This creamy cheesecake was one of the best I ever received.
—*Georgiann Franklin, Canfield, OH*

Prep: 30 min. + cooling
Bake: 50 min. + chilling
Makes: 12 servings

- 1¼ cups graham cracker crumbs
- 3 Tbsp. sugar
- ⅓ cup butter, melted

FILLING
- 2 cartons (15 oz. each) ricotta cheese
- 1 cup sugar
- 3 large eggs, room temperature, lightly beaten
- 2 Tbsp. all-purpose flour
- 1 tsp. vanilla extract
  Cherry pie filling, optional

1. Preheat oven to 400°. In a medium bowl, combine the graham cracker crumbs and sugar; stir in butter. Press onto the bottom and 1 in. up the side of a greased 9-in. springform pan.
2. Place pan on a baking sheet. Bake for 6-8 minutes or until crust is lightly browned around edge. Cool completely on a wire rack.
3. For the filling, beat ricotta cheese on medium speed for 1 minute. Add sugar; beat for 1 minute. Add eggs; beat just until combined. Beat in flour and vanilla. Pour into crust.
4. Place pan on a baking sheet. Bake at 350° for 50-60 minutes or until center is almost set. Cool on a wire rack for 10 minutes. Carefully run a knife around edge of pan to loosen; cool 1 hour longer. Refrigerate overnight.
5. Remove side of pan. If desired, serve with cherry pie filling. Refrigerate any leftover cheesecake.

1 PIECE: 234 cal., 11g fat (6g sat. fat), 81mg chol., 163mg sod., 29g carb. (23g sugars, 0 fiber), 6g pro.

TURTLE TART WITH CARAMEL SAUCE

This tart has a nutty crust, gooey caramel sauce, and a whole lot to love!
—*Leah Davis, Morrow, OH*

Prep: 15 min. + chilling
Bake: 15 min. + cooling
Makes: 12 servings

- 2 cups pecan halves, toasted
- ½ cup sugar
- 2 Tbsp. butter, melted

FILLING
- 2 cups semisweet chocolate chips
- 1½ cups heavy whipping cream
- ½ cup finely chopped pecans, toasted

CARAMEL SAUCE
- ½ cup butter, cubed
- 1 cup sugar
- 1 cup heavy whipping cream

1. Preheat oven to 350°. Place pecans and sugar in a food processor; pulse until pecans are finely ground. Add melted butter; pulse until combined. Press onto bottom and up side of a 9-in. fluted tart pan with removable bottom. Bake until golden brown, 12-15 minutes. Cool completely on a wire rack.
2. For the filling, place chocolate chips in a bowl. In a saucepan, bring cream just to a boil. Pour over chocolate; stir with a whisk until smooth. Pour into cooled crust; cool slightly. Refrigerate until slightly set, about 30 minutes.
3. Sprinkle pecans over the filling. Refrigerate, covered, 3 hours or until set.
4. For sauce, in a large heavy saucepan, melt butter over medium heat; stir in sugar until dissolved. Bring to a boil; cook for 10-12 minutes or until deep golden brown, stirring occasionally. Slowly whisk in cream until blended. Remove from heat; cool slightly. Serve with tart.

1 PIECE WITH 2 TBSP. CARAMEL SAUCE: 632 cal., 51g fat (24g sat. fat), 82mg chol., 93mg sod., 47g carb. (43g sugars, 4g fiber), 5g pro.

TURTLE TART WITH CARAMEL SAUCE

LEMON BREAD PUDDING

LEMON BREAD PUDDING

Sweet raisins and a smooth hot lemon sauce make my bread pudding extra special. Even today, I get requests for the recipe from people who tasted this traditional dessert years ago.
—*Mildred Sherrer, Fort Worth, TX*

Prep: 15 min. • **Bake:** 50 min.
Makes: 6 servings

- 3 slices day-old bread, cubed
- ¾ cup raisins
- 2 cups 2% milk
- ½ cup sugar
- 2 Tbsp. butter
- ¼ tsp. salt
- 2 large eggs
- 1 tsp. vanilla extract

LEMON SAUCE
- ¾ cup sugar
- 2 Tbsp. cornstarch
- 1 cup water
- 2 tsp. grated lemon zest
- 3 Tbsp. lemon juice
- 1 Tbsp. butter

1. Preheat oven to 350°. Toss bread and raisins in a greased 1½-qt. baking dish. In a small saucepan, combine the milk, sugar, butter and salt; cook and stir until butter melts. Remove from the heat.
2. Whisk eggs and vanilla in a small bowl. Stir a small amount of hot milk mixture into the egg mixture; return all to pan, stirring constantly. Pour over the bread and raisins.
3. Place baking dish in a larger baking pan. Fill larger pan with 1 in. hot water. Bake, uncovered, for 50-60 minutes or until a knife inserted in center comes out clean.
4. For the sauce, in a small saucepan, combine sugar and cornstarch. Stir in water until smooth. Bring to a boil over medium heat; cook and stir until thickened, 1-2 minutes. Remove from heat. Stir in lemon zest, juice and butter until butter is melted. Serve over warm or cold pudding. Refrigerate leftovers.
1 CUP: 385 cal., 10g fat (5g sat. fat), 84mg chol., 280mg sod., 71g carb. (58g sugars, 1g fiber), 7g pro.

BLUE-RIBBON APPLE CAKE

A friend from New Hampshire gave me this recipe for her cake, which won a blue ribbon at the county fair.
—*Jennie Wilburn, Long Creek, OR*

Prep: 15 min. • **Bake:** 55 min. + cooling
Makes: 16 servings

- 3 cups all-purpose flour
- 2¼ cups sugar, divided
- 1 Tbsp. baking powder
- ½ tsp. salt
- 4 large eggs
- 1 cup canola oil
- ⅓ cup orange juice
- 2½ tsp. vanilla extract
- 4 medium tart apples, peeled and thinly sliced
- 2 tsp. ground cinnamon
  Confectioners' sugar

1. Preheat oven to 350°. Combine flour, 2 cups sugar, baking powder and salt. In a second bowl, combine the eggs, oil, orange juice and vanilla; add to the flour mixture and mix well. In a third bowl, toss apples with cinnamon and the remaining ¼ cup sugar.
2. Spread a third of the batter into a greased 10-in. tube pan. Top with half the apples. Repeat layers. Carefully spread the remaining batter over the apples.
3. Bake until a toothpick inserted in the center comes out clean, 55-65 minutes. Let cool for 15 minutes before removing from pan to a wire rack; cool completely. Dust with confectioners' sugar.
1 PIECE: 353 cal., 15g fat (2g sat. fat), 53mg chol., 165mg sod., 51g carb. (32g sugars, 1g fiber), 4g pro.

BLUE-RIBBON
APPLE CAKE

SLOW-COOKER PINA COLADA
BANANAS FOSTER

SLOW-COOKER PINA COLADA BANANAS FOSTER

I took bananas Foster one step further and combined it with the flavors of my favorite tropical drink. Make sure your bananas are not super ripe—choose ones that are still nice and firm.
—*Trisha Kruse, Eagle, ID*

Prep: 10 min. • **Cook:** 2 hours
Makes: 6 servings

- 4   medium firm bananas
- 1   can (8 oz.) pineapple tidbits, drained
- ¼   cup butter, melted
- 1   cup packed brown sugar
- ¼   cup rum
- ½   tsp. coconut extract
- ½   cup sweetened shredded coconut, toasted
     Optional: Coconut ice cream, vanilla wafers and cream-filled wafer cookies

1. Cut bananas in half lengthwise, then widthwise. Layer sliced bananas and pineapple in the bottom of a 1½-qt. slow cooker. Combine butter, brown sugar, rum and coconut extract in a small bowl; pour over the fruit. Cook, covered, on low until heated through, about 2 hours.
2. Sprinkle individual servings with toasted coconut. Serve with optional ingredients as desired.
½ CUP: 358 cal., 11g fat (7g sat. fat), 20mg chol., 95mg sod., 63g carb. (53g sugars, 3g fiber), 1g pro.

MADEIRA CAKE

MADEIRA CAKE

This classic British cake is often served with Madeira wine, which is how it got its name. Similar to a pound cake, it is commonly flavored with lemon and can be served with sweet liqueurs or tea.
—*Peggy Woodward, Shullsburg, WI*

Prep: 15 min. • **Bake:** 45 min. + cooling
Makes: 12 servings

- 1   cup unsalted butter, softened
- 1   cup plus 2 Tbsp. sugar, divided
- 2   tsp. grated lemon zest
- 3   large eggs, room temperature
- 2¼ cups all-purpose flour
- 2   tsp. baking powder

1. Preheat the oven to 325°. Line the bottom of a greased 8x4-in. loaf pan with parchment; grease the parchment.
2. Cream butter and 1 cup sugar until light and fluffy, 5-7 minutes. Beat in lemon zest. Add eggs, 1 at a time, beating well after each addition. Whisk the flour and baking powder; gradually add to the creamed mixture.
3. Transfer batter to the prepared pan. Sprinkle with remaining 2 Tbsp. sugar. Bake until a toothpick inserted in center comes out clean, 45-50 minutes. Cool in pan 10 minutes before removing to a wire rack to cool completely.
1 PIECE: 304 cal., 17g fat (10g sat. fat), 87mg chol., 100mg sod., 35g carb. (17g sugars, 1g fiber), 4g pro.

GOLDEN M&M'S BARS

Our family loves to take drives, and I often bring these bars along for snacking in the car.
—*Martha Haseman, Hinckley, IL*

- -

Prep: 15 min. • **Bake:** 25 min. + cooling
Makes: 2 dozen

½ cup butter, softened
¾ cup sugar
¾ cup packed brown sugar
2 tsp. vanilla extract
2 large eggs, room temperature
1½ cups all-purpose flour
1 tsp. baking powder
½ tsp. salt
1 cup white baking chips
1¾ cups plain M&M's, divided

1. Preheat oven to 350°. In a large bowl, cream butter, sugars and vanilla until light and fluffy, 5-7 minutes. Beat in eggs, 1 at a time. Whisk together the flour, baking powder and salt; gradually add to the creamed mixture. Stir in chips and 1 cup M&M's.

2. Spread batter evenly into a greased 13x9-in. baking pan. Sprinkle with the remaining ¾ cup M&M's. Bake until golden brown and a toothpick inserted in center comes out with moist crumbs, 25-30 minutes. Cool on a wire rack. Cut into bars.

1 BAR: 233 cal., 10g fat (6g sat. fat), 29mg chol., 123mg sod., 34g carb. (27g sugars, 1g fiber), 2g pro.

Test Kitchen Tips

- To keep these bars chewy, check them 5 minutes before the end of the recommended baking time to make sure they haven't dried out. Also, be sure to use the right size baking pan; too large of a pan can create a thin, dry bar.

- Try adding other mix-ins, such as caramel candies, Oreos, chocolate or toffee chips, or nuts.

- You can store these bars for up to 5 days in an airtight container.

GOLDEN M&M'S BARS

BAKED PUMPKIN PUDDING

Even after you eat your favorite dinner, you'll find room for this perfect pudding dessert—a treat served hot or cold. Mildly spiced, it will leave you sweetly satisfied but not overly full.
—*Gerri Saylor, Graniteville, SC*

Prep: 10 min. • **Bake:** 40 min.
Makes: 5 servings

- ½ cup egg substitute
- 1 can (15 oz.) pumpkin
- ¾ cup sugar
- 1 Tbsp. honey
- 1 tsp. ground cinnamon
- ½ tsp. ground ginger
- ¼ tsp. ground cloves
- 1½ cups fat-free evaporated milk
- 5 Tbsp. reduced-fat whipped topping

1. Preheat the oven to 425°. In a large bowl, beat the egg substitute, pumpkin, sugar, honey and spices until blended. Gradually beat in milk. Pour into five 8-oz. custard cups coated with cooking spray. Place in a 13x9-in. baking pan. Pour hot water into the pan to act as a water bath.
2. Bake, uncovered, for 10 minutes. Reduce heat to 350°. Bake until a knife inserted in the center comes out clean, 30-35 minutes longer. Serve warm or cold. Garnish with whipped topping. Store in the refrigerator.

1 SERVING: 244 cal., 1g fat (1g sat. fat), 3mg chol., 141mg sod., 52g carb. (46g sugars, 3g fiber), 9g pro.

BAKED PUMPKIN PUDDING

MAGIC BARS

MAGIC BARS

These rich bar cookies will melt in your mouth—like magic! They're ideal to have on hand for a snack.
—*Pauline Schrag, Theresa, NY*

Prep: 15 min. • **Bake:** 30 min. + cooling
Makes: 16 bars

½ cup butter
1 cup graham cracker crumbs
1 cup sweetened shredded coconut
1 cup semisweet chocolate chips
1 cup chopped nuts
1 can (14 oz.) sweetened condensed milk

1. Preheat oven to 350°. Melt butter in a 9-in. square baking pan. On top of the melted butter, sprinkle the crumbs, then coconut, then chocolate chips, then nuts. Pour condensed milk over all. Do not stir.
2. Bake 30 minutes or until a toothpick inserted in the center comes out clean. Let cool for several hours before cutting.
1 BAR: 279 cal., 18g fat (9g sat. fat), 24mg chol., 138mg sod., 28g carb. (22g sugars, 1g fiber), 5g pro.

TART & TANGY LEMON TART

Our family adores lemon desserts. I like to make this lemony tart for brunch. For extra-special events, I bake it in my heart-shaped tart pan.
—*Joyce Moynihan, Lakeville, MN*

Prep: 15 min. + chilling
Bake: 45 min. + cooling
Makes: 14 servings

¾ cup butter, softened
½ cup confectioners' sugar
1½ cups all-purpose flour
FILLING
¾ cup sugar
1 Tbsp. grated lemon zest
¾ cup lemon juice
3 large eggs
3 large egg yolks
4 oz. cream cheese, softened
1 Tbsp. cornstarch
    Sweetened whipped cream, optional

1. Preheat oven to 325°. In a large bowl, cream butter and confectioners' sugar until smooth. Gradually beat in flour. Press dough onto bottom and up the side of an ungreased 11-in. fluted tart pan with removable bottom. Refrigerate for 15 minutes.
2. Line unpricked crust with a double thickness of foil. Fill with pie weights, dried beans or uncooked rice. Bake until edge is lightly browned, 18-22 minutes. Remove foil and weights; bake until bottom is golden brown, 5-7 minutes longer. Cool on a wire rack.
3. In a large bowl, beat the sugar, lemon zest, lemon juice, eggs, egg yolks, cream cheese and cornstarch until blended; pour into crust. Bake until filling is set, 18-22 minutes. Cool completely on a wire rack. If desired, serve with whipped cream. Refrigerate leftovers.
1 PIECE: 254 cal., 15g fat (9g sat. fat), 114mg chol., 125mg sod., 27g carb. (16g sugars, 0 fiber), 4g pro.

FROSTY WATERMELON ICE

For a different way to serve watermelon, try this make-ahead frozen dessert. It's so refreshing on a summer day—and you don't have to worry about seeds while you're enjoying it.
—*Kaaren Jurack, Manassas, VA*

Prep: 20 min. + freezing
Makes: 4 servings

1 tsp. unflavored gelatin
2 Tbsp. water
2 Tbsp. lime juice
2 Tbsp. honey
4 cups cubed seedless watermelon

1. In a microwave-safe bowl, sprinkle gelatin over water; let stand 1 minute. Microwave on high for 40 seconds. Stir and let stand until the gelatin is completely dissolved, 1-2 minutes.
2. Place the lime juice, honey and gelatin mixture in a blender. Add 1 cup watermelon; cover and process until blended. Add the remaining watermelon, 1 cup at a time, processing until smooth after each addition.
3. Transfer to a shallow dish; freeze until almost firm. In a chilled bowl, beat with an electric mixer until mixture is bright pink. Divide among 4 serving dishes; freeze, covered, until firm. Remove from freezer 15-20 minutes before serving.
¾ CUP: 81 cal., 0 fat (0 sat. fat), 0 chol., 3mg sod., 21g carb. (18g sugars, 1g fiber), 1g pro. **DIABETIC EXCHANGES:** 1 fruit, ½ starch.

Test Kitchen Tip

Working with gelatin requires a balance between temperatures. Before gelatin can be mixed with other ingredients, it first needs to absorb some cold water, a process called blooming. Then it needs to be added to a warm mixture, or heated, so it doesn't set too fast.

FROSTY WATERMELON ICE

PEANUT BUTTER
& JELLY ICE CREAM

½ **CUP:** 393 cal., 28g fat (14g sat. fat), 77mg chol., 231mg sod., 32g carb. (29g sugars, 1g fiber), 7g pro.

HEAVENLY BLUEBERRY TART

Mmm—this tart is bursting with the fresh flavor of blueberries! Not only do I bake berries with the crust, but I also top the tart with more fruit after I take it out of the oven.
—*Lyin Schramm, Berwick, ME*

Prep: 20 min.
Bake: 40 min. + cooling
Makes: 6 servings

    1   cup all-purpose flour
    2   Tbsp. sugar
    ⅛   tsp. salt
    ½   cup cold butter
    1   Tbsp. vinegar
FILLING
    4   cups fresh blueberries, divided
    ⅔   cup sugar
    2   Tbsp. all-purpose flour
    ½   tsp. ground cinnamon
    ⅛   tsp. ground nutmeg

1. Lightly grease a 9-in. tart pan with removable bottom; set aside. Preheat oven to 400°. In a small bowl, combine flour, sugar and salt; cut in butter until crumbly. Add the vinegar, tossing with a fork to moisten. Press mixture onto bottom and up the side of prepared pan.
2. For the filling, lightly smash 2 cups blueberries in a bowl. Combine sugar, flour, cinnamon and nutmeg; stir into the smashed blueberries. Spread the mixture evenly into crust; sprinkle with 1 cup whole blueberries. Place tart pan on a baking sheet.
3. Bake until crust is browned and filling is bubbly, 40-45 minutes. Remove from the oven; arrange the remaining berries over the top. Cool on a wire rack. Store in the refrigerator.
1 PIECE: 380 cal., 16g fat (10g sat. fat), 41mg chol., 173mg sod., 59g carb. (36g sugars, 3g fiber), 3g pro.

PEANUT BUTTER & JELLY ICE CREAM

What could be tastier than peanut butter and jelly ice cream? Use crunchy peanut butter if you like extra texture.
—*Taste of Home Test Kitchen*

Prep: 20 min. + chilling
Process: 20 min. + freezing
Makes: 5 cups

    1½ cups whole milk
    ⅔   cup packed brown sugar
    ½   tsp. salt
    1   large egg, lightly beaten
    ⅔   cup creamy peanut butter
    2   cups heavy whipping cream
    2   tsp. vanilla extract
    ½   cup grape or strawberry jelly

1. In a large heavy saucepan, heat the milk, brown sugar and salt until bubbles form around side of pan. Whisk a small amount of the hot mixture into the egg. Return all to pan, whisking constantly.
2. Cook and stir over low heat until the mixture is thickened and coats the back of a spoon. Remove from the heat; whisk in the peanut butter. Quickly transfer to a bowl; place bowl in ice water and stir for 2 minutes. Stir in the cream and vanilla. Press waxed paper onto surface of the custard. Refrigerate for several hours or overnight.
3. Fill the cylinder of ice cream maker two-thirds full; freeze according to the manufacturer's directions.
4. When ice cream is frozen, spoon into a freezer container, layering with jelly; freeze for 2-4 hours before serving.

HEAVENLY
BLUEBERRY TART

AIR-FRYER
COOKIE PIE

AIR-FRYER COOKIE PIE

My mom used to make cookie bars for every school event when I was growing up. My updated version takes half the time, and tastes just like hers.
—*Ashley Long, Mission, KS*

Prep: 15 min. + cooling
Cook: 10 min. + cooling
Makes: 12 servings

- ½ cup unsalted butter, cubed
- ½ cup sugar
- ½ cup packed brown sugar
- 1 large egg
- 1 Tbsp. vanilla extract
- 1½ cups all-purpose flour
- ½ tsp. sea salt
- ½ tsp. baking soda
- 1 cup brickle toffee bits
- ½ cup Nutella
  Confectioners' sugar, optional

1. In a small heavy saucepan, melt butter over medium heat until golden brown, 5-7 minutes, stirring constantly. Remove from heat. Transfer to a large bowl. Cool completely until butter is solid.
2. Preheat air fryer to 350°. Grease an 8-in. round baking pan that will fit in the air fryer; line it with greased parchment. Add sugars to browned butter; beat until crumbly, about 2 minutes. Beat in the egg and vanilla. Whisk flour, salt and baking soda; gradually beat into butter mixture. Fold in the toffee bits.
3. Press half the dough onto bottom and up side of prepared pan. Spread Nutella over dough to within ½ in. of edge. Press the remaining dough between sheets of parchment into an 8-in. circle. Remove paper and place dough over Nutella; pinch edge to seal. If desired, sprinkle with additional sea salt.
4. Cook until a toothpick inserted in the center comes out clean, 10-12 minutes. Loosen side from pan with a knife. Cool in pan for 10 minutes before removing to wire rack; remove paper. If desired, dust with confectioners' sugar before serving.

LEMON-LIME BARS

1 PIECE: 369 cal., 18g fat (8g sat. fat), 43mg chol., 261mg sod., 49g carb. (36g sugars, 1g fiber), 3g pro.

LEMON-LIME BARS

I baked these bars for a luncheon, and a gentleman made his way to the kitchen to compliment the cook who made them.
—*Holly Wilkins, Lake Elmore, VT*

Prep: 20 min. • **Bake:** 20 min. + cooling
Makes: 4 dozen

- 1 cup butter, softened
- ½ cup confectioners' sugar
- 2 tsp. grated lime zest
- 1¾ cups all-purpose flour
- ¼ tsp. salt

FILLING
- 4 large eggs
- 1½ cups sugar
- ¼ cup all-purpose flour
- ½ tsp. baking powder
- ⅓ cup lemon juice
- 2 tsp. grated lemon zest
  Confectioners' sugar

1. Preheat oven to 350°. In a large bowl, cream butter and confectioners' sugar until light and fluffy, 3-4 minutes. Beat in lime zest. Combine the flour and salt; gradually add to the creamed mixture and mix well.
2. Press into a greased 13x9-in. baking dish. Bake just until the edges are lightly browned, 13-15 minutes.
3. Meanwhile, for filling, in a large bowl, beat eggs and sugar. Combine flour and baking powder. Gradually add to the egg mixture. Stir in the lemon juice and zest; beat until frothy. Pour over hot crust.
4. Bake for 20-25 minutes or until light golden brown. Cool on a wire rack. Dust with confectioners' sugar. Cut into squares. Store in the refrigerator.
1 BAR: 88 cal., 4g fat (2g sat. fat), 28mg chol., 60mg sod., 12g carb. (7g sugars, 0 fiber), 1g pro.

CARAMEL-PECAN COOKIE BUTTER BARS

I love cookie butter and used to spread it on toast, vanilla wafers and graham crackers. One day I was thinking about another way to use it and came up with these bars, and they were an instant hit in my house. They freeze well—they are so tempting to remove from the freezer one by one until there are no more left!
—*Sheryl Little, Cabot, AR*

Prep: 15 min. • **Bake:** 15 min. + cooling
Makes: 2 dozen

½ cup butter, softened
½ cup sugar
½ cup packed brown sugar
½ cup Biscoff creamy cookie spread
1 large egg, room temperature
1¼ cups self-rising flour
2 cups pecan halves, coarsely chopped
1 pkg. (11 oz.) caramels
3 Tbsp. half-and-half cream
1 tsp. vanilla extract
1 cup (6 oz.) dark chocolate chips
1 Tbsp. shortening

1. Preheat oven to 375°. In a large bowl, cream butter, sugars and cookie spread until light and fluffy, 5-7 minutes. Beat in egg. Gradually beat in flour. Spread onto bottom of a greased 13x9-in. baking pan. Sprinkle with pecans; press lightly into dough. Bake until the edges are lightly browned, 15-20 minutes.
2. Meanwhile, in a large saucepan, combine caramels and cream. Cook and stir over medium-low heat until caramels are melted. Remove from the heat; stir in vanilla. Pour over crust. Cool completely in pan on a wire rack.
3. In a microwave, melt chocolate chips and shortening; stir until smooth. Drizzle over caramel; let stand until set. Cut into bars.

1 BAR: 285 cal., 17g fat (6g sat. fat), 20mg chol., 149mg sod., 34g carb. (25g sugars, 2g fiber), 3g pro.

"These bars are fabulous. There are several steps to this recipe but [they are] well worth it."
—**MARINEMOM_TEXAS, TASTEOFHOME.COM**

CARAMEL-PECAN COOKIE BUTTER BARS

LIMONCELLO
TIRAMISU

4. For the filling, in a large bowl, beat cream until it begins to thicken. Add sugar; beat until stiff peaks form. Fold Mascarpone cheese and whipped cream into the lemon curd.

5. Arrange a third of the ladyfingers on the bottom of a 9-in. springform pan. Drizzle with a third of the syrup; spread with a third of the filling. Repeat layers twice. Cover and refrigerate overnight. Carefully run a knife around the edge of the pan to loosen. Remove side of pan. Sprinkle with cookies and lemon peel.

1 PIECE: 396 cal., 20g fat (11g sat. fat), 128mg chol., 57mg sod., 51g carb. (37g sugars, 0 fiber), 4g pro.

BANANA FRITTERS

Soon after I made these fritters for the first time, my husband began requesting them on a regular basis. I also like to serve them to overnight guests as a sweet breakfast treat.
—*Laurel Cosbie, Palm Desert, CA*

Takes: 30 min. • **Makes:** 16 fritters

- 2 large eggs
- ½ cup 2% milk
- 1 tsp. canola oil
- 1 cup all-purpose flour
- 1 tsp. baking powder
- 1 tsp. salt
- 4 large firm bananas
  Additional oil for deep-fat frying
  Confectioners' sugar, optional

1. In a bowl, beat eggs, milk and oil. Combine flour, baking powder and salt; stir into egg mixture until smooth. Cut bananas into quarters (about 2 in. long). Dip each banana piece into batter to coat.

2. In an electric skillet or deep-fat fryer, heat oil to 375°. Fry bananas, 2-3 pieces at a time, until golden brown.

3. Drain on paper towels. If desired, dust with confectioners' sugar.

1 FRITTER: 124 cal., 7g fat (1g sat. fat), 24mg chol., 190mg sod., 14g carb. (5g sugars, 1g fiber), 2g pro.

LIMONCELLO TIRAMISU

We love everything about this terrific dessert—from the light lemon flavor and creamy Mascarpone to crushed macaroons on top.
—Taste of Home *Test Kitchen*

Prep: 30 min. + chilling
Makes: 16 servings

- ½ cup sugar
- ¼ cup water
- 2 Tbsp. limoncello

LEMON CURD
- 1½ cups sugar
- ⅓ cup plus 1 Tbsp. cornstarch
- 1½ cups cold water
- 3 large egg yolks, lightly beaten
- 3 Tbsp. butter, cubed
- ½ cup lemon juice
- 2 tsp. grated lemon zest

CREAM FILLING
- 1½ cups heavy whipping cream
- ¾ cup sugar
- 1 carton (8 oz.) Mascarpone cheese

ASSEMBLY
- 3 pkg. (3 oz. each) ladyfingers, divided
- 4 macaroon cookies, crumbled
  Candied lemon peel, optional

1. In a small saucepan, bring sugar and water to a boil. Cook and stir until sugar is dissolved. Remove from the heat. Stir in limoncello; set aside.

2. For lemon curd, in another saucepan, combine sugar and cornstarch. Stir in water until smooth. Bring to a boil; cook and stir until thickened, about 1 minute. Remove from heat.

3. Stir a small amount of the hot mixture into the egg yolks; return all to the pan, stirring constantly. Bring to a gentle boil; cook and stir 2 minutes longer. Remove from the heat. Stir in butter. Gently stir in lemon juice and zest. Cool to room temperature without stirring.

CHERRY CREAM CHEESE PIE

My mom is known for her scrumptious desserts, including this easy-to-make pie. It's one of my favorite desserts any time of year. I love the combination of cream cheese and cherry pie filling.
—Cindy Kufeldt, Orlando, FL

- -

Prep: 10 min. • **Bake:** 40 min. + chilling
Makes: 8 servings

- ¾ cup all-purpose flour
- 3 Tbsp. plus ⅓ cup sugar
- ¼ tsp. salt
- ¼ cup butter, softened
- 1 can (21 oz.) cherry pie filling
- 1 pkg. (8 oz.) cream cheese, softened
- 1 large egg, room temperature
- 1 tsp. vanilla extract

1. Preheat oven to 350°. In a small bowl, combine flour, 3 Tbsp. sugar and salt. Add butter; stir until combined. Press onto bottom and up the side of a 9-in. pie plate. Bake until lightly browned, 10-12 minutes. Pour pie filling into crust.
2. In a large bowl, beat cream cheese, remaining ⅓ cup sugar, egg and vanilla until smooth. Carefully spread around the outside edge of pie, leaving a 3-in. circle of cherries exposed in the center.
3. Bake until the edge begins to brown, 30-35 minutes. Cool pie on a wire rack. Refrigerate the pie for several hours before serving.
1 PIECE: 329 cal., 16g fat (10g sat. fat), 67mg chol., 232mg sod., 42g carb. (29g sugars, 1g fiber), 4g pro.

Test Kitchen Tip

To ensure a lump-free pie, allow cream cheese to soften at room temperature before mixing so it blends in smoothly with the rest of the batter.

PEACH POUND CAKE

Our state grows excellent peaches, and this is one recipe I'm quick to pull out when they are in season. It's a tender, moist cake that receives rave reviews wherever I take it.
—Betty Jean Gosnell, Inman, SC

- -

Prep: 10 min. • **Bake:** 1 hour + cooling
Makes: 16 servings

- 1 cup butter, softened
- 2 cups sugar
- 6 large eggs, room temperature
- 1 tsp. almond extract
- 1 tsp. vanilla extract
- 3 cups all-purpose flour
- ¼ tsp. baking soda
- ¼ tsp. salt
- ½ cup sour cream
- 2 cups diced fresh or frozen peaches
  Whipped cream, optional

1. Preheat oven to 350°. Grease and flour a 10-in. fluted tube pan; set aside. In a large bowl, cream butter and sugar until light and fluffy, 5-7 minutes. Add the eggs, 1 at a time, beating well after each addition. Beat in extracts. In another bowl, combine flour, baking soda and salt; add to batter alternately with sour cream, beating well after each addition. Fold in peaches.
2. Pour batter into prepared pan. Bake until a toothpick inserted in the center comes out clean, 60-70 minutes. Cool in pan for 10 minutes before removing to a wire rack to cool completely. If desired, serve with a dollop of whipped cream and additional peaches.
1 PIECE: 335 cal., 15g fat (9g sat. fat), 106mg chol., 178mg sod., 45g carb. (27g sugars, 1g fiber), 5g pro.

PEACH POUND CAKE

CLASSIC CREME BRULEE

This is my favorite dessert, so I quickly learned how to make it. I have attended parties where the guests finished off their own desserts by broiling the sugar on their portions with a small torch.
—*Joylyn Trickel, Helendale, CA*

Prep: 30 min. • **Bake:** 25 min. + chilling
Makes: 8 servings

- 4 cups heavy whipping cream
- 9 large egg yolks
- ¾ cup sugar
- 1 tsp. vanilla extract
  Brown sugar

1. In a large saucepan, combine the cream, egg yolks and sugar. Cook and stir over medium heat until mixture reaches 160° or is thick enough to coat the back of a metal spoon. Stir in vanilla.
2. Transfer to eight 6-oz. ramekins or custard cups. Place cups in a baking pan; add 1 in. boiling water to the pan. Bake, uncovered, at 325° until centers are just set (mixture will jiggle), 25-30 minutes. Remove ramekins from water bath; cool for 10 minutes. Cover and refrigerate for at least 4 hours.
3. Place the custards on a baking sheet 1 hour before serving. Sprinkle each with 1-2 tsp. brown sugar. Broil 8 in. from the heat until the sugar is caramelized, 4-7 minutes. Refrigerate leftovers.
1 SERVING: 551 cal., 50g fat (29g sat. fat), 402mg chol., 53mg sod., 22g carb. (22g sugars, 0 fiber), 6g pro.

CLASSIC CREME BRULEE

DATE PUDDING
COBBLER

DATE PUDDING COBBLER

There were eight children in my family
when I was a girl, and all of us enjoyed
this cobbler. I now serve it for everyday
and special occasions alike.
—*Carolyn Miller, Guys Mills, PA*

Prep: 15 min. • **Bake:** 25 min.
Makes: 8 servings

- 1   cup all-purpose flour
- 1½ cups packed brown sugar, divided
- 2   tsp. baking powder
- 1   Tbsp. cold butter
- ½   cup 2% milk
- ¾   cup chopped dates
- ¾   cup chopped walnuts
- 1   cup water
      Optional: Whipped cream and
      ground cinnamon

1. Preheat oven to 350°. In a large bowl,
combine the flour, ½ cup brown sugar
and baking powder. Cut in the butter
until crumbly. Gradually add the milk,
dates and walnuts.
2. In a large saucepan, combine water
and the remaining 1 cup brown sugar;
bring to a boil. Remove from the heat;
add the date mixture and mix well.
3. Transfer to a greased 10-in. cast-iron
skillet or 8-in. square baking pan. Bake
for 25-30 minutes or until top is golden
brown and fruit is tender. Serve warm,
with whipped cream and cinnamon
if desired.
1 SERVING: 347 cal., 9g fat (2g sat. fat), 5mg
chol., 150mg sod., 65g carb. (50g sugars,
2g fiber), 4g pro.

GLAZED LEMON CHIFFON CAKE

This fluffy cake is a real treat drizzled
with the sweet-tart lemon glaze.
—*Rebecca Baird, Salt Lake City, UT*

Prep: 15 min. • **Bake:** 45 min. + cooling
Makes: 16 servings

- ½   cup fat-free evaporated milk
- ½   cup reduced-fat sour cream
- ¼   cup lemon juice
- 2   Tbsp. canola oil
- 2   tsp. vanilla extract
- 1   tsp. grated lemon zest
- 1   tsp. lemon extract
- 2   cups cake flour
- 1½ cups sugar
- 1   Tbsp. baking powder
- ½   tsp. salt
- 1   cup large egg whites (about 7)
- ½   tsp. cream of tartar

LEMON GLAZE
- 1¾ cups confectioners' sugar
- 3   Tbsp. lemon juice

1. Preheat oven to 325°. In a large bowl,
combine the first 7 ingredients. Sift
together the flour, sugar, baking powder
and salt; gradually beat into the lemon
mixture until smooth. In a small bowl,
beat egg whites until foamy. Add the
cream of tartar; beat until stiff peaks
form. Gently fold into lemon mixture.
2. Pour batter into an ungreased 10-in.
tube pan. Bake for 45-55 minutes or until
cake springs back when lightly touched.
Immediately invert pan; cool completely.
Remove cake from the pan to a serving
platter. Combine the glaze ingredients;
drizzle over cake.
1 PIECE: 230 cal., 3g fat (1g sat. fat), 3mg
chol., 189mg sod., 47g carb. (33g sugars,
0 fiber), 4g pro.

GLAZED LEMON
CHIFFON CAKE

ANGEL
BERRY TRIFLE

ANGEL BERRY TRIFLE

I usually serve this in the summer when fresh berries are bountiful, but I recently prepared it using frozen cherries and some light cherry pie filling instead. It was just as delicious!
—*Brenda Paine, Clinton Township, MI*

Takes: 25 min. • **Makes:** 14 servings

- 1½ cups cold fat-free milk
- 1 pkg. (1 oz.) sugar-free instant vanilla pudding mix
- 1 cup fat-free vanilla yogurt
- 6 oz. reduced-fat cream cheese, cubed
- ½ cup reduced-fat sour cream
- 2 tsp. vanilla extract
- 1 carton (12 oz.) frozen reduced-fat whipped topping, thawed and divided
- 2 prepared angel food cakes (8 oz. each), cut into 1-in. cubes
- 1 pint fresh blackberries
- 1 pint fresh raspberries
- 1 pint fresh blueberries
  Fresh mint leaves, optional

1. Whisk the milk and pudding mix for 2 minutes. Let stand until soft-set, about 2 minutes more. Meanwhile, beat yogurt, cream cheese, sour cream and vanilla until smooth. Fold in the pudding mixture and 1 cup whipped topping.
2. Place a third of the cake cubes in a 4-qt. trifle bowl. Top with a third of pudding mixture, a third of the berries and half the remaining whipped topping. Repeat layers once. Top with remaining cake, pudding and berries. If desired, garnish with additional whipped topping and mint leaves. Serve immediately or refrigerate.

¾ CUP: 234 cal., 6g fat (5g sat. fat), 10mg chol., 342mg sod., 34g carb. (10g sugars, 3g fiber), 6g pro.

VEGAN TROPICAL MAGIC BARS

VEGAN TROPICAL MAGIC BARS

Magic bars are one of the easiest treats you can make, and I decided to give them a couple of twists. By using plant-based butter and condensed coconut milk, I made them completely vegan. I also added some macadamia nuts and dried pineapple and mango to give them a tropical spin.
—*James Schend, Pleasant Prairie, WI*

Prep: 10 min. • **Bake:** 30 min. + chilling
Makes: 16 bars

- ½ cup vegan butter-style sticks
- 1 cup graham cracker crumbs
- 1 cup sweetened shredded coconut
- 1 cup dairy-free white baking chips
- 1 cup macadamia nuts, chopped
- ½ cup dried pineapple, chopped
- ½ cup dried mangoes, chopped
- 1 can (11.6 oz.) sweetened condensed coconut milk

1. Preheat oven to 350°. Melt butter in a 9-in. square baking pan. Over melted butter, sprinkle, in order, the crumbs, coconut, baking chips, nuts, pineapple and mango. Pour well-stirred coconut milk over all. Do not stir.
2. Bake until a toothpick inserted in the center comes out clean, 30-35 minutes. Refrigerate at least 4 hours or overnight. Cut into bars and serve.

1 BAR: 323 cal., 20g fat (9g sat. fat), 2mg chol., 188mg sod., 34g carb. (27g sugars, 2g fiber), 2g pro.

RECIPE INDEX

FROZEN MARGARITAS P. 30

FETTUCCINE WITH SAUSAGE & FRESH TOMATO SAUCE P. 161

FETA CHICKEN BURGERS P. 238

CORNED BEEF
HASH & EGGS P. 54

ICON INDEX

SPANISH-STYLE
PAELLA P. 271

🍲 SLOW COOKER

BLUE-RIBBON APPLE
CAKE P. 290

ONE-DISH TURKEY
DINNER P. 264

🍴 5 INGREDIENT

PRESSURE-COOKER SALSA
LONDON BROIL P. 217

🍎 HEALTHY

FALAFEL P. 234

⏰ OVERNIGHT

❄ FREEZER FRIENDLY

SPRING PEA
SOUP P. 72